Libey and Pickering on RFM and Beyond

MeritDirect Press

MeritDirect Press publishes books that assist multi-channel direct marketers to become more successful and profitable. Established by the partners of MeritDirect, a leading business-to-business list brokerage and management firm, the mission of MeritDirect Press is to bring knowledge and wisdom of multi-channel direct marketing to clients and the direct marketing community.

MeritDirect Press
333 Westchester Avenue
White Plains, New York 10604
Telephone: (914) 368-1000
www.meritdirect.com

Editorial Offices
280 South 79th Street Suite 1401
West Des Moines, Iowa 50266
Telephone: (515) 537 2307

Manuscripts for books on multi-channel direct marketing are welcomed and may be sent to the editorial offices by email or CD.

To order books direct from the publisher:
www.MeritDirectPress.com

Libey and Pickering

on

RFM

and Beyond

How to Improve Multi-Channel
Customer and Prospect Profits
Using Advanced Recency, Frequency
and Monetary Value

Donald R. Libey
and
Christopher Pickering

Introduction by Jack Schmid

MERITDIRECT PRESS
WHITE PLAINS, NEW YORK

Acknowledgements

The authors wish to thank the partners of MeritDirect for their desire to publish books that will lead the way to Higher Ground and benefit the direct marketing profession.

The authors and publisher wish to thank Jack Schmid for his generous Introduction and his always-valuable wisdom regarding the practice of multichannel direct marketing. Jack Schmid is a legend in the direct marketing world, and the fine organization he and his colleagues have built over the years, J. Schmid & Associates, continues as a pre-eminent consulting practice dedicated to the success of direct marketing companies worldwide.

The authors wish, most appreciatively, to thank Andrea Stewart for her editorial talents and skills in isolating and resolving problems in the fine points of content and style throughout the book. If it were not for Andrea's intelligence, experience and wisdom, the book would not have been possible, and the authors are both eternally grateful for her dedication and expertise.

ISBN 9765172-1-30 (acid-free paper)

Published in the United States by MeritDirect Press

Sales and Customer Service Offices:
333 Westchester Avenue
White Plains, NY 10604
(914) 368-1000

Editorial Offices:
280 South 79th Street Suite 1401
West Des Moines IA 50266
(515) 537 2307

Printed on acid-free paper. Manufactured in the United States of America.
First Edition

Design by Angela Schmitt

*This book is dedicated to my father, James, the first direct marketer
in our family and my mother, Linda, a friend, mentor, partner,
and direct marketer without peer.*
—Christopher H. Pickering

Contents

Foreword

For several years, I've been urging Don Libey to update his 1994 book, *Libey on RFM*. This 139-page gem was written in an almost Socratic style and sold nearly fifteen thousand copies. The book was considered by many the 'last word' on recency, frequency and monetary value analysis.

I didn't think a straight reprint made sense, although the material is ageless. Frankly, I always considered it a tad too intellectual for my learning style. I wanted a new edition that melded the conceptual with the real world of profitable RFM execution and one that included the hand-drawn flip-charts Libey had used in hundreds of RFM seminars worldwide.

Ever proactive in his search for prime aged beef and a good Zinfandel, Libey suggested we discuss the project over dinner at Morton's in White Plains. One of my partners and a key marketing database consultant to our clients, Christopher Pickering, joined us for the dinner in early 2005. Out of that evening came the plan for this book. Don would tee up the topics conceptually, and Christopher would bring them into the real world of application. The unique, hand-drawn flip-charts and other visuals were agreed upon with the overall intent of making *Libey and Pickering on RFM and Beyond* the standard textbook and research resource on the subject.

Since we announced our plan to publish this book and a few other direct marketing titles each year, I've received many puzzled inquiries from people asking why MeritDirect, a list and marketing database services firm, would want to be a publishing house, as well. The most obvious reason is that we have a long-standing strategic partnership with Don Libey, one of the world's pre-eminent speakers, teachers and writers on the direct marketing discipline. Thus, we are leveraging our Libey relationship to move into another form of direct marketing service. If MeritDirect was a public company, that would suffice—the good old profit motive. However, the reason for the formation of MeritDirect Press is quite a bit more complex and is woven into the education and service culture of our company.

For me, the formative experience came in 1975 when I attended the first Co-op produced by Direct Media. I was marketing director for Kole Enterprises, a business-to-business cataloger of shipping and material handling supplies, and working for one of the legendary business marketers, Gary Brown. Up to that point, I had never taken a college course or a seminar on any topic dealing even remotely with direct marketing. But there I was, sitting in the dining room of the Apawamis Club in Rye, New York, with twenty-five or thirty business-to-business mailer clients of Direct Media, absorbed in a fascinating six-hour lecture by the direct marketing guru of the day, Dan Harding.

It was a memorable experience during which I had the opportunity to meet a few mail order entrepreneurs like George Mosher, Ed Baker and Mike Siegel. Our hosts, Dave Florence and Bob Foehl, had hit on a responsive chord for many of us who had never been exposed to so much direct response erudition as was on display that day. The lecture was rigorous but allowed plenty of interactive questions and often the answers came from other participants. The social aspect was also compelling, and thus was born DMI's almost annual Business Mailer's Co-op Conference.

Over the following decade, I attended the Co-op several times as a mailer and consultant and was always well rewarded by the excellent educational presentations and the social interaction, which gave a certain sense of community to the business-to-business catalog sector, a group underserved by the DMA, an association, until recently, dominated by large consumer catalogers and publishers.

By 1988, as the mysteries of time and place would have it, I found myself on the staff of Direct Media as a business-to-business list broker. Since I was building my clientele, I found that getting my prospects to attend the Co-op was a veritable icebreaker. Exposed to so much good information, provided by so many credible and relevant practitioners and consultants, the Co-op was, by far, my best client recruiting tool.

When Bob Foehl, DMI's long-time president and Co-op chairman, announced that there would be no program in 1991, citing several personal scheduling and time conflicts, I volunteered to keep the tradition going out of enlightened self-interest. Bob was receptive and I plunged into the process of planning the summer 1991 Co-op with the aid of my intrepid assistant Nancy Patterson Lynch.

At the first meeting, in which Bob passed the torch to Nancy and me, he off-handedly mentioned that a fellow named Don Libey had expressed interest in doing a keynote speech. Libey, he said, had been a client of his for a number of years at Rapidforms and elsewhere, and was a very smart guy. However, Bob said he had never heard him speak.

Thus it was that I met Don Libey for the first time. He delivered a sparkling invocation to the record crowd of some two hundred business-to-business catalogers. He was a unique combination of educator, comedian, preacher and thespian, and for sixty minutes he held our audience in thrall to his topic. Don's keynote was, for me, cathartic, having been very much on pins and needles about every aspect of the Co-op. But after Libey spoke, the attendees were supercharged, motivated to learn more and follow his exhortation, familiar to us all today, that we should, "Go forth and multiply."

Thereafter, I was the Co-op chairman until early 2000 when Mark Joyce and I, along with seven other partners formed MeritDirect.

Producing the Business Mailer's Co-op Conference is time consuming and expensive (it is free to our clients and guests). It spans three days, featuring twenty-five to thirty speakers, several receptions, breakfasts, lunches and dinners. Over two hundred direct marketers from seventy or eighty client companies take part in the Co-op. To execute the Co-op properly is a major commitment on many levels. However, even though the fledgling MeritDirect was but a six months old start-up, we could not imagine a July without the Co-op. And, we have continued each year since, bringing greater relevancy by adding many interactive topics, so the name has changed to the Business Mailer's Co-op and Interactive Marketing Conference. Additionally, over the years we have attempted to return value to our clients through a variety of other programs:

> we have sponsored a number of Libey-presented programs, such as the *Lunch with Libey* telephone conference calls with over one hundred sites participating;

> a series of one-day seminars by Libey at our headquarters auditorium on topics, such as product sourcing and management, lifetime value, RFM, creative and offer development;

> MeritDirect is a sponsor of the Amtower Government Marketing Town Hall series featuring Mark Amtower, the leading advisor to direct marketers selling to the federal government;

we publish the *Libey-Concordia Economic Outlook and Secrets of the Catalog Master*, a sixteen- to twenty-page newsletter, issued eight to nine times per year, and distributed to over four hundred catalog executives and CEOs;

we sponsored the best-selling video interview of Don Libey by Tad Clark, in conjunction with *DM News*, titled *The Wal-Martization of America and the Rebirth of Direct Marketing*;

and every year we donate generously to the Direct Marketing Educational Foundation.

This is more than just a laundry list of educational efforts. MeritDirect produces and sponsors these endeavors to educate, update and provide the vital connective tissue every community requires to remain relevant and stay ahead of the game.

I hope it is evident that MeritDirect is committed to the world of ideas as they relate to our direct marketing profession. Ideas need a habitat to take on their full meaning, to reveal unexpected new facets for change, to unpeel, examine and understand new concepts and future trends.

It is within this context and for these purposes that MeritDirect Press has been formed. It is another medium by which we can serve our clients and the direct marketing industry at large by always encouraging and facilitating the essential movement to Higher Ground.

Ralph Drybrough, CEO
MeritDirect
White Plains, New York
August 2005

Preface

Don Libey:

The idea for an expanded revision to *Libey On Recency, Frequency and Monetary Value* was first discussed in 2001 when Ralph Drybrough, CEO of MeritDirect, and I were thinking of ways we could help clients become better direct marketers. Over the next three years we believed that Christopher Pickering had an abundance of practical information to contribute that improves the first edition's concepts and transforms this second edition into a feast of practical application of RFM and beyond. Early in 2005, Ralph, Christopher and I decided to get to work, and the book that has resulted is the first of what we hope is to be a beneficial and growing collaboration that will produce a series of valuable books preserving the wisdom found in the Higher Ground of direct marketing.

For readers who have been kind enough to obtain the original book—the first book written on RFM—I am grateful. For all who are now reading this second book, we are grateful. Perhaps a slight explanation of its format will be of value as you explore the concepts and applications of RFM and the areas beyond. The keywords are *concepts* and *applications*. I have rewritten or revised my original sections on RFM concepts and added fresh conceptual thinking in the new, added chapters. Christopher has written all of the new sections and chapters on applications and has, truly, taken the book to the Higher Ground Beyond. My original book was well received by the direct marketing world, but Christopher has skillfully added the banquet to my mere appetizer. So, as you read, you will find flavors, textures and colors, as any good feast should offer. Our approach is simple: Libey sets the table; Pickering cooks; and Drybrough picks up the tab. So little has changed in the twenty years and more we have been associates.

Multi-channel direct marketing is a formulaic business. It is consistently predictable, and financial results can be projected with a high degree of accuracy and reliability in all channels. Knowing the formulas across all channels is the hallmark of the experienced practitioner of multi-channel direct commerce, the largest of all go-to-market forms of commerce. Applying those formulas with sufficient capital to create above average earnings is the hallmark of the master investor in multi-channel direct marketing. You may have plenty of money, but if you don't know the formulas and apply them with absolute accuracy, then earnings will elude you absolutely.

Many formulas exist in multi-channel direct marketing. They change based on channel variables and externalities; however, only the percentages and ratios change. The relativities and unities of the data transformed to knowledge and finally distilled to wisdom remain constant. Understanding and applying the wisdom derived from the knowledge derived from the data is the key to creating above average earnings in this complex business.

This is a book about the formulaic nature of multi-channel direct marketing. It is a book about the cardinal formulas: recency, frequency and monetary value. And it is a book about the cardinal concepts and applications found beyond RFM, in the expansion realms of product, channel, position and market.

The original 1994 book was written as a response to the surprising recognition that few direct marketers, either business-to-business or consumer, thoroughly understood or expertly applied even the basics of recency, frequency or monetary value. In the eleven years since the first edition, it remains jarringly evident that, still, few direct marketers thoroughly understand or apply RFM. And during those years an entire generation of new, multi-channel direct marketers has emerged and *they* do not fully understand or apply RFM in any of the channels they are managing. Over the thirty years I have been in this business, I have had over twenty thousand seminar and conference attendees in my RFM courses. Less than ten percent of them are using full RFM, and perhaps only ten percent of those who do are exploring fully optimized RFM and its applications to product, channel, position and market. For too many marketers, the elusive answer lies in building models and more models. Yet, the Master Marketer—in any channel—must have an intimate and tactile understanding of fully optimized RFM if there is to be any hope of above average earnings. No direct marketer can be fully furnished without a facile understanding of and ability to apply recency, frequency and monetary value in concert with analyses of product, channel, position and market. To conceive of such a skills void is analogous to a physician having no understanding of temperature, pulse, respiration and blood pressure.

The advances in multi-channel direct marketing and Internet marketing have brought large numbers of new players to the direct marketing world. Private equity groups have invested hundreds and hundreds of millions of dollars in catalog and web-based businesses in their search for scalable market sectors that will return high earnings and allow them to achieve a higher than normal rate of return for their investors. Similarly, large consolidators have bought up hundreds of catalog companies and are attempting to drive earnings through a strategy of dominance. But both the financial and strategic operators of multi-channel direct marketing companies will be at risk unless they have mastered and applied the concepts of recency, frequency and monetary value and beyond. Without mastery of the concepts and applications described in this book, those operators will simply be throwing money on the altar of Higher Earnings. How much simpler and better it would be for them to feast on the wisdom found in the land of Higher Ground.

In an ideal world, recency, frequency and monetary value calculations would flow seamlessly from order creations in all channels in real time. At any time, managers could obtain constantly refreshed, accurate, comparative information concentrated to useful knowledge about how their customers are responding and behaving. Unfortunately, most multi-channel direct marketers are only able to complete analyses of recency, frequency and monetary value in retrospective isolation. After a quarter century of ever-evolving analytic sophistication in our industry, we still only know what happened three, six or twelve months in the past. We have no idea what is happening right now. While it is true that analytic time can be shortened by selling on the web, direct marketers in all channels are still reacting to historical marketing results, not immediately influencing future outcomes. One-time pictures are taken, but those pictures often cannot be replicated. Starting over requires freezing customer and prospect segments in time and waiting weeks or months to obtain comparative data upon which to base decisions which are, unfortunately, made too late with too little current knowledge. Nothing is less useful than knowing what happened six months ago and not knowing what is happening today and what will happen tomorrow. To be useful in the shifting multi-channel future, recency, frequency and monetary value must evolve in ever-shortening segments of time that will analytically reveal current conditions as well as the changes and trends in customer behavior over time. And for multi-channel direct marketing analysts who are passionate, the only acceptable goal for the generation of data, information and wisdom will be real time, immediate and accurately predictable and replicable.

The ultimate benefit of multi-channel marketing is its immediacy, applied as instantaneous and corrective web changes that offset real-time competitive and external conditions. To get there, we require an entirely new generation of analytic capability and capacity. Rather than continuing to stumble down the spurious road of CRM systems that lead us nowhere and devour outrageous amounts of money while self-perpetuating analytic mediocrity, we need to advance to immediate, real time, absolute metrics that actually *tell* us something. It is time to stop attempting to measure speculative, subjective *relationships* and start once again measuring real, numeric, monetary events that beneficially drive increased earnings. RFM is a great place to start. Or, I should say, RFM is a great place to get back to.

And so it is my personal hope that this revised edition will first serve and benefit our many clients in the business-to-business and the consumer multi-channel direct marketing world. It is they who move our industry forward. But, also, it is my hope that this book will become a relied-upon textbook for the growing number of colleges and universities with established and developing direct marketing programs. Woven into these pages is not only recency, frequency and monetary value, but also lifetimes of insights and, perhaps, a small bit of wisdom worthy of being passed on to the future.

A final comment about the illustrations in this edition is necessary. First, there *are* illustrations. In my original book there were none and I asked the reader to work through the material with a pad and pencil to actually figure out the conceptual structures for themselves. That is still the very best way to master a discipline. In this edition, however, we are including illustrations in a slightly less Zen-like approach to attaining wisdom. Christopher will include classic tables, charts, and other forms of illustrations. I have opted for my old seminar and conference stand-by: flip charts, hand-drawn. For so many of you who have seen these drawings over the years, perhaps they will rekindle the familiar touch and comfort of an old friend for you. But my primary reason for hand drawing them myself is that it is cheaper, thereby increasing the margins. Some things never change.

Donald R. Libey
West Des Moines, Iowa
August 2005

Christopher Pickering:

If you have read the foreword in *Elements of Style* by Strunk and White, you will appreciate my position. E.B. White studied under William Strunk in college. In his professional life he was asked to edit his teacher's book. He was cognizant of the responsibility and quite honored. It has been required reading for many high school and college students for nearly one hundred years.

On my first day at a computer service bureau, I found *Libey On RFM* waiting for me on my desk with my stapler and tape dispenser. I read it, re-read it, and re-read it. I have constantly kept it as a reference for all these years. It is a touchstone for me, particularly when faced with a complex task or challenge. The basics provide a guide to navigate uncharted waters, and I leaned on this extensively.

I was quite humbled when Don decided to revise his book and asked me to join him. I envisioned adding some background data and behind-the-scenes help. Don's magnanimous gesture to include me as a partner is the height of grace; I am eternally grateful for his assistance, guidance, patience, and good nature.

Over my career, and continuing at an increasing rate, people working in direct marketing circulation positions have not had the benefit of a few years of tutelage under a seasoned old pro. This book is part of a continuing effort of mine personally, and Merit-

Direct's efforts as a company, to add to the fund of knowledge in our industry. The number of direct marketing programs in colleges in the U.S. today doesn't number more than a few. Thus, as an industry, we need to make an effort to develop our own system of continuing education.

Since I first received Don's book much has happened in direct marketing. Several shocks to the system like the Internet boom and subsequent bust, 9/11, the anthrax scare, a war, and economic downturns. There have been changes in customer preferences in terms of products and in terms of methods of purchasing. Through that all, RFM is a consistent set of principles, a structure of thinking, that helps the Master Marketer focus on what is important. RFM gives those who practice it a framework with which to work the problems and, with persistence, the answers will certainly become apparent.

Don does the difficult part: setting the agenda of how to go about studying and applying RFM. Don is the strategist in this endeavor. Don is as comfortable in his role as he is as being a jazz drummer. I accompany by adding some real-world anecdotes, tactics, and a bit of data.

There are many, many people that I have to thank in my endeavors. First and foremost are the clients that I have worked with and for over these fifteen or so years. Many have also become friends. I am grateful for the opportunity to associate with you.

My partners at MeritDirect have put together a company that makes one proud to be associated with it. Especially helpful in my work in general, and in this book specifically, were Ralph Drybrough for encouraging it; Blair Barondes for enormous forbearance and sharing much knowledge; Mark Joyce for being a student of the game and coaching me; and Linda Pickering for spending nearly a lifetime teaching me about direct marketing and client service.

I have had the honor to work with a great many talented people and I have tried to learn all that I could from each of these folks. Simon Zreczny at Audio Consultant taught me much about business from the retail end. Sally Coughlin at Direct Media had enormous patience with me in my first job, Eric Worazek and Roy Wollen taught me the basics of database marketing at Direct Marketing Technology. Mike Antognoli, Curtis Larkin, David Ramon, and I learned much about direct marketing working together at Discover Financial Services. Dan W.C.A.S. Kendt, James Clifford Shuler III, and Wayne Randall Smith, Jr. have been an important help in all things. I owe an enormous debt to those in VT-8, especially. Thanks to you all.

My sister, Jenny, and my wife, Holly, have both had to put up with my adolescence. I love you both.

I am hopeful that you are able to learn from the principles laid out in this book and successfully implement them. Ours is an industry that can give very much to those who work within it; we must be good custodians of the industry.

Christopher Pickering
White Plains, New York
August 2005

Introduction

Jack Schmid

I vividly remember my very first direct marketing conference. Eagerly attending every session, I was keen on learning more about the key metrics of direct marketing—those tried and true benchmarks that gave this business the edge in tracking and measuring results. During one particular session on maximizing results from one's customer list, the speaker casually mentioned 'RFM.' He further indicated that there wasn't a better, more reliable way to segment the customer list than using RFM. I was dumbfounded! What was this magical RFM that he referred to and how could I learn what it stood for and how to apply it?

Wow, does that recollection seem like ancient history. Today, many years later, having taught the basics of direct marketing to numerous direct marketing clubs and associations in the United States and Canada and having taught a full-day workshop at the last twelve catalog conferences as well as having written *Growing a Profitable Catalog (and Internet) Business,* RFM (recency, frequency and monetary value) seems like an old friend. It is a tried and true technique that many companies are under-using or not using at all.

1

I am delighted to provide a brief introduction to this book that should be a 'must-read' for every multi-channel direct marketer.

Multi-Channel Direct Marketing

A new terminology that is becoming well accepted is *multi-channel direct marketing*. I have always believed that CRM was a meaningless buzzword that someone concocted who really didn't understand database marketing. After all, isn't sound management of one's database all about segmenting the customer list, identifying problem or opportunity clusters, and personalizing offers that can be tested to each segment to improve response, average order values (AOV) and ultimately sales per piece mailed? With the maturing of the Internet, we are moving away from the land of 'pure-play' marketers. For a number of years in the past decade, we saw pure-play Internet companies that rose like shooting stars, only to flame out. They quickly discovered that they needed to get people to their websites, much like traditional retailers. On the other hand, catalog and direct mail companies lumbered along in their well-buttoned up silos, seldom thinking about other channels, except perhaps how to open retail stores. Catalog companies like Sharper Image, Brookstone Tools, Williams-Sonoma, Talbots, Walt Disney, etc. embraced the store concept in a major way and aggressively sought to combine the two channels.

One of the lessons learned during the Internet-only era, was that the web business is *passive*, much like a retail store, and it needs to get people or businesses to the website to generate sales. Pure-play Internet sites came to be replaced with businesses that used direct marketing and catalogs to drive traffic. These companies had to learn direct marketing principles and understand that fulfillment and customer service were an integral part of their business.

The pendulum will continue to swing to the point where there will be *no pure-play catalog companies.* Every catalog needs a fully functional website to support its business. With greater than forty to fifty percent of orders being placed via the Internet, it doesn't take a rocket scientist to see where the Internet will take us for the future. But remember, the Internet is still a passive marketing channel. Research has proven that the catalog and direct marketing are the number one drivers of web traffic.

Historically, the third selling channel—retailing—is the most interesting. Retailers have discovered in the last twenty years that they are the most dinosaur-like, the most mature or over-built channel and have slowly sought direct marketing/catalog skills and capabilities to help drive store traffic. Today the retailers are crying, woe is me! How can we ever compete in the new catalog/Internet revolution? The answer is quite simple—join the fray. Don Libey puts it succinctly, "Retailers have discovered something new: direct marketing is profitable" and he predicts that there will be an invasion of catalog and Internet channels by retailers.

My conclusion is quite simple: we are moving rapidly into an era of *multi-channel direct marketing* where the boundaries are becoming blurred, and retail and direct will be joined at the hip. Consumer marketing in the next decade will be driven by multi-channel efforts with the shift to integrated databases and communication oriented to letting customers decide where, when and how they might like to shop. Future multi-channel direct marketing that retailers must understand will be driven by information, facts, and measurability.

A Formulaic Business

There is little doubt that the most significant driver of multi-channel direct marketing is that the business is trackable, measurable and predictable. With proper capture of customer transaction history and intelligent testing of offers, product, formats, seasonality, etc, the industry can effectively project future results with a high degree of accuracy. The direct marketing industry has always used RFM, in one way or another. Now in a multi-channel environment it can be taken a noticeable step further. Beyond recency, frequency and monetary segmentation, the industry can now look to further modeling refinements that involve:

1. <u>Product</u> purchase information by category, price point, seasonality, margin, old vs. repeat items, affinity clusters and more.

2. Source or <u>Channel</u> that drove the inquiry or purchase, i.e., catalog, Internet, store, search engine, affiliate program, wholesale, etc.

3. <u>Positioning</u> or what drives transactions relative to price, product quality, service, selection, speed of delivery, or ease of access and ordering.

4. <u>Market</u> that can be divided into core, adjacent or concentric segments

The chart below **(Figure S.1)** demonstrates one of the challenges of multi-channel direct marketing. It is integration of data from various selling channels. This Shop.org study shows the evolution from one set of customer data with no integration to adding a second channel's data, i.e., a catalog and finally a third channel's data, i.e., the Internet. Ultimately for a retailer to become an 'advanced' multi-channel direct marketer, it needs to integrate all three channels for testing and active use.

A further study on customer service by Modalis Research found that multi-channel customers will demand greater customer service. The research particularly concluded that:

- 90 percent of multi-channel customers don't want to be asked the same questions from different channels

- 73 percent of multi-channel customers expect the company's agent (telemarketer, store salesperson or Internet chat or customer service) to know everything about them

- 72 percent of multi-channel customers will stop doing business with the company if they have poor customer service.

Most Retailers Start With Integrated Marketing

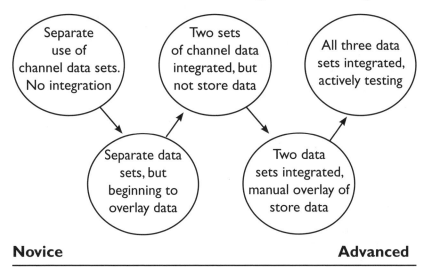

Novice　　　　　　　　　　　　　　　　　　　　　**Advanced**

Evolution of Data Use and Integration

Figure S.1　　　　　　　　　　　　©2001, J. Schmid & Associates, Inc.

The Database Drives Customer Marketing

As multi-channel direct marketers track customer orders and maintain the all-important transaction history, they are able to start differentiating between poor, average, good and great customers. A typical starting place in segmenting customers is the building of a simple RFM model for all buyers. This model will be different for every marketer in that each promotion has different price points, which affect the monetary range in the chart. The model will also be different in measuring frequency of purchase. For example, an office or computer supply catalog might get six or more purchases a year from good customers. A gift catalog is likely to get only one to two orders per year.

Today's computer technology has made the building of a multi-channel direct marketer's database more cost-effective and user-friendly. Further, applications in personalized printing, highly targeted email campaigns, in-line message affixing, dot whacks, cover changes, etc., allow catalogers to personalize the message and take customer communication to a new level. One word of caution—historically, tracking of source codes and buyer information in the mail and phone environment was benchmarked at the ninety percent plus level. With today's multi-channel order setting, direct marketers have had to become expert in match-back techniques to track Internet, fax and retail orders. Forget about data mining until you really can track where orders are coming from.

The Customer List: A Multi-Channel Direct Marketers Most Valuable Asset

Most mature direct marketers will tell you that their customer list is their most important and valuable asset. But the customer list is perishable. The old expression 'if you don't use it, you'll lose it' is most appropriate here. Recency of names is critical. If a list is more than twelve months old, it deteriorates dramatically in value. Records must be maintained, updated with recent purchase history and have current addresses. Business names are especially difficult to maintain with the quantity of changes that occur in the workplace. It is estimated that as many as eighty to ninety percent of business names have some type of change in a twelve-month period.

A Buyer is Not a Buyer is Not a Buyer

The hierarchy of a customer **(Figure S.2)** is especially important when a company looks at its customer list. One-time buyers must be converted to two-time buyers. Two-time buyers must be promoted to advocates or loyal customers. Both two-time buyers and advocates, who haven't purchased in more than twelve to eighteen months, must be reactivated. The process of maintaining, updating and actively promoting the customer file is one of the critical drivers and core competencies of a profitable catalog. The bottom line in looking at one's customer list is that successful multi-channel direct marketers don't treat all buyers alike. As the chart illustrates, there is not one customer, but literally dozens that must be communicated with in a more personal manner.

The Hierarchy of a Customer

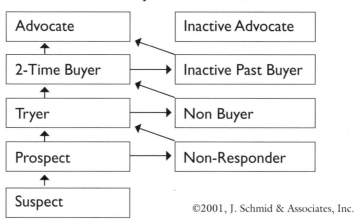

©2001, J. Schmid & Associates, Inc.

Figure S.2

Why the Buyer List is Important to Bottom Line Results

The chart below (**Figure S.3**), helps explain the tremendous leverage that the buyer list exerts on multi-channel direct marketing economics. While prospecting normally costs direct sellers money, the buyer list generates the profitability needed to:

1. Pay the shareholders.

2. Finance the growth of the business.

3. Fund the investment in prospecting or new customer development.

4. Pay overhead, salaries and general and administrative costs.

The fact that buyers are more apt to be repeating purchasers from the catalog accounts for the fact that you can expect higher response rates and higher average order values from this group. The buyer list will out-perform non-buyer and rental names by a factor of two to four to ten times. In effect, buyers are far more profitable if they are current and repeat buyers.

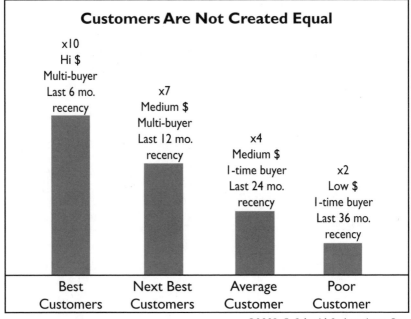

Figure S.3

©2001, J. Schmid & Associates, Inc.

Customers can often be likened to a staircase with the best ones—those who are multiple buyers, have spent more with the catalog in the past and have purchased recently—being the very top segment. The next best customer segment is that which has multiple buyers who have spent less and purchased in the last seven to twelve months (i.e. they are not as recent.) The third customer segment has one-time buyers who have spent higher dollars and are also less recent—maybe in the thirteen to twenty-four-month last purchase category. The lowest buyer segment is those who have produced low revenues, are one-time purchasers and haven't purchased in quite a while. Naturally, there are a number of gradations in this chart that can be made, but the point of a hierarchy is always present. What this chart displays is the simple concept of RFM or recency of purchase, frequency of purchase and lifetime monetary value of purchases.

Let me demonstrate this concept with an example. Several years ago, when working on the circulation plans for a craft catalog client, we were able to go into the catalog's database and quantify the customer RFM segments and use them for test mailings. A simple RFM segmentation not unlike the one in the chart was mailed with the following results:

1. The top customer segment pulled thirty-two percent with a $69 AOV or $22.08 sales per catalog mailed.

2. The second best customer segment pulled seventeen percent with a $63 AOV or $10.71 sales per catalog mailed.

3. The third customer segment pulled seven percent with a $57 AOV or $3.99 sales per catalog mailed.

4. The lowest customer segment pulled just slightly better than outside rental names with a two-and-a-half percent response and a $53 AOV or $1.33 sales per catalog mailed.

5. The best outside rental lists, the continuations, pulled just over two percent with a $52 AOV while new test rental lists were substantially lower.

This 'stair step' phenomenon occurs with customer mailings over and over. Understanding this principle is critical to working the buyer list harder.

Customer Problems

Smart multi-channel direct marketers look at their RFM data and identify groups of customers that are problems, i.e., those that need specialized or personalized communication including the following groups:

1. First-time buyers who must be aggressively promoted to obtain a second purchase.

2. Customers with low average order values.

3. Inactive buyers with all levels of past purchase activity, i.e., one-time, two-time or three-time plus purchases who have not made a purchase for twelve to eighteen months. These customers need a special reactivation message.

4. Customers who only purchase in one season, not year around.

5. Buyers who only purchase from a single product line when many other categories are being offered

Customer Opportunities

There are also segments of customers that represent an opportunity for the company, i.e., groups that could generate greater or additional sales and profits. Examples include:

1. A loyalty program for customers that have the best long-term lifetime value. Remember that the more unique your company's products are, the less a loyalty program is needed. In fact, you may be incentivising customers (or spending dollars on customers) who would continue to purchase from your catalog without any special loyalty program. The more that your firm's products are a commodity, the more a loyalty program is needed to keep solid customers from buying elsewhere. The database can help you identify the customers to whom a loyalty program should be mailed. Remember, it is difficult to test a loyalty program—either you have one or you don't. Think about your exit strategy up front, not after you're in the mail.

2. Add extra units per order with effective cross sells and up-sells, thus increasing the average order value.

3. Identify cells that should receive additional contacts. Most catalogers do not contact their customers often enough. It makes a great deal of sense to re-mail or email those cells that have the highest RFM values. A good industry rule of thumb is that re-mailings of the same catalog or one with minor cover changes will pull fifty to sixty percent of the original mailing.

4. Move good customers into the 'best' customer category.

5. Create buying incentives for commodity products that are purchased each month or each quarter.

6. Say thank you to good customers. When is the last time you sent your best customers a note saying thank you for their business and loyalty? The RFM segmentation can identify them immediately.

Contact Your Customers More Often

Most multi-channel marketers under-contact their customer list. Marketers who have done head-to-head tests typically find that more contacts actually improve the response of customer names. Multi-channel buyers like to receive mail, email and shop in stores. And many shop in all channels. Obviously this is where the customer hierarchy comes in. If a multi-channel marketer is contemplating one or two additional contacts for the quarter, it is more logical to direct those contacts to people or companies at the top of the buyer hierarchy and those that have previous channel-specific activity. .

A Fingerhut Success Story

While working at Fingerhut in the 70s, a group of statistical analysts that worked for me raised the question about increasing the number of mailings to the customer file from twenty to thirty times per year. I thought they were crazy until I looked at their numbers and logic. By segmenting the customer list based on past purchase activity, especially product category, recency, frequency and dollars spent with Fingerhut, we set up a year-long test using last twelve-month buyers, with at least two purchases. The control group got the standard twenty promotions for the year. The test group received thirty promotions. Merchandising supported the test with quality products and the creative team (which also reported to me) developed ten additional mailings to their already hectic creative schedule. We knew that we would increase sales, but the primary criteria for judging the test was whether we would dilute the bottom line results with marginal promotions.

The Rest of the Story! Everyone pitched in and the yearlong test was conducted. Sales increased, but more importantly, the contribution to overhead and profit met the corporate goal. The test was an overwhelming success and helped Fingerhut leapfrog to a new sales plateau from which it continued. By the time I left the catalog company, it was promoting its list over fifty times a year and looking for ways to double that number of promotions.

Changing Paradigm: Getting Greater Profits from Your Customer List

The two charts shown below **(Figure S.4)** & **(Figure S.5)** contrast the traditional method of planning a catalog campaign and a new integrated method of thinking about multi-channel customer contacts. Let us examine the two processes.

This chart shows the way many catalogs have historically thought about campaign planning. The *merchandising team* reviews the past catalog's results normally looking at the seasonal product indicators. (holiday last year compared with holiday this year, etc.) Likewise, the *creative team* kicks off the campaign about ninety days or so from the mail date, receiving input from the product people as to new items and suggested changes in creative approach. Togeth-

The Old Paradigm: Traditional Catalog Campaign Planning

TRADITIONAL CATALOG CAMPAIGN PLANNING

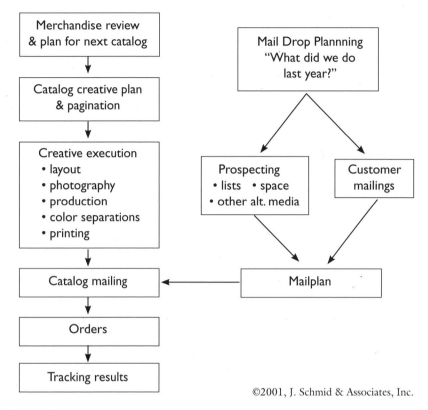

©2001, J. Schmid & Associates, Inc.

Figure S.4

er, these two groups generally develop the pagination and proceed with the catalog design, copy, photography and page production.

On another planet, (or so it would seem), the marketing department, or people responsible for *circulation planning*, look at the budget for the year and what occurred last year. The 'What Did We Do Last Year' syndrome is unfortunately the primary method of determining how a new campaign will be planned. There generally is little contact between circulation and creative until the production people (those responsible for printing the catalog) ask how many pieces are being mailed. That input usually takes place well along the creative process, with little or no thought about versioning, personalization or special offers. Circulation determines what prospect mailings, if any, will be mailed and similarly plans how many mailings will go to customers and how deep to mail the house list.

If everyone is quite good at doing their respective jobs, this process works okay. Each team pays strict attention to the results from the previous season's (or year's) activity and life is good, profits are reasonable and the catalog continues to grow.

The New Paradigm: Integrating Merchandise, Creative, Database and Circulation in Multi-Channel Campaign Planning

MULTI-CHANNEL CAMPAIGN PLANNING

REVIEW
previous year's catalog & Internet results

Merchandise Sales

Media & Email Results

Critique Creative (catalog, website & email)

ANALYZE DATABASE:
- consumer buyers
- business buyers
- house prospects (inquiries)
- lifetime value (LTV)

Merchandise & Creative Planning
- marked-up book
- squinch analysis
- web/e-email results

Preliminary Contact Strategy (mail & email)
- RFM
- No. of contacts, by media
- offers
- tests

Organization & paginization for new catalog

PRELIMINARY
Integrated Circulation Plan

Creative Execution (catalog, website & email)

Refined Contact Plan
- Customer mailings
- Push emails
- Outside lists
- Space advertising
- Affiliate marketing plan

FINAL
Integrated Circulation Plan

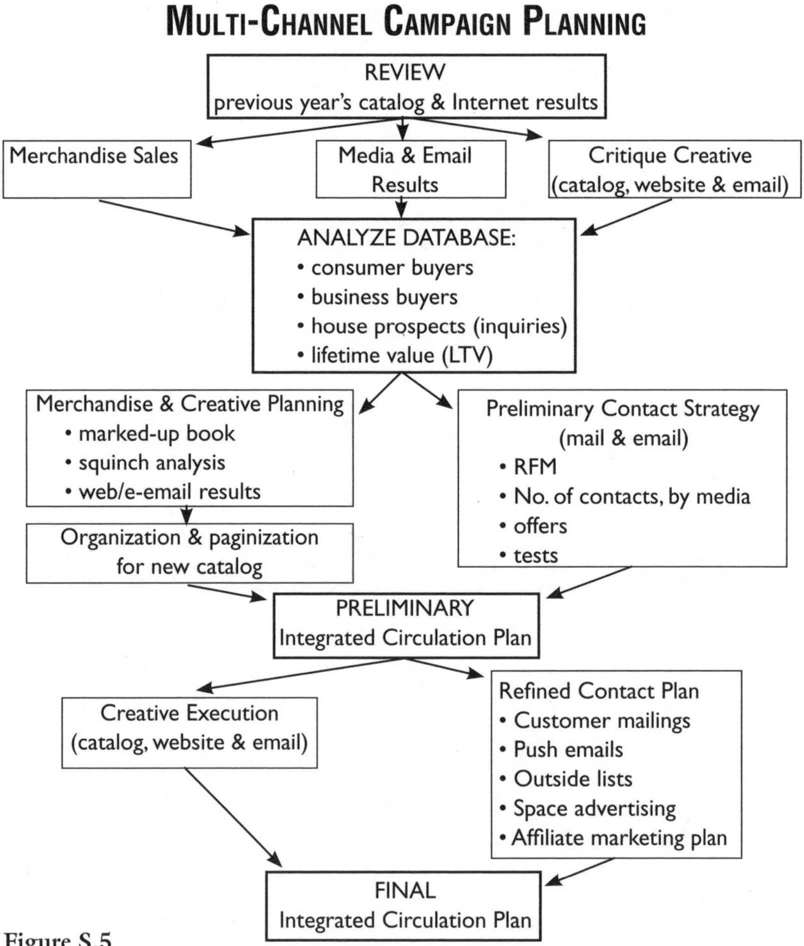

Figure S.5

©2001, J. Schmid & Associates, Inc.

14

This figure shows quite a different approach to planning a customer contact campaign. Let's review how this process differs from the traditional approach. The first difference is that instead of every team working in its own little world, the campaign planning is done on an integrated basis. Results of all aspects of last season's or last year's mail campaigns, email campaigns, Website activity, store promotions and other types of contacts are analyzed by:

1. Merchandise results (item sales, dollar sales and square inch analysis by item, product category, price point, etc.).

2. Media results from direct channels (list response, other new customer acquisition efforts via the Internet, space, email efforts, TV, package insert, card decks, customer referrals, etc.) and from store promotions.

3. Creative critique analyzing why certain design or photo treatments sold better than others and looking at square inch analysis to determine how to improve catalog, website, email and store promotion productivity.

A second difference that dramatically varies from the traditional planning is taking a step backward and looking at the customer database for key indicators of how the customer list can be better segmented to improve results. Building an RFMP chart (recency, frequency, monetary and product category) can provide inquiring marketers with amazing information with which to specialize their communication messages.

A third difference is to plan, as a team, the merchandising, creative and marketing approach to reaching customers. Instead of having a simple five-line mail plan, you will find that you're looking at problem and opportunity segments and totally changing the manner in which you communicate with customers. All selling channels, mail, email, Internet and store, need to be planned and integrated to produce optimum results.

Conclusion

The good news is that RFM works! It is a tried and true methodology that is infinitely applicable to the new concept of multichannel direct marketing. There is, however, some bad news. The bad news is that few direct selling companies are doing it well or have taken RFM to as complete a level as they might across all channels. This book has the chance to rectify all that by redefining RFM and going beyond past boundaries. Give it a good read and see if it doesn't change your way of thinking about how you keep in touch with your customers.

Jack Schmid, Chairman
J. Schmid & Associates, Inc.
Mission, Kansas
August 2005

Chapter 1 Recency

RECENCY CHARACTERISTICS: LIBEY

Recency is *when* a customer last purchased. It is an indicator of timing and freshness. As an aggregate of all customers, by individual channel and by all channels combined, it is a primary measurement of business vitality and, by extension, one indication of the valuation of the business. By itself, it is arguably the most important indicator of the cardinal three: recency, frequency and monetary value.

Recency describes a state of a customer's being. Customers exist in one of three states of being **(Figure L1.1)**. All businesses or people who have never bought from you in any channel are future customers and the state is *potential*. All businesses or people who have bought from you in any channel are current customers and the state is *active*. All businesses and people who bought from you in any channel in the past but are no longer buying are lapsed customers and the state is *inactive*.

Within the three states of being, there exist combinations of channel states. You may have a customer who is an active catalog channel customer, but an inactive web channel customer. Similarly, you may have an active catalog channel customer who remains a

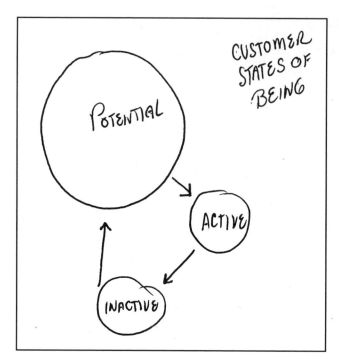

Figure L1.1

potential web channel customer. The state of recency in each channel can describe either a migration of the customer or a potential opportunity. If we accept the fact that a recent customer is good, then perhaps a migrated, multi-channel recent customer is better than a single channel recent customer.

The process of direct marketing uses the vast universe of potential customers to create a growing sub-universe of active customers. Keeping those active customers active is the constant objective; otherwise they dissipate into the inactive state. Keeping an active single channel customer active is, however, very different from keeping an active multi-channel customer active in all channels. A migrated customer may, in fact, have dissipated into the inactive state in one or more channels, and that may or may not be a bad thing depending on the current state of channel behavior. If a customer migrated from the catalog and retail channels to only the web channel, but doubled the level of spending in doing so, then the migration was positive and the state of being was improved. However, if that customer migrated and reduced the level of spending by half, then the migration was negative and the state of being was diminished. *The point: It is no longer enough to measure the state of recency of the customer alone. The customer's recency must be qualitatively and comparatively measured and evaluated across all channels.* And once the state of being is evaluated, it is necessary to determine where, when and how the customer should be directed in the future for a higher and more beneficial evolution of channel migration.

Only three sources exist from which to create active customers **(Figure L1.2)**: They are recruited from the universe of potential customers (businesses or people who have never bought from you); or they are enticed back from the inactive customer state (people who once bought from you but have stopped); or they are recruited inter-channel from competitors or intra-channel from existing customers (businesses or people who may buy from you in one chan-

Figure L1.2

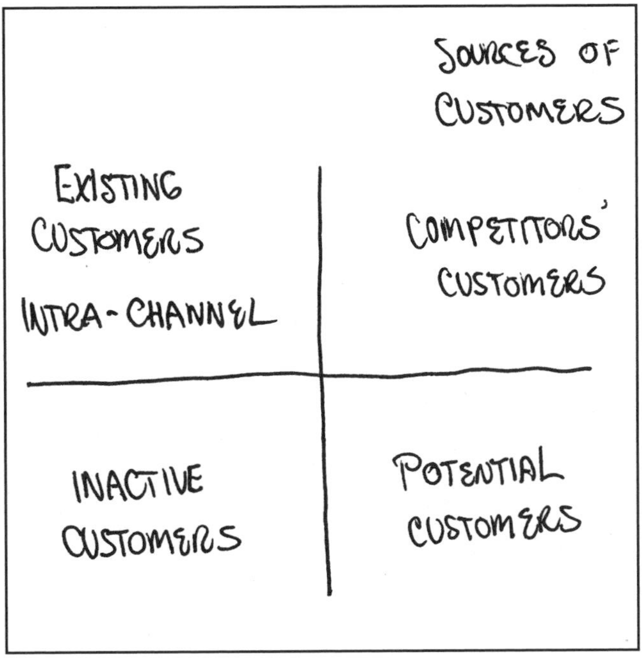

SOURCES OF CUSTOMERS

EXISTING CUSTOMERS INTRA-CHANNEL

COMPETITORS' CUSTOMERS

INACTIVE CUSTOMERS

POTENTIAL CUSTOMERS

nel but can be beneficially recruited into a new channel). This last source is new for most direct marketers and is an outgrowth of the multi-channel revolution. To some degree, it is either an external or internal cannibalization, but one that potentially both recruits and migrates customers beneficially. It also adds an entirely new level of complexity to the game.

Logic would dictate that the true definition of direct or any other channel of marketing is *creating and keeping customers*. The objective is to fill the active state with as many customers as possible, old and new. If every customer would buy every day, you would have a clockwork, perpetual motion money machine. Every customer would be recent and life would be simple, and all customers would be recent regardless of their channel.

Reduced to the essence of mastery, this is what the rare Master Marketer does: excels at recency. Only that rare rainmaker is able to squeeze thousands upon thousands of new and repeat customers into an ever-freshened active state of being, across each individual channel.

Recency also describes the state of the customer's awareness, that diffuse awareness that has come to be known as *top-of-the-mind*. Different levels and intensities of awareness of products, brands, vendors, prices and all other elements of recognition merchandising exist in the mind of the customer, and all at the same time. Say the word 'stapler' and I think Swingline; say 'ice cream' and I think butter pecan. Ice cream is a near-daily recurring awareness of a product; Swingline is a semi-annual awareness of a brand. They are very different types of awareness and are tied to very different types of recency. Plus, Swingline is a sometime business-to-business brand awareness, and butter pecan is a daily consumer product awareness. But both are, in their own way, top-of-mind.

A customer who routinely purchases *The Wall Street Journal* every morning exhibits a back-of-the-mind awareness that drives a *regular* state of recency. Reading *The Wall Street Journal* has become a habit. The same customer who purchases *The Financial Times* now and then based on impulse exhibits a middle-of-the-mind awareness that drives a *periodic* state of recency. And the same customer who hears about a special feature article in the latest issue of *Forbes* and rushes out to buy a copy exhibits a top-of-mind awareness that drives an *episodic* state of recency. The customer has a high recency level relative to *The Wall Street Journal,* a middle recency level relative to *The Financial Times,* and a low recency level relative to *Forbes.* However, that customer has a low intensity level for *The Wall Street Journal,* a middle intensity level for *The Financial Times,* and a high intensity level for *Forbes.* Interestingly, the high intensity purchase of *Forbes* may only consist of one issue a year while the low intensity purchase of *The Wall Street Journal* may consist of 250 daily issues a year. Recency that is episodic is generally the least valuable indicator of customer loyalty. Recency that is periodic is better, but not optimum. Recency that is regular is coveted by marketers (**Figure L1.3**).

Figure L1.3

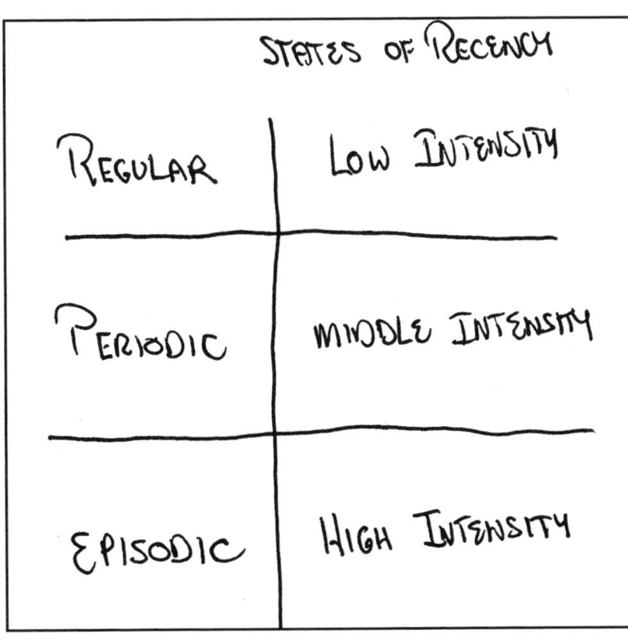

STATES OF RECENCY

REGULAR	LOW INTENSITY
PERIODIC	MIDDLE INTENSITY
EPISODIC	HIGH INTENSITY

Another way to conceive of recency is to think of it as affirmation. If a customer purchases a pair of shoes from your shoe company once in a lifetime, that customer has made an episodic affirmation of loyalty. If, however, that customer purchases a pair of shoes every ten years from your company, that customer has made a periodic affirmation of loyalty. But, if that customer purchases a pair of shoes from your company every year, that customer has made a regular affirmation of loyalty. You cannot count on the episodic affirmations of loyalty; you can only marginally count on the periodic affirmations of loyalty; however, you *can* count on the regular affirmations of loyalty and take them to the bank.

Marketers are constantly searching for ways to migrate customers from episodic and periodic affirmations of recency to regular, repeat affirmations of recency. Master Marketers elevate this process and search for ways to create high intensity, regular affirmations of recency. And, on the Highest Ground, Master Multi-Level Marketers are creating high intensity, regular affirmations of recency in multiple channels for *each* customer and for *all* customers.

A customer who buys *The Wall Street Journal* every day and exhibits a low intensity is simply affirming loyalty. Raised to the next level—high intensity—that customer will not only constantly reinforce self-loyalty but, when repeatedly satisfied, will bring additional, new customers into a state of regular recency. And, when that affirming, satisfied loyalty is recruiting or even cannibalizing across multiple channels, the levels of customer loyalty, affirmation, retention and value increase at a faster rate than was possible with only one channel. In this way, recency is regeneration. Every consecutive time a purchase is made in any channel, the customer is regenerating. If the regeneration process is static, the level of intensity is low. If, however, the regeneration process is dynamic, the level of intensity is high. And, when the regeneration process is dynamic across all channels, the level of intensity is optimal.

Customers who buy *The Wall Street Journal* every day only for news may exhibit a low intensity, static regeneration, affirmation of loyalty. But customers who buy because of a desire to track the price of their stock portfolios exhibit a higher intensity, more dynamic regeneration, affirmation of loyalty. Those customers *desire* to be recent. And if direct marketing companies will allow that desiring to be done sometimes in print, and sometimes online, and sometimes through television, and sometimes at a kiosk, and sometimes by telephone, and sometimes by retail stores, then the customers become more and more satisfied through multi-channels of self-selectable access and elevate their recency, frequency, monetary value, retention, regeneration and lifetime value. *These* are the customers coveted by companies; *these* are the companies coveted by customers.

Another differentiating and little-recognized aspect of recency is whether it is compelled. Compelled recency is preferable to non-compelled recency. Among coffee drinkers, dependency on caffeine compels regular recency of a higher intensity than that of non-coffee drinkers who purchase coffee only for periodic or episodic dinner guests. As a marketer of coffee, you can count on the daily, compelling need for caffeine to regenerate the regular affirmation of loyalty and the recency of purchase. In the business-to-business realm of multi-channel direct marketing, the labor law poster is a unique and interesting example of a product that compels recency. Whenever laws change, either federal or state, new labor law posters are compelled by legislation to be displayed. Fines for not displaying the posters in the workplace further compel purchase and, therefore, recency through compliance. In the consumer realm of marketing, deodorant is a socially compelled product. Smelling good is good; smelling bad is bad. Therefore, deodorant is compelled by society and regular purchases occur driving either product or brand affirmation and recency. In both realms, certain products must be purchased due to the demands of function. Business cards

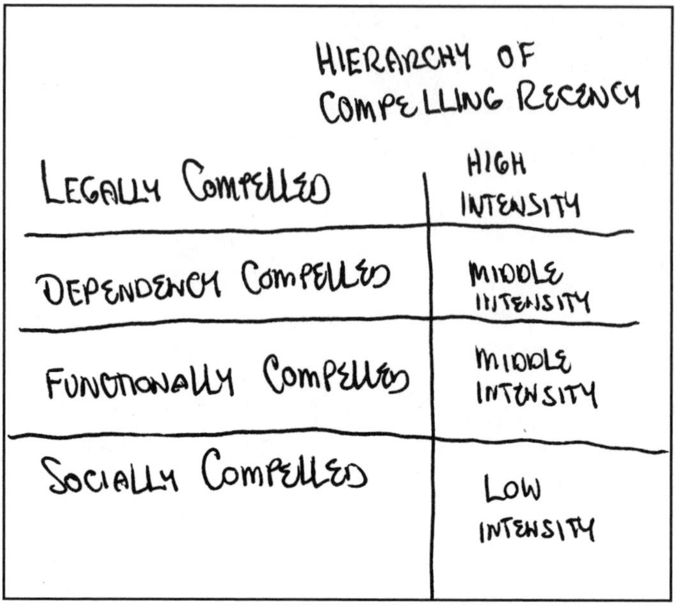

Figure L1.4

are functionally required; so are light bulbs. All compelled products and, therefore, compelled recency fall generally into four categories: legally compelled; dependency compelled; functionally compelled; and socially compelled. Further, this also appears to be the hierarchy of compelling recency (**Figure L1.4**). Legally compelled products have the highest intensity; dependency and functionally compelled products have a middle intensity; and socially compelled products have the lowest intensity. Yet, *any* compelled product has a potentially higher intensity of recency than a non-compelled product, absent fad or emotional demand characteristics. *The point: Businesses with products that are compelled are more attractive than business with products that are not compelled.* The attraction is due to recency and usually high gross margin driving above average earnings.

The recency ideal, then, is a high-margin, compelled, dynamic, high intensity, multi-channel, regular affirmation of satisfied loyalty. Customers who are energized and compelled to demonstrate their loyalty and satisfaction through continual purchases across multiple channels are superb customers and the ones you want to keep.

RECENCY CHARACTERISTICS: PICKERING

Recency is to the direct marketer what the pulse is to the human heartbeat. It is the measurement of the heartbeat, which in our business is the marketing effort. If you don't have a reasonably sized group that makes up your recent customer segments, little else matters.

For business-to-business marketers, recency can be looked at two different ways: it is when an individual last made a purchase or, as some companies do in parallel with individual level recency, it is when the *company* last made a purchase. (Companies that only maintain RFM at the company level are generally using legacy systems and are courting disaster.)

Why does individual versus company (or site) level recency matter? It matters because, unlike in consumer direct marketing, within one organization you could have many, sometimes many tens or hundreds of possible decision makers and purchasers. If a site is in your most recent segment, zero- to three-months, but you have several other individuals at the site who have recency of thirteen plus months or more, what does that say? If you generally have one decision maker at a buying site, it says that there have been several individuals who have moved on from the buying authority into other positions. If you can sell to more than one person within the organization it says that you have many lapsed buyers and you have to figure out if they are still there or if they have exited the organization.

Some products, particularly those that are more durable or higher in cost or complexity may have many people involved in the purchase decision-making process. There may be a technical product specifier, a technical approver, a business approver with authority to authorize a purchase above a certain cost level, or a purchasing agent. In this case, if you are only talking to the purchasing agent, you may not be getting all the information that you can into the hands of others who are playing key roles in the decision-making process and you may want to consider segmenting on the house file circulation side by company level RFM. If the company bought within the active time frame, all contacts on the database fall into the circulation plan.

On the prospecting side, for higher complexity or higher cost items, if you have a prospect at a recent buying site, you may want to take extra measures to make sure that they get into the circulation plan. As with many things in life, though, it is best to do this in moderation. If you have thirty percent or more of your prospecting circulation going to existing buying sites, you run the risk of not bringing in enough new sites. Balance is key and the proper balance can be determined through testing.

For products that have lower price points or lower costs, often consumable or commodity items, recency takes on a much different effect. If you are marketing office products into small- to medium-sized business and you have two buyers at a site, one with a three-month recency and one with a thirteen plus month recency, what you likely have is the current person in charge of purchasing and their predecessor. In this case, the older buyers at active buying sites will not perform as well, and any catalog (or flyer or telephone call or email) that might have been intended for them is probably better directed toward acquiring a new site.

With the different levels of recency (individual versus site) and how recency can mean different things for different types of products, it is critical for your understanding of the health of your buyer file to know how recency should be applied to your particular business. The principles are constant, but the correct application is the key.

RECENCY AND INTUITIVE KNOWLEDGE: LIBEY

To understand the future, look to the past. Our present multi-channel marketing sophistication is essentially a high volume, automated version of the intuitive processes used by nineteenth century peddlers. The peddler was, perhaps, the most efficient marketer in our commercial history. With virtually no technology, the peddler maintained a complex customer database in memory and updated it on every sales call and with every purchase. The peddler knew who purchased what on the previous trip through town, what was asked for on that trip, and could predict accurately what would most likely be bought on the next trip. For each customer on the circuit (*circu*-lation), the peddler amassed large amounts of information, from the customers themselves and from the gossip of the customers' neighbors. All of that knowledge was filed in memory and used to predict the next purchase of each customer and to gauge the likely product interest and dollar value of the sale. The end result was the peddler purchased inventory on an informed basis that assured having the exact products the customers wanted when they wanted them, and the peddler was assured of sales at every stop. The individual and aggregate customers were maintained at a high level of recency and were retained in the active, dynamic state. All of this data collecting *cum* analysis was the art of the peddler's business; transforming it into knowledge and, finally, into wisdom that created sales was the intuitive skill. And nothing yet has replaced intuitive knowledge of the customer as a primary characteristic of successful marketing. We are still traveling down a dirt road, driving a horse-drawn wagon, catching a glimpse of a farmhouse in the distance, and saying to ourselves, "Let's see . . . The last time we were here they bought two pots, an iron skillet, twelve spools of thread, six needles and a bottle of liver tonic."

The peddler asked a lot of questions. Information was the key to sales. The questions seemed innocent enough: questions about planting or harvest; about the children; whether a wedding was coming soon or a birth; and all of those same questions about neighboring farm families. Any information was welcomed and from all sources. Reflecting on what was heard, analyzing and pigeonholing it for future sales was the intuitive art of the Master Peddler.

Intuitive marketing information aimed at maintaining recency has evolved through several stages beginning with the peddler's near-perfect useful knowledge, changing to the mass market broad and generalized homogenization of pseudo-knowledge in the decades from 1950 to 1980, then to the 1990's frenzy for business demographic and consumer lifestyle data maintained in relational databases, to today's model-creating, data-mining, integrated multi-channel, customer relationship managing, cooperative prospecting and proprietary customer database building arsenal. Actually, all we have done is to become better peddlers. At least, we think we have progressed. If you compare the utility—that is, the benefit versus the cost—the peddler was efficient but could generate only limited size for the business. Today, we generate size but the utility cost is disproportionately high.

The peddler's understanding of recency was simple: Every customer had to buy on every trip. The wagon made the circuit only once or twice a year. Keeping each customer recent demanded making a sale on every pass. Today, we have multiple wagons, some arriving in the mail, some by telephone, some over the web, some through search engines, some through affiliate marketing, some through retail stores; we can make more trips; we can collect more knowledge; we can go to the farm, or the farm can come to us; intuitive knowledge is more precise; recency is more recent, or it is shifting in ways we either know about and understand or that are unknown to us and mysterious.

The resulting body of intuitive knowledge collected from the selling process used to be static; that is, it was 'one size fits all.' If we collected knowledge about a business or a consumer, it was a single view of that customer. Now, that body of intuitive knowledge is dynamic in each channel. A single business or a single consumer can have one 'look' as a result of using only the catalog channel, but 'look' entirely different when using the pure web channel, or even the catalog-assisted web channel. And the customer will look totally different again when using the retail channel. *The point: Recency characteristics and intuitive knowledge are different in each of the multiple direct marketing channels, as are frequency, monetary value and other optimal cardinal elements.* One recency size no longer fits all; the customer wears a different recency wardrobe for each channel. The peddler still sees a farmhouse in the distance, but there are five other different farmhouses inside the one farmhouse that is visible. Our industry used to be a game of dominoes; now it's a Rubik's Cube.

Intuitive knowledge also implies learning about recency behavior. As a customer's recency changes, in any and all channels, there is an implied demand that marketers know those changes. Recency is never constant; it is always shifting in and out in time, back and forth between channels, to and from competitors. Learning why recency changes, at the individual customer level and at the aggregated level of all customers, is an essential part of the intuitive knowledge quotient of not only recency, but of all of RFM and beyond.

RECENCY AND INTUITIVE KNOWLEDGE: PICKERING

There needs to be an addition to the list of endangered species: the founders, owners and presidents who are also the circulation and product managers of small to mid-sized multi-channel direct marketing companies. With the attractiveness of direct marketing companies to non-direct marketing companies and to private investment groups, and the logic (real or perceived) of conglomerates of direct marketing companies, there are fewer and fewer of these 'independents.' It is popular within the halls of business schools to refer to these folks as entrepreneurs.

Each entrepreneur's story is different, but there are many common threads. Frequently they were working in the profession or industry that is the one they are trying to sell into. They managed a warehouse and now they are selling boxes, packing supplies, and safety equipment. Or they were in the agricultural industry and saw a need to build better ag-widgets, which led to a catalog of ag-widgets and ag-widget-related devices. Some saw that their customers needed and were willing to pay a premium for specialty paper to put into their laser printers to make presentations that were eye-catching and unique.

These entrepreneurs had an intimate knowledge of the specifiers and users needs. They knew *who* was the right kind of person to buy the product, *what* type of products they needed, *when* they needed them, about *how* quickly consumables were consumed and durables wore out or became obsolete. They knew the competitors' offerings and where their strengths and weaknesses were. These abilities became so ingrained within the entrepreneur that they seemed to be able to divine or intuit what the next wave was going to be.

Another unique characteristic of entrepreneurs: they were there for the long haul. Making circulation or product decisions wasn't a two-year stint before moving into finance or operations. This was their job from now until they retired, or until someone made them an offer they couldn't refuse.

Today's business climate is different. Most of us work in companies started long ago and the entrepreneur has long since departed for warm climes. Where does that leave us? What can we do to acquire some of those skills that the successful entrepreneurs have? Consider the skill of intuition.

Intuition is simply knowing something without the need for conscious thought. Ancient Samurai warriors practiced their stance and their countermoves for hours on end. Their practice so ingrained these motions that they became second nature. They could intuit their opponents' moves and without conscious thought use the appropriate counter.

For the thinking direct marketing practitioner *intuition can be acquired*. To acquire this high skill level, you need access to the correct type of data and the time and commitment to study it. Learn the basics of both RFM and of the company that you work for and you will go far. And I posit that if you spend enough time learning something that it will work like intuition.

One of recency's strongest virtues is that it lets us, the marketers, know that the individual is there—alive—making decisions about purchases, and has the wherewithal to pay for those purchases. The better the recency, the more likely it is that the customer looks like they did when they made their purchase.

This may seem elementary, but the *first* battle the direct marketer has is getting the mail piece (or telephone call or email) delivered. Contrary to popular belief, getting the recipient to open the letter, catalog, or email is second. This is a challenge for consumer direct marketers as well as business-to-business direct marketers.

The consumer direct marketer has a climate and some tools that are more favorable than those that face the business-to-business marketer. Most consumer mailers are targeting households where there are only one or two people with purchase authority. If they move, the consumer direct marketer changes the address, often using address hygiene tools like the USPS provided National Change of Address (NCOA) file or the Address Correction Service (ACS). There are even proprietary Change of Address (COA) files that can use different sources (like periodical delivery) and looser matching rules than NCOA. And if a buyer or prospect moves, that may increase their likelihood to respond, especially if your offer is credit related or pertains to household furnishings or any of the myriad things someone who has just moved may need.

For the business-to-business marketer, there are two types of moves: the first is a company move; the second is when an individual exits the company (to go to another company, retire, etc.). These are very different circumstances and require different responses.

When an entire company moves, it often will do the same thing that consumers do: fill out a Change of Address form at the USPS. At one point this was not very meaningful for business-to-business direct marketers because of the changes returned about one-third were useful. The USPS has changed and improved the way that they maintain NCOA for businesses and today it can be helpful and effective.

The move of an individual out of a company is a much more urgent issue for the business-to-business direct marketer. In most instances there is a new individual who is taking over that job or at least taking on those responsibilities. The key is knowing how to find that new individual?

Intuition may lead you to look at the job title of the person who was in that position, or the job title that is most used among your recent customers. Intuition is a good thing and an effective way of keeping up with who is buying your product. It underscores a very important need, however: capturing as frequently as possible the job title.

You have a customer, John C. Waldron, and John is a good and regular customer. He will sometimes migrate from the one- to three-month segment to the four- to six-month segment, but John is usually good for two or three purchases a year.

Then you stop hearing from John. He eventually migrates into the seven- to twelve-month range. You pull his data and you see that he was the Human Resources director. So, the next time you get ready to mail him the addressing looks like this:

John C. Waldron
Or Human Resources Director
Hornet Enterprises
123 Main Street
Midway, TX 75850

This simple device, of ink jetting the title, can help get the catalog to the right desk at the right time and keep the recency recent. It starts with a conversation with the telesales representatives to impress upon them the need to capture title. And it continues with I.T. to make sure that they have fields set up to capture this data and, if you are very fortunate, to have the ability to codify it for analysis and selection purposes.

There are many different ways that following your intuition can help you become a more effective marketer. Intuition rarely involves making guesses detached from a basis of knowledge. The 'gut feel' may be attractive, but time spent understanding your customer file, understanding a single purchase—repeated thousands of times—will allow you to make decisions that seem intuitive, but are based on much hard work.

To paraphrase an old hand in direct marketing: *Prepare to be intuitive.*

RECENCY AND TIME: LIBEY

At what time interval should a customer purchase from you to meet the ideal goal of a compelling, dynamic, high intensity, regular, multi-channel affirmation of loyalty?

If you are *The Wall Street Journal*, recency time can be defined as daily for newsstand buyers or annually for subscribers. Recency time is a function of the preferred method of purchasing the product or the preferred method of delivery or fulfillment. For those who prefer to pick up the paper daily and pay cash, recency is daily; those who prefer to subscribe for a year and receive the paper in the mail, recency is annual. Viewed only this way, recency is when money is paid.

Right away, interesting things can be seen. If recency is daily, there is the risk that the customer will buy another paper instead. To reduce that risk, the annual subscription locks in short-term retention and eliminates the need for a daily reaffirmation of loyalty. Daily recency also requires that the customer has cash each day;

if not, a sale is missed. Annual recency eliminates lost sales due to lack of pocket change; the paper arrives regardless of cash on hand. Perhaps annual recency is more stable than daily recency.

But a newspaper is different from most other product purchases. It is, by definition, a *daily* recency product just as a weekly magazine is a weekly recency product and a monthly magazine is a monthly recency product. How do we equate recency and time to the thousands of business or consumer customer relationships and the products that drive those relationships? When in time must a customer buy to be optimally recent?

The optimal recency time for newspapers may be daily. But what if the product is bridges across the Mississippi River? In the bridge-building business, a recent customer may be every one hundred years. *Recency and time are directly linked to the product usage rate.* If there is no newspaper purchase in thirty days, the customer is probably reading Google News online. But if a state has not bought a bridge in fifty years, there may be an order coming sometime in the next five decades.

Thinking, then, only of recency and time, what would you say is an acceptable time period for reaffirming recency for the following products?

peanuts	automobile	gallbladder surgery
IRA	flowers	term life insurance
golf clubs	business checks	personal checks
termite control	bread	fly rod
watch	vitamins	forklift
carpet	diamond	toothpaste
opera tickets	puppy	gasoline
baby crib	cruise	wheelbarrow
headstone	cell phone	bottle of wine
postage	warehouse racks	mailing labels
chain saw	ski mask	cabin in the woods

Some products are only purchased once, such as headstones and gallbladder surgery. For those, recency becomes familial or multigenerational. Other products depend entirely on the consumption rate, such as a bottle of wine, bread, peanuts, toothpaste, gasoline or business and personal checks. Others are event driven, such as diamonds for engagements and anniversaries, baby cribs for births, or opera tickets for a special night out. Some products are causation-driven, such as termite control, carpet or warehouse racks. Yet, others are more impulse or interest-driven, such as golf clubs, puppies, fly rods, and cruises. A few products cross a number of boundaries, such as flowers which may be event-driven, as for anniversaries or illness, or could be causation-driven, as for landscaping a home, or possibly impulse-driven, such as a bouquet when you forgot an anniversary. *The point: Establishing acceptable recency time is measurable based on usage rates and the purchase drivers.*

Obviously, recency varies relative to time, product usage and the reason for the purchase. Understanding those variances relative to product selection, new product introduction, old product retirement, product mix, product pricing, and product positioning—by channel, by customer—is a distinguishing characteristic of a Master Marketer. If your customers purchase a large variety of products from you, they may be self-classifying the type of product and the usage rate and then self-determining which channel to purchase them from. For example, I'll purchase $35 fly fishing line from L.L. Bean's catalog. I may go to the website to purchase a $400 fly rod. I likely will want to go to the retail store to buy a $3,000 canoe **(Figure L1.5)**. Those purchases are, respectively, a consumption rate purchase, an event purchase, and a multigenerational purchase. Somehow, I need to be understood for recency based on all three individual purchases, not just the most recent purchase, particularly if it is the canoe. Sell me more fly line in three months via the catalog and email, entice me to the website for another rod in a year, but don't ask me to buy another

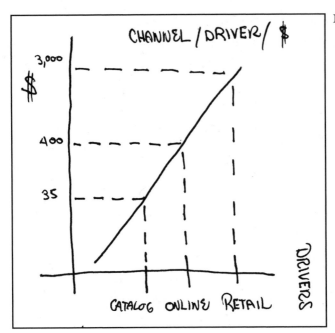

Figure L1.5

canoe soon on the web. And, above all, *learn* from what I buy, how I buy it, when I buy it, for whom I buy it, and what that all means and predicts.

Fully using recency as a foundation on which to hang so much intuitive information is complex. There has to be an acceptable method of categorization and classification of customers. There must also be an acceptable measuring protocol, device and universal terminology describing the multi-channel state of recency for each customer and all customers. There must be a reporting mechanism that allows 'what is' queries as well as 'what if' constructs. And these reports must be replicable at will. Recency has to be looked at from many points of view in all channels. More important, it must be understood—empirically—from the customer experience. In the simplest form, this translates to the customer database and the customer segmentation methodology.

RECENCY AND TIME: PICKERING

Why does time matter for the direct marketer? Time matters both in relative terms (like one to three month recency), and absolute terms (March or October). For example, time of year when the purchase is made makes a difference. If you are selling snow shovels, sidewalk de-icer and the like, your one- to three-month recency doesn't look so full in August. This does not mean the company is in trouble, this is how the business operates. So the propensity to purchase these products is based on the time of year. Frequently this effect is referred to as *seasonality*.

Many products can be classified as seasonal. Some easy examples are holiday greeting cards and wrapping paper, holiday food gifts, cold weather gear, warm weather gear, tax-related accounting forms; the list is probably longer than you first imagined. These are fairly obvious examples, and equally obvious is the appropriate time to mail. For products like de-icer, snow shovels and cold-weather items, sometime in the early fall is the best time to mail. And you may start the mailing sooner based on region: Maine will have demand for shovels and warm coats earlier in the fall than Missouri.

What about a consumable commodities mailer, like office products, packaging materials, gourmet coffee, janitorial and sanitation products? Don't people need paper and staplers in January as much as in June? Schools consume much in the way of office supplies, and their demand is often seasonal. October and January are great buying times for schools based on the availability of various federal funds as well as state and local tax transfers. Analogously, churches are in considerably better shape to make purchases in January (after large Christmas attendance) and in late Spring, after Easter. So, even a commodities mailer whose products seem to have no seasonality can have significant pockets of customers who have seasonality to them.

To illustrate the point, let's look at a typical distribution of buyers of office commodities (**Figure P1.1**). Let's compare the overall distribution to the distribution of a certain segment, in this case, education.

	Recency	Overall % of Active Buyers	% of Education Buyers
Q1	1-3	55%	65%
Q4	4-6	13%	11%
Q3	7-9	9%	9%
Q2	10-12	6%	4%
Q1	13-15	5%	3%
Q4	16-18	4%	3%
Q3	19-21	4%	3%
Q2	22-24	4%	2%
		100%	100%

Figure P1.1

We can observe several things. First of all, there is a high concentration in the most recent segments. This is good and is usually the indication of aggressive circulation. However, what jumps off the page the most is how much more of the education market is in the most recent bucket. A full ten percentage points more, or almost a twenty percent lift over the average of all buyers. This shows that promotions targeted toward the education market in the first quarter keeps these buyers recent and active.

As a corollary, the education market has a smaller percentage of records in prior quarters, even high response quarters like Q4 and Q1 because *many of those buyers were brought forward into the recent quarter.* Bringing those buyers forward is the goal of house file circulation. Easy to determine, not always as easy to achieve.

Recency will also vary based on what types of products you are selling. A high dollar, highly durable product, like home or office furniture, water coolers, fax machines, generators or lawnmowers will have a very different recency distribution than what we saw with consumables. Marketers whose product offerings consist mostly or entirely of durable products will often draw their line of active buyers at twenty-four months or even thirty-six months. Here is a typical recency distribution of customers of durable goods marketers: **(Figure P1.2)**

Recency	Percentage
1-3	8.0%
4-6	8.1%
7-9	8.4%
10-12	7.1%
13-15	11.5%
16-18	10.0%
19-21	9.9%
22-24	6.6%
25-27	8.6%
28-30	7.6%
31-33	8.3%
34-36	5.9%

Figure P1.2

As with the consumable example, we can see several things from this distribution. The most obvious is that there is a more even distribution of buyers between the quarters and that the distribution goes further back. Why is this distribution of recency so different between consumables marketers and durable marketers? This is where the linkage to other parts of RFM comes into play.

We can see from recency that it is likely that there is a greater interval between purchases for these buyers. How do marketers survive these longer time periods between purchases? Generally, because of somewhat better margins than many commodity consumable products and frequently because of higher average order values (AOV). We will see more of this in subsequent chapters.

With more time between purchases, the house file circulation problem changes. With more consumable and commoditized products it is frequently about circulating to existing buyers regularly and often. With more durable products the circulation problem becomes more one of timing: what is the optimal interval of catalog mailings that yields the most response? This is especially important as the cost of larger catalogs, which are more common for durables goods marketers, makes the costs of circulation high.

Many marketers have products with purchase cycles that are event driven to a degree. Consider those marketers who sell dated business forms. In the late 1990s, businesses were looking at their stocks of forms and noticed the date fields, which often had a space that looked like this:

_____, 19__

Obviously these wouldn't be as useful and time saving after December 31, 1999. Thus, the end of the millennium created a spike in demand for these types of forms to be replenished. This catalyst to purchase brought forward many buyers before their stocks would normally have been depleted. Thus, an event unrelated to the depletion affected the time between purchases and brought buyers into more recent time frames than normal. The skilled direct marketer sees this and makes adjustments to their house file circulation; this blip doesn't signal a change in the norm of recency distributions, rather, it is an extraordinary event.

What are other extraordinary events that could bring buyers forward? Or delay purchases? Here is a list of a few:

Natural disasters like hurricanes;

Changes to world security like 9/11 or the invasion of Iraq;

Changes to minimum wage or labor law;

New or modified mandates for safety equipment;

Introduction of new computer hardware or software;

Elections.

To gauge the difference between events that change the paradigm and extraordinary events, you have to be a student of recency. As an example, most catalogers who have been in their position four years or more can attest to the fact that October and early November are poor response months during a presidential election year. After the election (the delayed 2000 election results notwithstanding) pent-up demand will unleash itself. This manifested itself yet again in the fall of 2004 and will again in 2008. This is not to say avoid mailing in the fall of an election year. It may mean paying more attention to the in-home date and perhaps shifting some prospecting volumes toward later in the season.

RECENCY AND THE CUSTOMER DATABASE: LIBEY

Database technology is neither mystical nor arcane. There are those who would have the database seem mystical and arcane because they have a vested interest in keeping it that way. Actually, databases are nothing more than shoeboxes.

Years ago, peddlers scribbled customer information notes on 3 x 5 cards and filed them alphabetically by customer name in a shoebox. Every purchase was recorded, including the date, the product, the price, personal details to trigger future sales, gossip picked up from neighbors, and other details supporting future sales and recency. Every time a sale was made, the card was pulled and updated and refiled in the box. Before a sales call was made, the card was consulted and the intuitive knowledge brought top-of-mind for the crafty peddler. Children's names, color preferences, sizes, birthdays,

41

returns, income and all manner of useful information was recorded to assist the peddler in making another sale now, or on future trips. The hearts and souls of the customers were contained in those shoeboxes.

Now, it should be recognized that not every peddler used the shoebox method; only a few mastered this technology. The rest proceeded from place to place guided by the seat of their pants, relying on serendipity or luck. But the shoebox peddlers were successful where others failed. They employed knowledge rather than charm, and knowledge always wins. They were actually the first true merchandisers because they knew what the customer wanted before the customer knew and they knew where, when, why and how to present those products to each customer to assure a sale.

Today's advanced database technologies are basically file cards in a shoebox. For all of our sophistication and technological advancement we still scribble notations on the customer cards whenever we make a sales call and whenever someone buys from us. And, we are interested in the same information that the nineteenth century peddler captured. It is interesting that the peddlers experienced the same technology demands we experience today. At some point, they found they needed more memory for their shoebox databases. Their solution: they doubled the memory by moving up to 5 x 6 cards. Does anyone remember the early Remington Rand Cardex systems used for customer files?

The method of organizing the customer database is, essentially, alphabetically by name. We use phone numbers, customer numbers and other identification notations, but we find a single customer by sorting in one way or another. The end result is still the same: we get the information we need to make another sale. One component of that information is recency.

Where the peddler had one shoebox, we have multiple shoeboxes. We may have one for catalog customers, one for retail customers, one for web customers, one for email customers, one for infomercial customers, and so on. Where the peddler made notes on one card, we may be making notes on five cards, as well as cross-notes on all cards. When we get a catalog order, we note it on the customer's card in the catalog shoebox. We also note it on the customer's card in the web shoebox, because last time that customer bought through the website. And we note it on the card in the infomercial shoebox and the one in the retail shoebox, because the customer has bought in those channels also. It's important. We need to know everything. It just might come in handy. After all, we're obsessed with this stuff.

The peddler, preparing the wagon for a swing through the territory, would go through the customer cards and redistribute them into a logical route format—the *circulation plan*—that ordered the trip and the information about the customers to be contacted on that trip—or the *contact strategy*. Perhaps only those customers who had purchased every year for the past five years would be called on during that year's trip. Perhaps only those customers who purchased something two years ago but had not purchased anything during last year's trip would be called on. If the peddler was trying to expand the business, perhaps people who had never bought, living close to customers who had bought regularly, would be squeezed in between customer calls. A number of choices were available to the peddler depending on the business strategy and the accurate knowledge of customer history found in the shoebox.

Once the peddler had selected the customers to be visited, the cards were put in traveling order. Villages and settlements would be scheduled and allocated against the available number of days for the trip. Customers and prospects would be added or dropped to make the route efficient, particularly with regard to expected sales and profits. No successful peddler ever traveled a random route trusting to serendipity or luck; successful peddlers built marketing plans, predicted product purchases, calculated predictable sales and earnings, and managed inventory, just as we do today.

The peddler made a relationship between customer purchases and trips. Over time, patterns emerged that could be relied upon to repeat. One customer might buy every trip regardless of the trip timing. Another customer bought only on the fall trip after harvest when cash was in hand. A third customer bought only every other trip, sometimes in the fall and sometimes in the spring; and a fourth bought only every other trip in the spring. Thus, the peddler understood *seasonality*. The intuitive knowledge of these patterns was built into the customer cards and ordered in the mind of the peddler through the intimate and tactile understanding of the shoebox database.

The peddler's objective was no different from the objective of the database marketer of today: to optimize sales and to generate the greatest possible profit with the least possible expenditure of resources. The shoebox system worked then, and the database system works today.

Key to the success of the shoebox and the database, however, is the recognition that the primary purpose was and is *marketing;* that is, selling more stuff to more people. The prospecting and customer databases exist first and foremost to create additional sales and to keep customers buying. They do not exist for the convenience of accountants, for generating invoices, for managing inventory, or other purposes, although these are secondary by-products of the database. Too often, too many diversions interfere when data becomes organized into information; too many parasites attach themselves to the database and obstruct the primary purpose: selling. CEOs who embrace a formulaic approach to marketing, supported by sophisticated and accurate database practices, must first swear an unwavering allegiance to marketing to their customers and reject all other unessential, non-selling noise interfering with that one dominant purpose.

The Master Marketer having control of multiple channels also has control of multiple sub-databases that accurately portray the individual channels. It must be possible to fully understand database information for the catalog channel separately from the online channel and separate from any other channel. It must also be possible to fully understand the database information for the combined databases of all channels and to be able to see changes and trends intra- and extra-channel; otherwise, how do you know where to put your money?

RECENCY AND THE CUSTOMER DATABASE: PICKERING

Database technology is neither mystical nor arcane. So says my writing partner. I would make one small modification: database technology *should be* neither mystical nor arcane. In the everyday business world, however, your database workings are sometimes mystical or arcane.

To be certain, there are more choices out there for affordable and powerful database technologies than ever before. A new cataloger can get a reasonably powerful software package for a few thousand dollars. The disconnect generally comes in the use of the systems.

We are marketers, so we think that the systems should primarily support marketing. Unfortunately, our peers in order fulfillment and accounting think that the systems should work for them. Middle ground can be found.

Looking at recency, it seems obvious that it applies to the date of most recent purchase by an individual (or a site). What happens, though, when an existing customer calls to place another order and the customer service representative (CSR) cannot quickly find the existing customer record? Often it is easier for the CSR to create a *new* record.

This duplicate record creates several problems. First, it overstates the number of customers. Secondly, it misstates the recency of buyers on your file. It also creates additional work in setting up a new account, slows down the ordering process by making the customer give data that is already resident elsewhere in the ether of the database. The duplicate record problem is frequently exacerbated by the compensation structure for CSRs. It is typical for CSR compensation to be based on volume of calls handled. If their perception is that it is faster to set up a new account, then that is what they will do. To address this problem, many marketers work with their CSR group to develop ways to improve the ordering system. Using customer numbers and finder numbers are effective ways of addressing order input issues.

You likely assign your customers a customer number of some sort. This allows look-ups, enables your relational database to access their item loop (history of products purchased), and endless other useful things. And most enlightened direct marketers print their customer number on their catalogs, frequently in a colored box.

On the prospecting side a similar process can occur. A non-permanent number can be assigned to a prospect mailing piece, much like a customer number, that will allow the database to populate name and address information into the order screen when a call is received. The problem is that all too frequently the CSRs have not been trained to ask every time for the customer or finder number. Once trained, or incentivized, CSRs can capture these numbers, which yield many benefits:

> faster, more accurate order entry;
> fewer duplicate records added to the database;
> higher key code capture rates, particularly on new customers.

In addition to trying to ensure the accuracy of recency, marketers today have more channels to track, analyze, and follow. In some systems (generally newer) it is easy to add fields to track recency by channel and in legacy systems this is sometimes quite difficult.

If you have a system that can keep a recency by channel, by all means, do so. Also contemplate what other similar data you should keep:

database recency–the recency associated with the most recent
   purchase irrespective of channel;
channel of first purchase and channel of most recent purchase;
date of first purchase.

The database recency will be the easiest to use recency and will
drive much of the segmentation. Database recency should be the
recency used when measuring overall database performance, such
as house file counts by recency.

The channel of first purchase and last purchase will be critical to
see how your customers like to purchase from you. Many catalogers
with web presence find that they are most effective acquiring new
customers via the mail, but once the initial purchase is made repeat
buyers prefer to buy via the web. To confirm that theory, simply
look at recent two-time plus buyers whose first and most recent
purchases were through the same channel versus those that migrated from one channel to another. You cannot assess this, though,
unless you have your database set up to capture and report on this
vital information.

Date of first purchase is a little used nugget of information that
can be unbelievably useful in determining house file circulation
strategies. Drilling into customers by the year of first purchase allows you to do 'vintage analysis' to see if, for example, customers
acquired in a given year perform differently than those acquired in
another year.

Consider 1998 buyers versus 1999 buyers. There was no large
scale change or shock to the system in 1998, so we can treat that as
a 'normal' year. In 1999 we were on the cusp of a change, the New
Millennium. As discussed, this led to some accelerated buying. It
also led to some different buying habits. In 1999, those catalogers
who sold goods like camping equipment, freeze-dried foods, water
purification and survival equipment, fuel storage, first aid, and power
generation products had a better than average year. Some had their

best year ever. As these customers progress and attrite through the life-cycle, they cause anomalies. Many of the purchasers were making a one-time purchase: they aren't campers by nature, but they bought a few lanterns and sleeping bags. You won't see them again. In 2000 and 2001, as these buyers progressed down through the Recency cells, it looked as though the company was doing a poor job of retention. In 2002 and 2003 it looked like there were large pools of re-activation candidates. The problem was there was the 'glut' of event driven buyers.

By using date of first purchase and creating recency reports for each year, the Master Marketer can see these anomalies. Taking this information they then begin to develop house file circulation plans that treat those buyers differently, perhaps adding additional selection criteria or redeploying circulation from these segments to more productive ones.

These examples show that a big key to understanding your database technology is getting familiar with how the data is entered, rolled-up and updated, and extracted. The Master Marketer has an understanding of all of these.

RECENCY SEGMENTATION: LIBEY

Customers are either *active* or *inactive*. An active customer is buying; an inactive customer isn't buying. While there are also *prospective* customers who have never bought and *suspects*, who may have inquired, the active and inactive customers make up the bulk of the overall customer list.

An active customer is one who has bought at least once in the 'recent' past. The definition of recent past is variable from one business to the next and from one channel to the next. Some businesses define recent past as six months, some twelve months, some two years and others three years or longer. It depends on the product and the rate of product usage as discussed earlier. However, in most direct marketing companies, a definition of an active customer has not been made, either overall or by channel. It is common to find the circulation manager defining active in one way and the owner or CEO defining active another. Similarly, sales and customer service representatives have an entirely different definition of active, as do merchandisers and returns processors. At some point, a unified definition of active customer has to be made. The continuity of analyses overall and within each channel demands a consistent, oranges and oranges definition.

In my experience, an active customer in business-to-business is one who has purchased something in the last eighteen months. This would be a conservative norm for recency if all customers from all business-to-business market sectors were combined in a blender and reduced to a common recency period. For the consumer world, I believe the common recency period would likely be twelve months. If a business customer has not purchased from you in a year-and-a-half, it is probably not an active customer any longer. If a consumer has not purchased from you in a year, that customer is likely no longer active. I tend to define active in much stricter periods of time than most, however. *The point: You need to measure and find out what the period of time is for active customer status in your business.*

There are many business-to-business companies that classify customers as active with only one purchase in three years and, while this may challenge the imagination, there are reasons. The value of the active customer is a major asset of the company; this asset is important when companies are being valued for sale. List rental quantities are another factor in defining the active customer state. The most often found reason for keeping non-buying customers in the active customer segments is denial. It is common to find owners and CEOs who choose to ignore worsening customer attrition and who conveniently extend out their definition of recent and active until they reach their personal denial comfort level. Such denial is almost always fatal.

For a reality check of recency, the filling of a bathtub serves well. When you start, you close the drain and turn on the tap. This is exactly what a new business does in each channel. As long as water runs in, the tub fills. This is the same effect as new customers flowing in and no customers going down the drain. But, if the drain is opened and water runs out, you have to increase the flow of water just to keep the same level in the tub. If the tap is turned off and the drain opened, the tub empties. That is exactly how recency works in the customer base. If first-time buyers are flowing in and keep buying, your tub fills, maybe even overflows. But, if you're losing them down the drain faster than you can fill up, you are going to go dry. Customers 'fall off the back end' or 'go down the drain' constantly and that is normal. Customers move, die, get mad, go away, close up shop, declare bankruptcy, lose interest and find any of a thousand reasons for falling off the back end of recency. If one customer a day falls off, then one customer a day must be added just to maintain the customer base at a static level. If two customers a day fall off and only one is added, the business will soon lose fifty percent of the customers, a condition generally called *death*. In its absolute form, all marketing efforts are done to ward off death.

Now, re-read the paragraph above and wherever the words 'tub' or 'customer' or 'buyers' occur, insert the word 'channel' in front. The Master Marketer is maintaining multiple tubs, all with different levels, different drain rates, different faucets and water pressures, and different capacities. In each channel 'falling off the back end' is a completely different definition; "going down the drain" means something totally different. And, just to make things fun, one channel uses bubble bath and another has rusty water. It's not easy. Obviously, it is essential to know the exact attrition rate taking place at any moment—in any channel and overall—if you are to avoid the Grim Reaper. In part, that is discovered by recency segmentation.

For our purposes here, customers will be classified as one-year, two-year, three-year, four-year or five-year buyers. This is totally arbitrary and simply helps illustrate recency segmentation with some continuity. The segments could be three-month, six-month, twelve-month, eighteen-month, twenty-four-month; or thirty-day, sixty-day, ninety-day, one hundred twenty-day, or any other segment of time that makes sense for a particular business.

The one-year buyer segment of the customer database is, in reality, a small box inside the larger shoebox (**Figure L1.6**). Inside this smaller box are all the 3 x 5 cards of all the customers who have bought at any time in the last twelve months. If there has been a purchase of any kind in the past 365 days, those customer cards have been pulled, updated and re-filed in the smaller one-year box inside the larger shoebox. When the marketer wants to refresh the memory as to who has bought something in the last year, the little box can be lifted out of the shoebox, opened up, and all the customer index cards can be reviewed.

The two-year buyer segment of the customer database is, similarly, another small box inside the shoebox (**Figure L1.7**). It contains

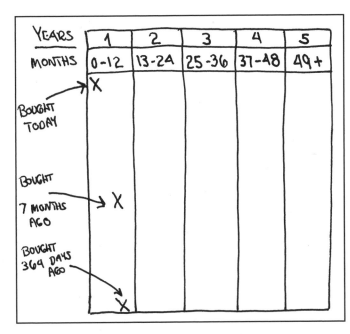

Figure L1.6

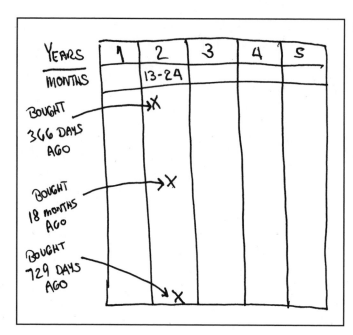

Figure L1.7

all of the cards of customers who bought sometime between thirteen and twenty-four months ago but who have not bought anything in the past twelve months (all of those customers have been moved into the one-year buyer box). Another way to say this is the two-year segment contains all customers who bought in the past twenty-four months but not in the past twelve months. This customer has not been heard from in one year. If one of those customers buys today, their card will be updated and moved into the one-year box. No record will remain in the two-year box because the customer has reaffirmed loyalty and has been promoted to the most recent segment, the one-year box. Being in the one-year box is good. In fact, the job of marketers is to cram all customers into the one-year box. If all of your customers are in the one-year box, you are either a rainmaker or you have been in business less than a year.

The three-year buyer segment is a third box inside the shoebox, and it contains all of the cards of customers who bought twenty-five to thirty-six months ago but have not bought in the past twenty-

Figure L1.8

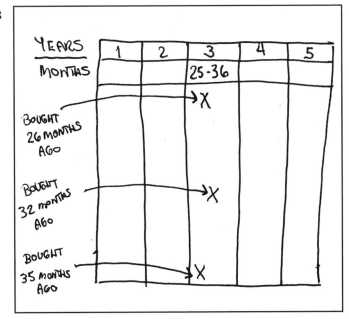

four months (**Figure L1.8**). In other words, these are customers you have not heard from in the past two years, although they bought something twenty-five to thirty-six months ago. This customer has not been heard from in two years. If one of these customers called and bought something today, the card would be updated and placed in the one-year box. Again, no record would be kept in the three-year box. The recency record works the way your medical records are supposed to work: They follow you wherever you go.

The four-year buyer segment is a fourth box inside the shoebox. It contains all of the customer cards for customers who bought something four years ago but have bought nothing in the past thirty-six months. Their last purchase was sometime between thirty-seven and forty-eight months ago and they have made no purchase in the past thirty-six months. This customer has not been heard from in three years.

The five-year buyer segment is the last small box inside the shoebox. The customers in this collection of cards bought something forty-nine to sixty months ago but have not bought again in the last forty-eight months. This customer has not been heard from in four years.

Many companies have a sixth box inside the shoebox. It contains all the customers who bought sixty-one months ago and more. These are customers who have not been heard from in six years or longer, often going back ten years or more. The dust is usually extremely thick on this box because there is so little activity and because owners never open it up to dump out the bones; they just keep adding bodies to it. In fact, many companies keep mailing these customers, whether through a special, secret strategy or just forgetfulness I have never quite determined. From time to time, this little treasure chest is trotted out and paraded as a corporate asset, generally when the owner is trying to sell the company.

The minute a customer from any box makes a purchase, that customer is automatically pulled and reclassified as a one-year buyer. They have bought in the most recent twelve months and are, therefore, the *most* recent of all customers. Their cards are rooted out of their respective boxes and re-filed in the one-year box. For customers from the one-year box who purchase again, their cards are updated and they go to the head of the box, the one-day recency position **(Figure L1.9)**.

But, any customer who buys once and never buys again slowly begins the descent through the boxes from day one of one-year of recency, sliding through the one-year box and erupting into day one of the two-year recency box, and sliding through the two-year box to splat into day one of the three-year recency box, and sliding from there successfully to the four- and five-year recency boxes until finally being disgorged from the bottom of the five-year box on the 1,825th day to plop into the Treasure Chest of Old Bones, there to molder and decay into faintly magnetic dust **(Figure L1.10)**.

Again, we have to remember that the Master Marketer is managing multiple shoeboxes with multiple one, two, three, four and

Figure L1.9

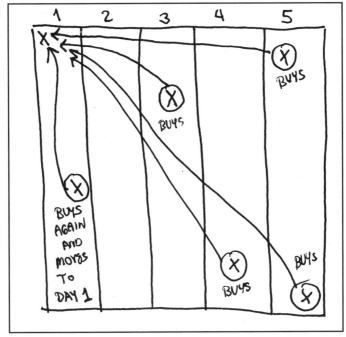

Figure L1.10

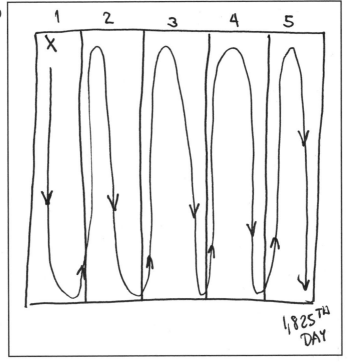

five-year boxes inside. A customer in the catalog channel will be moving from the three-year box to the one-year box; a customer in the online box will be moving from the two-year box to the one-year box; a customer from the infomercial box will be moving from the middle of the one-year box to the head of the one-year box; and it's possible that all three of those different channel recency events will be for the *same* customer. And the aggregate shoebox with all channel boxes and all aggregate year boxes will keep track of *all* customer recency by *all* channels. It's a Rubik's Cube.

It is important to recognize that each of the boxes inside the shoebox—and the shoebox itself—are continually moving forward in time. If today is April 1, then the one-year box will extend back to March 31 one year ago; tomorrow, the box will be between April 2 and April 1 a year ago. All of the year boxes are moving through time. *The point: The customer database is dynamic; it never stands still in time.*

It is also important to recognize that individual *buying* customers can only move one direction in recency: forward. A one-year customer can never move to the two-year box if a purchase has been made sometime in the past 365 days. A one-year customer can move to the two-year box only when no purchase is made in the past 366 days. *The point: Buying is the catalyst for recency.*

Combining these two cardinal points, then, leads to the following conclusion:

*A customer must make repeat purchases in one or,
preferably, more channels in some acceptable length of time
for the company to be profitable.*

That conclusion—simple as it may seem—is the heart and soul of multi-channel direct marketing. From just this rudimentary knowledge about recency, one or two insights can be obtained. If *all* of the customers are in the one-year box in all channels, the company is quite tasty (**Figure L1.11**). But if all of the customers are in the five-year box in all channels, the company has been out of business for the past four years and nobody has told them (**Figure L1.12**). Most companies have some logical and normal distribution pattern of customers across the recency boxes and channels (**Figure L1.13**). The difference between great companies and not-so-great companies is in the awareness of the profitability of the patterns and the channels and the ability to optimally shift the weight in both the patterns and the channels. Mediocre companies have too few customers in the one-year box and too many in the two, three, four and five-year boxes in some or all channels. In other words, more customers are going down the drain than are coming in at the faucet. The tub is draining. Sometimes it is hard to tell how much leakage there really is; and sometimes there is a whirlpool around the drain and you can hear the sucking noise. The real problems, however, are the companies who don't even know there is a bathtub.

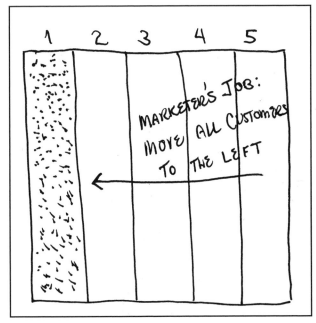

Figure L1.11

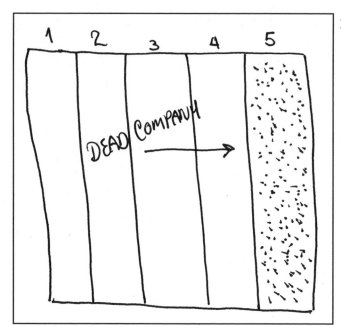

Figure L1.12

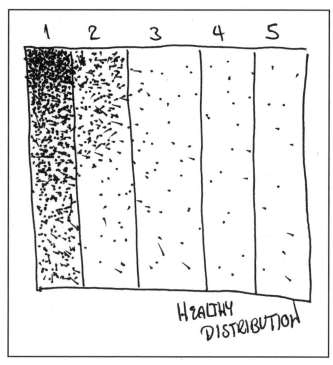

Figure L1.13

RECENCY SEGMENTATION: PICKERING

Active versus Inactive, or (with apologies to The Bard): 'Am' versus 'Was.'

Active does indeed mean different things to different businesses. If you are selling consumables you could make the argument that a customer is inactive at the point in time when they have consumed all of your product and have not yet reordered. This would obviously vary by quantity ordered; if two businesses ordered the same product, let's say envelopes, and ordered different quantities (assuming the same rate of depletion) the business that ordered the lesser quantity would be inactive first. Whether or not that makes sense, it isn't very practical in application. It does show, however, that this is not a black and white issue.

If you remember your microeconomics, the profit maximizing point of production is $MC=MR$ or, in English, when Marginal Cost (the cost of producing or selling one additional unit) is equal to the Marginal Revenue (revenue generated by producing or selling one additional unit).How might your definition of active and inactive change if you defined active as those segments of your house file that you can mail down to break-even? This may be an easier concept to test than you may think.

Break all of your house file into the various cells. Mail a portion from each cell, large enough to generate about fifty orders each, at least. When the mailing is closed and you have tabulated all the results, how many (and which) segments perform at break-even or above, with all costs considered? If so, you may want to consider this your active file. Another school of thought has been to mail your house file to the level that the lowest performing segments are equal to the best segments of the prospecting efforts.

There is enormous variability to what is active or not (by definition) from business-to-business consumable to business-to-business durable. Most marketers today are using a definition of active and inactive that they have inherited. As my colleague stressed above:

You need to measure and find out what the period of time is for active customer status in your business. I would only add that you need to find out what this is today; what worked in the past may have changed. Also, there will be differences by channel. Older than twelve months may very well be inactive for the web channel and not yet inactive for customers who purchase via mail or telephone. After you have arrived at your definition of active, you mail the actives and prospect. There are some traps to avoid.

Many mailers mail from a database where their house file is resident (for suppression purposes) or include their house file in suppression in a merge/purge. *Be certain to suppress from your prospecting circulation only that portion of your house file that you are mailing at that time or in the near future.*

It is common to use the standard definition of 'active' and suppress those records from prospecting. If that definition is thirty-six months, that is the file suppressed. If the house file selection is only taking twenty-four month names, or only portions of the thirty-six month file, you don't want to suppress the entire thirty-six month period for this reason: a buyer in the twenty-five to thirty-six month segment that you were not planning to mail may also appear as a hotline (one- to three-month) buyer on one of your core continuation lists. If you indiscriminately suppress all thirty-six month buyers you could be missing a great opportunity to get this a catalog in that hotline buyer/twenty-five to thirty-six month customer's hands and re-acquire them as a customer.

RECENCY VELOCITY: LIBEY

Recency velocity is the speed at which the next purchase—the affirmation of loyalty—is made, by a single customer, in a specific channel. As an example, a daily buyer of *The Wall Street Journal* has a recency velocity speed of 1, the fastest velocity possible. That customer is renewing the one-year recency on a daily basis. A buyer of house paint may have a recency velocity speed of 1,459, a slow velocity representing 1,459 days since the last purchase, or four years. If a customer purchases five times a year, the recency velocity speed is 73. These are the days between purchases, and the change in velocity speed becomes important when the number of days changes either direction.

Customers have different recency velocity speeds. One customer may be a 110, another, a 56, and a third a 250. In the aggregate, customers combine to determine an *average recency velocity speed*. The three customers above have an average recency velocity speed of 138.7. Another way of saying this is the average customer reorders 2.63 times a year, about every 139 days (**Figure L1.14**).

The example above may be for catalog customers. Online customers may have recency velocity speeds of 87, 42, and 92 for an average speed of 73.7. These customers order 4.95 times a year, about every 74 days.

Figure L1.14

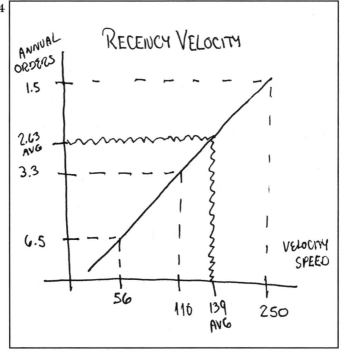

The recency velocity speed for both of these channels combined is 106.2, or 3.44 orders a year, about every 106 days. The multi-channel comparisons become interesting when analyzed for average order value, gross margin, marketing costs, fulfillment costs, net profits, customer retention, and return on investment.

Recency velocity describes the dynamic movement of the individual customer and averages of groups of customers in each channel, as well as overall. Ideally, recency velocity speed will constantly increase; buyers will speed up their rate of next purchase. The higher the velocity speed, the higher the number of orders. If all customers can be moved closer to a velocity speed of 1, then the whole customer base will move closer to daily ordering and all of the customers will be in the one-year box. At a constant or growing average order value, this is good. If, however, the recency velocity speed for individual customers and for all customers on average across all channels is slowing, then the company is experiencing decreasing dynamism; the business is slowing down or the tub is draining. This is not good.

Recency velocity speed direction for a single customer can be signified by a directional arrow (**Figure L1.15**). If speed is increasing, the arrow points up; if staying the same, the arrow points sideways; if decreasing, the arrow points down. Note that only one direction is acceptable.

Recency velocity speed will vary by segment. The speed of reaffirming one-year customers may be 83; two-year segment customer recency velocity speed may be slower at 97; three-year segment customer recency velocity speed may drop to 156. Here, we have an example of an overall slowing of recency velocity speed in aging recency segments (**Figure L1.16**).

Studies of speed may produce surprises. If the example immediately above produced a three-year customer recency velocity speed of 48 (**Figure L1.17**), it would indicate that between twenty-five and thirty-six months, customers buy twice as quickly. In that one

Figure L1.15

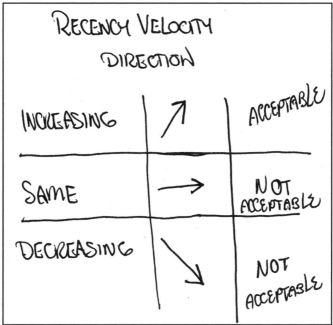

Figure L1.16

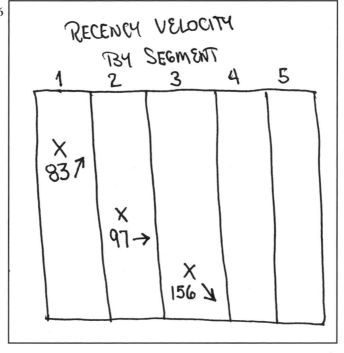

cell of recency segmentation, the arrow is suddenly pointing up; the question must be asked, "Why is that?" The answer will be found in product, usage rate or promotion.

Figure L1.17

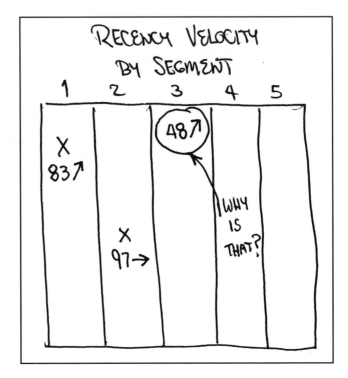

RECENCY MOMENTUM: LIBEY

Recency momentum is the force of the change in recency velocity. If recency velocity has improved from a score of 130 to 120, or said another way, if the number of days between orders has improved from 130 to 120, then the recency momentum is positive at +10. If the change in velocity scores was from 130 to 60, then the recency momentum is a greatly positive +70. If recency velocity is deteriorating from 120 days to 130, then recency momentum is negative at -10. Positive momentum is a good thing; negative momentum is a bad thing. Generally, momentum is concerned with the positive or negative direction of large customer groups. In office products, for example, days to reorder may be improving in specific SICs or large market groups, such as financial services and banks. The rate of change of momentum can range from slow to fast, from low momentum to high momentum.

If the peddler goes out selling along the route, the recency velocity is going to speed up as customer after customer buys. The recency velocity average for all customers will also speed up even though many customers are not being called on during that trip. For a brief period—the length of the trip—the recency momentum will increase positively. When the trip is over, the recency momentum will decrease negatively.

The same experience occurs when the direct marketer mails out or emails an offer. Both the recency velocity and the overall recency momentum increase as orders flow in; both decrease as the mailing ends. Recency momentum exists in each channel. Momentum may be increasing in the online channel, but decreasing in the retail channel. This is an indication that customers are migrating from retail to online, or that online promotions are more attractive than retail, or any of dozens of possible explanations. The Master Marketer is examining the velocity arrow directions in all segments of all channels, and is equally examining the momentum arrow directions in whole segments of whole channels.

It is the ebb and flow of recency velocity and recency momentum that is significant. If the recency velocity speed is faster with each successive offer, then the overall recency momentum will achieve successively higher and positive levels, maintaining the business in the pink of recency health. Over long periods of time, say, forty rolling quarters, the ebb and flow of recency velocity and recency momentum should slope upward when displayed on an *x-y axis* chart. Only a sufficiently long view will allow for the smoothing of marketing efforts to provide a clear picture of the state of true customer recency (**Figure L1.18**).

The overall business health is determined by the macro velocity and momentum of recency, but an equally important micro view

Figure L1.18

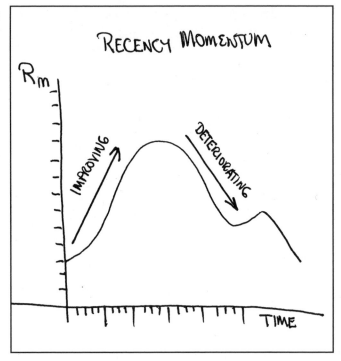

of velocity and momentum for individual customers must be developed, as well. Understanding a direct marketing company begins with understanding a single customer thousands of times. If you have the luxury of individual customer knowledge, you have the luxury of understanding your business with the same degree of tactile intimacy the peddler knew. Actually, few direct multi-channel marketers have that knowledge and, as a consequence, even now with all of our sophistication and technology, still operate their businesses with an obsolete and irrelevant mass marketing strategy. Too often, they attempt to fix the problem by spending huge amounts of money on the vagaries of customer relationship marketing systems (whatever that means) rather than actually studying customer behavior by looking at real customers in real time and finding out real information that makes a difference. If you do not know the individual customer's reasons for positive or negative changes in recency momentum, in all channels, you are flying by the seat of your pants and there is a big mountain top ahead in the fog.

RECENCY VELOCITY AND RECENCY MOMENTUM: PICKERING

Recency velocity and momentum are so closely linked that I am taking them as two parts of the same thought.

Recency velocity and recency momentum are overlooked by almost all of today's direct marketers, even the more seasoned ones. They are overlooked for two main reasons: most systems have not been set up to calculate these measures and they are not used in even the most sophisticated RFM*X* segmentations. To be sure, it isn't easy to do date comparisons that calculate recency velocity measured in days on most database systems. It isn't much of a trick to calculate the recency momentum once you have the velocity calculated. recency momentum also is not used in segmentation because of the difficulty of obtaining this calculation and because most circulation managers wouldn't use it. Truth be told, it probably wouldn't change how house file circulation decisions are made to a large extent.

This being said, recency momentum and recency velocity are a *critical* measure of the health of the buyer file. Many business leaders say that they would rather have an eighty percent solution today than a one hundred percent solution tomorrow. Here is the eighty percent solution.

Rather than looking at recency momentum and velocity with the precision of the number of days to a purchase, in this example we will look at recency by month. Obviously that is less precise by a factor of about thirty, but it is more easily done. Simply take your update report that shows the distribution by month. (The zero month is the current month and, as that is by definition incomplete, we start looking at those who purchased in the most recent, complete month.) For one-month buyers, multiply by one, for buyers who purchased two months ago, multiply by two, and so on.

If you do not get monthly update reports from your in-house or external marketing database, you can achieve the same thing by taking counts on your database the same time each month. And if you have a marketing database that updates in real time (or nightly) you may want to take a 'snapshot' of the database every month and archive it. This is invaluable as it gives you the ability to do trend analysis.

Below (**Figure P1.3**) is a simple example showing how to calculate velocity. It is done on a month level and once you have the data, it takes about five minutes to put everything together in your favorite spreadsheet program.

Month	Customers	Customers X Months Since Purchase
Month 1	20,689	20,689
Month 2	13,320	26,639
Month 3	7,359	22,076
Month 4	5,649	22,595
Month 5	3,331	16,653
Month 6	3,589	21,531
Month 7	2,937	20,556
Month 8	2,943	23,546
Month 9	2,838	25,543
Month 10	2,677	26,773
Month 11	2,519	27,704
Month 12	2,696	32,353
Month 13	2,275	29,570
Month 14	2,778	38,889
Month 15	2,356	35,346
Month 16	2,291	36,662
Month 17	1,164	19,796
Month 18	1,267	22,805
	82,677	469,728
Velocity	5.68 or 1 purchase every 5.68 months	

Figure P1.3

A couple of important things stand out. First of all, there is a tight grouping of customers in the most recent months. This could be due to a recent campaign of new customer acquisition, or house file mailings to the active or inactive portions. It could also be a combination of new customer acquisition and house file circulation that helped move many buyers forward.

Secondly, the velocity of under six says that we will, on average, get about two purchases per customer within any twelve month period. If the mailer is dependent upon the second purchase to make money, i.e. prospecting at an investment, this is a sign that the strategy is working. To cleave apart what is driving this recency velocity you can also split it up between one time purchasers and two time plus purchasers.

Does it make sense to look at the recency velocity and momentum of two-time plus customers separately from one-time purchasers? It does. This way you can see if the velocity is being kept low by a large influx of new, recent buyers or by bringing existing buyers forward in recency by house file promotion. If the portion of recent, one-time buyers is large, and the business is dependent upon the second purchase to become profitable, this can obscure an unhealthy business. On the other hand, by only promoting to the house file, the house file will become stagnant and miss the opportunity to sell to new businesses or businesses newly convinced of the need for the product. The key is a balance between new and existing customers.

Once you have the ability to calculate recency momentum, velocity is relatively easy. You take two month's worth of momentum reports and create velocity. Again, we will be using the expedient of looking at this on a month-by-month level rather than calculating days. After calculating the recency momentum you compare current month's results to the prior month's results. If you have improved .15 (that is to say that the average record is .15 months more recent), that is shown as a positive. If your recency momentum has declined, that is to say the average record is .15 months older in the current update compared to the last update, that is shown as a negative.

For the example below (**Figure P1.4**) we just examined an active eighteen-month file. As we discussed, your business may dictate a shorter or longer period of active status.

Month	Customer Count	Customers X Months Since Purchase	Prior Mo Customers	Customers X Months Since Purchase
Month 1	20,689	20,689	21,345	21,345
Month 2	13,320	26,639	10,935	21,870
Month 3	7,359	22,076	7,545	22,635
Month 4	5,649	22,595	4,301	17,206
Month 5	3,331	16,653	4,363	21,815
Month 6	3,589	21,531	3,523	21,137
Month 7	2,937	20,556	3,377	23,642
Month 8	2,943	23,546	3,197	25,578
Month 9	2,838	25,543	2,997	26,972
Month 10	2,677	26,773	2,740	27,403
Month 11	2,519	27,704	2,949	32,435
Month 12	2,696	32,353	2,462	29,539
Month 13	2,275	29,570	2,972	38,638
Month 14	2,778	38,889	2,490	34,856
Month 15	2,356	35,346	2,421	36,311
Month 16	2,291	36,662	1,220	19,521
Month 17	1,164	19,796	1,324	22,507
Month 18	1,267	22,805	1,985	35,722
	82,677	469,728	82,145	479,131
Velocity 5.68 or 1 purchase every 5.68 months			5.83 1 purchase every 5.83 months	
Momentum +015 Months or The Velocity has improved that the average buyer is 15 months more recent.				

Figure P1.4

If this were the only recency velocity and momentum information available to us, the file would look as though it is healthy (shown by a concentration of buyers in the recent months) and improving (shown by the positive recency momentum). What we do not see is a plot of velocity and momentum for sixty rolling months nor could we see in this short of a time frame any effects of seasonality. It is critical to look at this sixty month period to get the complete idea of the health of the file.

In the course of corporate acquisitions, many acquiring companies do some form of due diligence on the house file: comparing the profitability of customers, response rates and $/M of circulation on recent prospecting efforts, analyzing the overlap between the customer files, etc. I have yet to see a study of the velocity and recency and that could uncover critical weaknesses (or hidden strengths) of a business. More acquisitions within direct marketing don't work because of lack if understanding of what they are buying than from any other reason.

RECENCY RECONCILIATION: LIBEY

At any moment in time, a precise number of customers exists which is the sum of all the customers in all the recency segmentation boxes, for all channels, inside the big shoebox. Each day the number of customers changes and individual customers move between the recency segmentation boxes. A customer in the three-year recency segment—who has not been heard from in the past twenty-five to thirty-six months—makes a purchase today. That customer moves from the three-year box to the one-year box, a loss of one customer from the three-year box and a gain of one customer in the one-year box. At the end of today, the one-year recency segmentation box will have added all of the existing customers who bought today from the two-year, three-year, four-year and five-year and older boxes. At the same time, all of the first-time buyers or new customers who have come in through the faucet will have been added to the one-year box. All customers in the one-year box who aged beyond one year today without buying will be moved to the two-year box. The one-year box has gains and losses and, when reconciled, a net gain or loss. But every customer can be accounted for through reconciliation.

At the end of today, all the customers in the two-year box who purchased today will be moved to the one-year box. And all of the customers who have aged beyond twenty-four months without buying will be moved to the three-year box. The two-year box has a precise net gain or loss; no customer 'leakage' or 'shrink' is possible with proper reconciliation. It's like a checkbook. Every penny went somewhere.

Similarly, at the end of today, the three-year box will lose customers who purchased today to the one-year box. Customers who aged beyond forty-eight months today without buying will be moved to the four-year box. Again, reconciliation accounts for every customer.

The four-year box sends customers to the one-year box if they bought today and to the five-year box if they aged beyond sixty months today without buying. The net gain or loss is accounted for to the individual customer, in all channels, and in the aggregate.

The five-year and older box may send a few customers to the one-year box, but mostly it receives aging customers from the four-year box. This is a terminal box. It doesn't send customers further down the line because this *is* the end of the line. This is the old customer graveyard.

By calculating the net gain or loss in each of the segmentation boxes, in each channel, and in the aggregate, an accurate reconciliation of the total customer count is accomplished. If the day began with 123,342 existing customers and 311 new customers were added with 115 customers dropped due to inactivity, the reconciliation count is 123,538. But to get to this reconciled number, all boxes in all channels must be reconciled. Also, removals from the customer list by request, bad debt, or other reasons must also be factored into the reconciliation.

Beyond the total number of customers and the need for accurate accounting of this asset, a number of interesting things can be revealed by the reconciliation process. If, suddenly, there is greatly diminished movement of customers from the older boxes to the one-year box, something is seriously wrong. The customer base has stopped repeat buying and the reason why needs to be uncovered. Or, perhaps all of the movement is between boxes and no new customers are coming into the one-year box. New customers have stopped flowing in through the faucet, another serious problem requiring explanation and accountability.

Over time, the reconciliation process can track a large concentration of customers through the recency process. Suppose you offer a product totally free. As a result, you attracted 5,000 new customers and only 32 ever bought from you again. What you would see is a big lump of 4,986 freeloaders moving through the boxes for five years (**Figure L1.19**). Being able to spot large boluses of useless customers in the recency data is a helpful skill when evaluating companies for acquisition. Without adequate recency segmentation in all channels, these indigestible hair balls would simply be hidden in the overall customer count and the business would be artificially valued.

Many other intricacies can be learned through studies of recency reconciliation. When marketing efforts are uniformly focused on the two-, three-, four- and five-year customers, the response rates for each group should be relatively consistent although declining in the older segments. If the customer count in the three-year box suddenly drops, only three possibilities exist to explain the drop. The first is that possibly a large number of three-year customers has suddenly purchased. This can be verified through reconciliation by confirming that the one-year box increased by the same number. The second possibility is that a large number of three-year customers aged as a

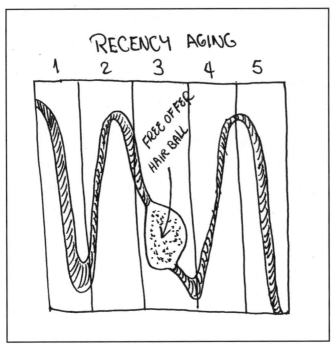

Figure L1.19

group and dropped into the four-year box. This can be verified by confirming that the four-year box had a net gain of a like number. The third possibility is that an error in recency reconciliation occurred, a common problem when tracking large numbers of customers.

The necessity for reconciling all segments in all channels is required because of the need to understand extra-segmental, inter-channel transfers of customers. If, suddenly, online promotions are disproportionately attracting catalog customers, the shift from the catalog recency segments to the online recency segments can be seen through detailed reconciliation.

The percentage of customers moving to the one-year box compared to the percentage moving to the next box in the aging process is another interesting intricacy. If the three-year customers, over time, average a sixteen percent movement to the one-year box and an eighty-four percent movement to the four-year box, what does it mean when, in one month, forty percent of the customers show up in the one-year box? Obviously, there was a successful marketing effort that reactivated three-year customers. A change in the percentage rate of movement, either forward or backward in recency, is an indication of something going on in the business you should know about. The only way to get this information is to accurately track the changes in movement in each recency segment, in all channels, every month, over a minimum of twenty rolling quarters, and to look for changes and trends in customer activity.

Similarly, the percentage of customers moving to the one-year online channel box from the next box in the aging process of the catalog channel is interesting. If the three-year catalog channel customers, over time, average a sixteen percent movement to the one-year catalog channel box, and suddenly forty percent of the customers show up in the online channel one-year box, what does *that* mean? Obviously, there was a reason for the inter-channel switch and it requires explanation and understanding, especially if it wasn't planned.

The admonition that accuracy is the hallmark of the Master Marketer is particularly true in recency reconciliation. Any discrepancy must be explained, understood and corrected. Customers do not appear out of thin air or disappear into vapor. They went somewhere, for a reason, and that movement and reason must be accounted for precisely.

RECENCY RECONCILIATION: PICKERING

Many direct marketers choose to house the marketing database at a service bureau vendor. Frequently, choosing an external vendor is a good decision as it enables marketers to use more state-of-the-art systems without having to bear all the costs and efforts of building a database in-house. The decision to house this data externally leads to some needs for quality assurance, and recency reconciliation is one of the points that should be analyzed.

Often the inputs (feeds) to these external marketing databases are coming from the in-house fulfillment or accounting systems.

These updates of transactions are then added to the marketing database. In the instance of a new customer, the recency date is populated from the date of purchase field. In the instance of an existing customer the purchase date on the incoming transaction is compared to the existing recency and the more recent date is kept as the recency.

As part of the database design process, the more skilled database providers will prepare reports that show recency distribution of the current update compared to the prior update and sometimes the same month of the prior year. Although this generally isn't enough to do the velocity and momentum measurements to the precision of number of days, they can generally work to the precision of one month. Also, reviewing these reports will help identify any anomalous changes. These changes often point to an error in the update process and should be investigated.

RECENCY AND LIST RENTALS: LIBEY

Under the assumption that a one-year recency customer is a better customer than a two-year or three-year recency customer, recency segmentation is an essential pillar of list rentals (your customer list rented to other companies) and list renting (you renting other companies' customer lists).

Renting your customer lists can result in attractive income, essentially 'found money.' A list of 500,000 names may rent for $100 per thousand. The one-year file may rent for $125 per thousand. If that consists of 100,000 names, the rental would be $125 x 100 = $12,500 plus 400,000 names at $100 per thousand, or $100 x 400 = $40,000. The total for all names would be $52,500. If the entire list could be rented twenty-six times a year, the total rental would be $1,365,000 annually less twenty percent to your list brokerage firm (money well spent) for a total income of $1,092,000.

Renters of customer lists are interested in the quality of potential response. Therefore, a one-year segment of the list is more desirable than a four-year segment of that list. Typically, renters pay more to rent the most recent names, or the 'quarterly hots' list, customers who have purchased in the past ninety days. Customers from the second, third and fourth quarters back do not bring as high a rental rate as the most recent quarter names.

For list rental purposes, quarterly recency segmentation is essential. This is a further segmentation of the one-year box inside the shoebox, for each channel. Of course, this requires moving customers back and forth between *quarters* as well as years, and it requires quarterly reconciliation in the one-year box. Ideally, the perfect company is one with all customers in the one-year box and, within that box, all customers in the first quarter sub-box. Of course, that doesn't happen, but it's nice to contemplate the perfect money machine (**Figure L1.20**).

As a list owner, you want to rent *all* of your customer names; as a list renter, though, you usually want the most recent buyers. Experienced direct marketers will rent quarterly names from one,

Figure L1.20

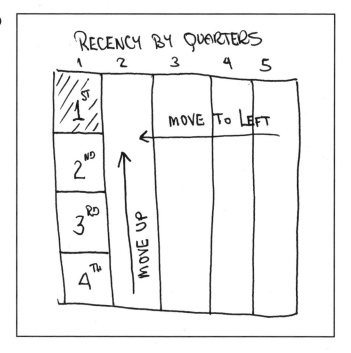

two, three or four quarters back, as well as the hots. The reason is that the most recent quarterly names receive many contacts because many marketers are renting those names while those in the older quarters receive less; therefore, it may be easier to get their attention for your offer. For some products and services, this strategy works well; for others it doesn't.

Recency is only one element of an overall list strategy; many other segmentations and attributes are considered when creating a contact plan for each channel. In most instances, the initial cut is made based on recency. A recently active customer has the greatest future potential and that potential diminishes over time, regardless of the channel.

RECENCY AND LIST RENTALS: PICKERING

Where some say that recency is the most important part of RFM on a house file, in many instances recency is the only one of the three available when renting a list. The *hotline* is what matters to most direct marketers and that is generally ninety days for business-to-business marketers and often thirty days for consumer marketers. In many instances, these outperform the other segments of the file; if nothing else, their recent activity shows that they are deliverable at that address and have buying authority at this time. So if you have exhausted all the hotline names and frequency and monetary aren't available, you have exhausted all options, right?

Direct marketers who use a private or some shared/public prospecting databases may have another option. They can use the 'database recency' meta data. Database recency is the most recent date of activity for that individual from anywhere on the database. This is calculated without respect to which list it came from, so no list specific information is used.

The Master Marketer can use database recency to plumb the older segments of the core continuation files for those good names that are still active. You can look at the seven- to twelve-month portion of a continuation file and only select those names that have zero- to three-month database recency.

Use of data from multiple list sources may incur additional charges or require a multi-buyer calculation. Your list broker should be able to assist you to determine what is the ethical way to use and pay for this information. Remember, this industry is small and based on a high level of trust. Your good reputation is invaluable, treat it as such.

There are also other special situations where recency can be used. New telephone connection files are available for both consumer and business-to-business marketers. The thought is to get an offer into the hands of people who have just activated phone service. The focus is on the thirty-day segment of the file.

Many savvy marketers use those same new telephone connections lists five or six months after the connections have been made. The individual or business after five or six months has had time to get settled, make all of those initial purchases that are needed when moving into a home or opening an new office, and now they can think about more long-term or more expensive purchases. And as a bonus, you can usually get the older segments of these lists for less than the hotline segments rent for.

Another special circumstance is when the continuation list is based made up in large part or entirely by seasonal buyers. With these lists a hotline segment may be too small to be useful or relevant.

Consider the core continuation list whose purchases come mostly in the fall, from September to November. This could be true of many types of businesses like greeting cards, gifts, cold weather gear, etc.

If your product is non-seasonal, you may want to use these names as soon as they are available, generally in January. You may also want to test using them again in the fall simply because these buyers have not had the need to purchase more holiday cards or snow shovels through the spring and summer, but they likely still have the same affinity characteristics as when they made the purchase. The Master Marketer will even use database recency to key separately and read different segments within those seasonal lists.

RECENCY AND CONTACT STRATEGY: LIBEY

Returning to our peddler, how many trips a year can be made to the customers? It costs money to make a trip, whether by wagon, mail, Internet, email, telephone, television, or retail store.

If every customer buys on the annual trip, the peddler will ask, "What if I made two trips a year?" If every customer buys on each of the two trips, the question becomes, "What if I made three trips a year?" And, if every customer buys on each of the three trips, the question becomes, "What if I made four trips a year?" As long as enough customers buy on each trip so that the trip is profitable, the number of trips can increase.

Multi-channel direct marketers ask the same question, "How many catalogs (or solos, or emails, or pay per clicks, or inserts, or phone calls) can I mail to a customer every year?" The answer is the same: as long as enough customers buy so that a profit is produced, the number of catalogs (channel contacts) can increase. There are those who believe in the old adage: you can mail your customer one more time provided that mailing is more profitable than your worst prospect mailing. Personally, I have always subscribed to the strategy of increasing mailings (channel contacts) until dropping to break-even, then back down one or two mailings and test regularly to see if the ceiling moves. The same applies to online contacts or any other channel. The justification process remains the same: *You market to those who buy from you regularly and, if you are smart, you market to them often, up to the point where profits are optimal and no further.*

In the early days of cataloging, marketers would send out one catalog a year. With positive experiences, that grew to two, three and four catalogs a year sent to active customers. Today, the number of catalogs sent by both business-to-business and consumer marketers can be as high as twenty-six a year, occasionally more. It is a reasonable assumption that those marketers are making money on that number of mailings.

A hierarchy of contacts exists based on the profitability of the customer response. The best customers receive the most contacts; the others receive less. If a one-year customer receives twenty-six catalogs a year, a two-year customer may receive only eighteen, a three-year twelve, a four-year eight, and a five-year customer only four catalogs **(Figure L1.21)**. Similar hierarchies exist in each channel of the multi-channel direct marketing company. The contact logic is clear: the more recent the customer, the more contacts. However, even in today's age of sophisticated analytics, there are marketers who simply send every customer four, fourteen or eighteen or however many catalogs that are being mailed this year. They send the same amount to every customer regardless of recency. The reason can usually be tracked to a lack of ability to segment, although sometimes it is simply naiveté. Some people just don't understand this stuff.

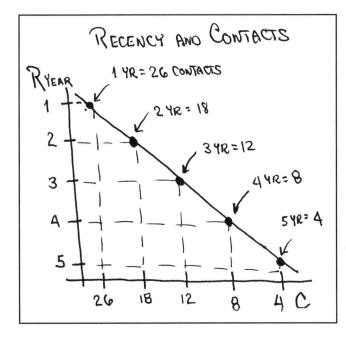

Figure L1.21

While profitability drives contact strategy, so does new customer acquisition. Recency begins with a new customer coming through the faucet. It does little good to over mail existing customers at the expense of acquiring new customers. Without new customers coming in every day, the tub will run dry—even with great buying from existing customers. This is a business of balance between investing in customers and investing in prospects. Unless an aggressive new customer acquisition program is managed, all of the customer contacts will not prevent eventual decline. Generally, if a choice has to be made between investment prospecting and deeper contacts to existing customers in older recency boxes, the strategy of investment prospecting makes better long-term sense. When prospecting stops, so does the business.

For the Master Marketer, the balance is more complex. It is necessary to micro-balance investment prospecting and existing customers in not only optimal recency configurations, but also in optimal channel proportions. And, while search engine marketing, search engine optimization, pay per click, pay per sale, and other online prospecting tactics aggressively compete for prospecting dollars, it has to be noted that a high percentage of all online orders are driven by paper catalogs.

RECENCY AND CONTACT STRATEGY: PICKERING

Contact strategy used to be geared towards answering one question: how many catalogs do I send to my house file? And the answer was generally: more to the more recent vintages and fewer to older segments.

Today the question is more like: how many communications do I send to my customers, and what is the most profitable mix of mail/email/telephone/fax?

As contact strategy becomes a question that is as much 'how' (via what channels do I send my promotions?) as 'how much' (how frequently do I promote?), it pays dividends to look at what channels your recent buyers are buying from.

For example, several years ago it was generally the larger companies that were purchasing online, because of the cost savings involved. The smaller businesses were reluctant, for whatever the reason, to purchase via the web. That has recently changed; smaller businesses are now more likely to purchase via the web than large businesses. There will continue to be changes.

It also pays to look at contact strategy within the context of time. Most mailers, for example, mail at the same times of year every year without giving it much thought or testing. Only a few very learned mailers that I have seen have tested mailings (prospect and house file) every month to see when are more productive times. It is probably a good investment of catalogs to test your off months, unless you are a very seasonal mailer.

Even seasonal mailers have contact strategy testing that can be done. Is it more productive to begin mailing a few weeks earlier than conventional wisdom? Or perhaps an additional contact late in the season, to pick-up the last minute buyers that are more conscious of availability and deliverability than of price?

Contact strategy can also be applied to prospect mailings. How many times do I want to circulate to a given site or individual within a certain time frame? Although this makes much intuitive sense, this mindset on the business-to-business side is generally not driven based on any results. It is either based on what number of contacts makes sense to those who are budgeting or based on a goal of acquiring X number of new sites within Y budget of mail pieces. There is not much science behind this approach, and it is not recommended.

Frequently marketers use contact history files to drive contact strategy. This is a file that tracks how many times a promotion has been sent to an individual, household or business site within a period of time.

Contact history-driven strategies are best used within a prospect database environment and can hold much value for consumer mailers. They can be used to find that point of diminishing returns. If you have mailed an individual seven times in the previous year and you are sending them the eighth promotion, you may see that this segment has a lift of twenty to thirty percent over the average. And you will likely also find that any number of promotions over that number is wasting catalogs. Since contact history is made best use of in a sophisticated database with large prospect universes, it lends itself more to the more broad-based consumer offers than more vertical consumer markets or business-to-business markets.

RECENCY AND INQUIRIES: LIBEY

Direct marketers are not sure how to treat inquiries. Should they be treated as customers? Or should they be treated as suspects until they actually buy something?

An inquiry is more recent and more qualified than a complete unknown. The act of making an inquiry has qualified the person to some extent, at least more so than a name on a prospect list. Because of that, an inquiry should be offered the opportunities to purchase for a period of time before discarding the name. How long contacts should be made without a purchase is the question.

In some companies, inquiry names are added to the one-year recency file and treated as one-year customers. Perhaps six months of frequent contacts are made and, when no purchase occurs, the inquiry is removed from the one-year box and discarded or is sent to the Treasure Chest marked *Old Inquiries* where nothing ever happens again. More aggressive companies give the inquiry only one or two contacts to make a purchase before sending it down. Products have an influence in inquiry strategy. Some products take forever to win a buying decision; some take ten seconds. One company may have to contact an inquiry twelve times before a purchase is made; another only once. *The point: Tracking and measuring the response and profitability of inquiries, at variable lengths of recency, by channel, is essential to a fully optimized inquiry strategy.*

Generally, in business-to-business direct marketing, the length of time and number of contacts an inquiry is given to make a purchase is less than in consumer direct marketing. If, after a reasonable period of time, the business inquiry has not purchased, the name can be returned to the prospecting pool. One strategy is to maintain a list of inquiries and add them to prospect mailings as you would a prospect list. The assumption is that a non-buying inquiry is better than a total unknown. That may or may not be true since the inquiry has seen your offer and rejected it several times. Another strategy is to move the inquiry contact from one channel to another. If there is no purchase from a catalog, contact them online by email or incent them to visit a retail location. After no response in one or more channels after a logical period of time, delete them, rent them or store them.

Inquiry names should be maintained separately in the shoebox. Moving buyers from the inquiries to the one-year recency box has to be figured into the database schematic. I can't tell you how many companies I have been to that cannot separate the inquiry management, strategy and performance from the rest of the names. They have no idea how the inquiries are performing.

Of course, one must always look for inquiries that are simply added to the customer list and treated thereafter as a customer. This is usually a tactic used by companies planning on selling the business and attempting to make the customer list growth look good. The telling symptom of this is, of course, a drop in average order value without a drop in line items per order.

If there is one factor that influences inquiry performance and, therefore, recency and new customer acquisition more than any other, it is the marketer's response time. The inquiry may cost the direct marketing company fifty dollars to obtain, yet *forty percent or more of all inquiries never receive a response*. If a prospect asks for information, get it to them immediately. If it is a catalog request, send it first class mail if not priority. In some cases, where average order values are high, catalog requests are responded to with overnight delivery. Wherever possible, first convert that request to a website visit while the inquirer waits for the catalog to arrive.

RECENCY AND INQUIRIES: PICKERING

God save me from my friends. I can protect myself from my enemies.
—Marshall de Villares

Marshall de Villares probably wasn't thinking about direct marketing inquiries when he made his quote, but we can take something from it.

As mentioned above, an alarmingly high number of marketers never respond to an inquiry or catalog request. Not only is this missing an opportunity to sell something, it is actively creating a bad impression of your organization. I have seen one foolproof system for handling inquiries: all were routed to one person in the organization who took the name, wrote it on the envelope, put a catalog in, and mailed all packages out at the end of the week. They didn't make it to the database, but there was a one hundred percent effort to fulfill the request.

After you have set up a foolproof system for getting information to requestors, you have to consider what to do with the name. One rule is for sure: if your goal for your promotion is to generate buyers, and you can *only* add inquirers to your system as a buyer, then *do not* add them as a buyer. Develop a different system. Don't corrupt your most important source of business intelligence (your buyer file) with non-buyers. Once done, it can only be undone with great difficulty.

Inquiries are a small number for almost every marketer, consumer and business-to-business. The numbers are generally so small as to hardly be worth spending much effort on managing. Let us be clear, though, that this is different than lead generation. If your goal is to generate leads for additional contact, usually by a person, then this does not apply to you.

Maintain your inquiries separately. Fit them into the circulation plan under house file circulation but above prospects. It generally doesn't make sense to mail them more than one year unless you have processed them through an address change routine like NCOA. If that is the case, you may want to promote to them an additional time.

RECENCY AND CUSTOMER ATTRITION RATES: LIBEY

What is the attrition rate of customers in multi-channel direct marketing? The other side of this question is what is the customer retention rate in multi-channel direct marketing? It is the same question. Attrition is the negative case; retention is the positive case. I prefer attrition because there is more attrition than retention; it is what it is, and we should call it that.

In all of commerce there is a maxim that says, "You turn your customer base one hundred percent every seven years." This seems to be fairly consistent, whether you are a doctor, a hardware store, a barber, a restaurant, a direct marketer, or— and here you have to forgive my lowly and wretched example—a lawyer. If you obtain one hundred customers today, seven years from now those customers will all be gone. There will always be the life-long customers, but they are the exception. You lose customers constantly at some relatively stable rate of attrition barring disasters. That is why you have to constantly invest in prospecting for new customers.

As an example of recency and attrition, a hypothetical example may be helpful. For some direct marketing companies, this model will be representative; indeed, I have found it to be accurate across many business-to-business and consumer direct marketing companies. For other companies, it will not be representative, but we are more concerned with the concept than the accuracy; accuracy is for you to discover.

Today the company receives one hundred first time orders (**Figure L1.22**). These are new customers and are placed in the one-year recency box. Over the next year, fifty percent, or fifty, of those customers reorder and are retained in the one-year recency box. The other fifty customers do not reorder, age and pass to the two-year box. The one-year attrition rate is fifty percent.

During the second year, twenty percent of the original fifty customers still retained in the one-year recency box do not reorder and move to the two-year box. In other words, forty of the original customers reorder and are retained in the one-year recency box; ten customers move to the two-year box.

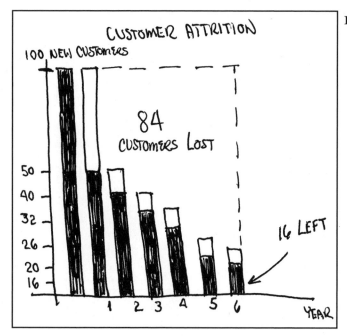

Figure L1.22

During the third year, another twenty percent, or eight, of the remaining forty original customers fail to reorder and go to the two-year box, leaving thirty-two of the original one hundred customers in the one-year recency box.

During the fourth year, twenty percent of those remaining thirty-two, or about six customers fail to reorder and move to the two-year box, leaving about twenty-six of the original customers in the one-year box.

During the fifth year, twenty percent of the remaining twenty-six customers fail to reorder and are sent to the two-year box. This leaves about twenty recent customers in the one-year box.

In the sixth year, another twenty percent, or four, of the remaining twenty, original customers fall to attrition and are sent to the two-year box, leaving only sixteen customers from the original one hundred as retained, one-year recency customers.

Attrition has totaled eighty-four of the original customers. Retention totals sixteen. In this example, attrition is fifty percent the first year and twenty percent of the remainder each year thereafter. Of course, a few customers who age out of the one-year box will eventually reorder and return to the one-year box from the two-, three-, four-, or five-year boxes, but their number is relatively few. The bottom line is only about sixteen percent of the original customers are retained; attrition claims eighty-four percent of the customers. Another way of looking at this is that you have to replace eighty-four percent of your customers just to stay even. But that is not all. You have to bring in another one hundred customers every year on top of the replacement fifty the first year and ultimately the eighty-four in the full six years, and that simply keeps the tub filled at a stable level. If you want to really soak up to your chin, you've got to do a lot better.

Attrition rates vary from company to company, industry to industry, marketing strategy to marketing strategy *and* channel to channel. What never varies, however, is the fact that attrition is a dynamic process; it cannot be denied and it does not go away, no matter how much it is ignored. The glaring recognition to be etched on the direct marketer's mind is that, unless new customers are prospected for and brought in at a rate greater than the outgoing rate of attrition, the company is going out of business every day.

The ability to know the exact attrition rate in each year of recency on a monthly, quarterly, annual and over twenty rolling quarters, plotted on a uniform *x* and *y* axis chart is essential for any direct marketing company. Moreover, the attrition rates must be plotted for every channel and the relationships between channel attrition rates examined and understood **(Figure L1.23)**. The question, "In what channel do we have the least attrition?" has to be answered, as well as, "In what channel do we have the most attrition?" Perhaps more important is the recognition of the changes and trends over time in attrition rates by segment, by channel and the reasons for those changes and trends. Only three possibilities exist for the

Figure L1.23

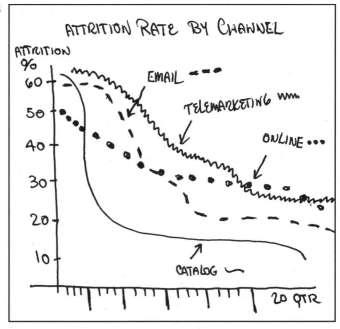

direction and trend of attrition: improving, remaining the same, or getting worse. There are no other choices and there is only one acceptable direction and trend.

A measurement of the effectiveness of marketing to individual segments of recency, such as two-year versus three-year, or two-year catalog versus two-year online, is the change in the rate of attrition in one segment over another. If the four-year segment is performing better than the two-year segment, relative to attrition, what has caused that improvement? *The point: The goal of the Master Marketer is to move all customers into the one-year box in all channels: zero attrition.*

RECENCY AND CUSTOMER ATTRITION RATES: PICKERING

There are more marketers that I have worked with who invest in prospecting (i.e. lose money acquiring a new customer) than marketers who prospect at a profit. For those marketers, winning the battle of attrition is the difference between making money and losing money, between prospering and closing the doors. For most marketers there are few issues more important to survival than attrition and retention.

In medicine there is a term, the 'Golden Hour,' that refers to a period of time during which the patient, if treated promptly and properly, stands a substantially higher chance of making a recovery. There is also a period like this in direct marketing.

If you examine your two-time plus buyers created over the last several years, and you can measure the interval between first purchase and second purchase, you will find a tipping point, perhaps it is at the three-month mark or the six-month mark, but it is there. That point will show this: if you can get a purchase within that tipping point time period, the majority will go on to make a third and subsequent purchase. Past the tipping point, they are less likely to make a third purchase.

To this end, many companies have created committees charged with acquiring second purchases. They examine contact strategies and special offers, merchandising and special account managers. Some of these may move the needle a bit. However, the Master Marketer is like a chess player, thinking several moves ahead. If you are not acquiring the right types of customers to begin with, this is largely an exercise in futility. In practice, to acquire the right types of customers, this means that sometimes you have to walk away from prospects that have high response rates but poor propensity to repurchase. Sometimes this is based on a list or employee size or income range, but they are there, and you can identify them.

As discussed earlier in this chapter, vintage analysis can be particularly helpful. Recall, vintage analysis looks at the customer database by year (or any more minute segmentation) of first purchase. For the last five years, by year of first acquisition, is the twelve-month retention rate increasing, decreasing, or staying the same? If it is changing significantly from year to year you must investigate what is (are) the driving force(s) behind this. It could be a shift in the product mix, or a change of focus on acquiring customers from large companies to smaller ones. It could be an offer change from one with a premium to one without—or vice versa. Either will dramatically affect your retention.

Attrition is closely allied with momentum and velocity, but they all have the same goal: finding and retaining the customers. For consumer marketers, in general, it makes sense to measure retention at the individual level. For items that are bought for oneself, you are not replaced as the buyer. This can change if the product can be given as a gift, in which case it makes sense to look at household level retention.

For business-to-business marketers the level of measurement is a bit more complex. First of all, it generally makes more sense to measure retention at the site (business) level. With the propensity to pass along catalogs within a company and in larger companies with purchasing departments, it only makes sense to measure at the site level.

For larger business organizations you may also want to track how many buyers you have at a site. In an organization of nine people, having only one buyer is sufficient and you are probably not missing out on too many selling opportunities. In an organization of one hundred or one thousand at a site, having only one buyer is likely leaving money on the table.

What does this have to do with recency? It is all aimed at keeping buyers in that top recency bucket.

RECENCY AND REACTIVATION: LIBEY

Perhaps the greatest promise of recency improvement is found in customer reactivation, or attrition recovery. During year one, some fifty percent or so of all new customers are lost to attrition and never order again. I have seen the first-year attrition rate as high as ninety percent and as low as twenty percent. Business-to-business marketers seem to fall in the forty to fifty percent attrition area, and consumers in the fifty to sixty percent attrition range, although these figures vary by market niche. More often than not, marketers—when asked for their attrition rates—don't know. And for those model-building addicted marketers who are constantly looking for the next 'decile high' and say, "RFM is too simplistic, too basic, too obsolete," my response is, "Perhaps if you *actually* mastered just recency you would be making far more earnings than you are now with all of your arcane models and abstruse wizardry." One thing is clear: there is enormous waste due to attrition, and it is very expensive. Actually, we pay for these customers twice—once when we acquire them, and again when we replace them. What if, instead of losing fifty percent of the customers in the first year, you lost only twenty-five percent? The end result would be a fifty percent gain in customer retention in the sixth year. Rather than keeping just sixteen of every one hundred new customers, you would wind up with twenty-four. What would that do to your earnings? Do the math. It's astounding.

Reactivation of lapsed customers is both a science and an art. Knowing the numbers cold and applying them optimally relative to return on investment is the science. Knowing the customers cold and creating an attractive dialogue and offer that brings them back is the art. And the science and the art are very different in each channel. Reactivation in the catalog channel is unlike reactivation in the online channel. Reactivation in the catalog-assisted online channel is different from the pure online channel. Retail reactivation is different from telephone reactivation. Plus, the recency segments in each channel that respond best to reactivation efforts may be totally different. In one channel, you will find you obtain the highest reactivation in the twenty-five to thirty-six month segment; in another channel, the eighteen to twenty-four month segment works best.

After observing reactivation initiatives seriously for about two-thirds of my career in direct marketing, it is puzzling to me that we learn so little. A lot of money has been spent in reactivation over the past two decades, but the first-year attrition rates have not changed. Perhaps a fifty percent attrition rate is organic to multi-channel direct marketing, but I am unwilling to accept that conclusion. Rather, I believe that there has been, almost always, insufficient focus, money and time dedicated to doing the testing and research necessary to understand *why* customers go away and don't return. For all of our channel technology and sophistication, the age-old maxim is still true: *People buy from people they like*. You begin there in establishing a permanent reactivation program, and you marry it to all of the recency measurements. Why? Because if you improve attrition by fifty percent you will be *four times* as profitable.

RECENCY AND REACTIVATION: PICKERING

I have never seen a reactivation that didn't work. There are no guarantees in life, but that is as close as I can come.

Many direct marketers invest to acquire a customer. If you are a marketer that invests in acquisition, then you have already paid the freight on these inactive customers; make the most of them. There are easy ways to do this. If you use a prospecting database, load the inactive buyer file separately from the active customer file. Then select your inactive buyers who show recent database activity using the database recency field. Those lapsed customers who show recent database activity (within the last three months or so) generally respond at a rate three or more times higher than the segment that has no indication of recent activity. Frequently these reactivation segments out-pull the best prospect lists and have been known to do as well as the active file segments.

If you still operate within a merge/purge environment (if you do, you are probably reading this book by candlelight), you can add a segment of inactive buyers and only mail those that dupe to the recent buyer lists in your merge.

As said before, using this data will frequently obligate you to pay a data charge or make a multi-buyer calculation to be fair to the list owners. This is money well spent.

These are examples of the most basic ways to use reactivation, there are more complex methods as well. These frequently involve using demographic or firmographic or other data external to the house file. Some marketers even develop models, though you must carefully and accurately measure the cost benefit to this option.

RECENCY AND MULTIPLE CUSTOMERS: LIBEY

Keeping customers in their correct boxes is complicated. For business-to-business and consumer direct marketers, a decision about who the customer is has to be made. While it sounds simple, that decision can complicate the recency segmentation beyond belief.

Who was the peddler's customer? Was it the mother, the father, the children, or was it the family unit, the farm itself? Did the peddler decide to include a particular farm on the route based on which family member purchased last? How did the peddler notate and manipulate the 3 x 5 cards when several members of the same farm family bought on different trips? What if there were two farms in the family?

A business is an *entity*. It continues usually without regard for the people who are the employees. Employees come and employees go; the business is the stable entity. If a business has several employees who are customers, which is the *customer of record*, the individual people or the business entity? The answer to that question has a lot to do with how the recency segmentation boxes are set up and maintained.

The peddler would have noted the purchases from each family member on the same card. The family unit itself would have been the customer of record. It made little difference to the peddler who bought as long as someone bought—and paid—each trip. The farm family was the target.

But does that work in multi-channel direct marketing? If an employee is the customer, do both the business *and* the individual employee continue to be carried in the one-year box, or only the employee, or only the business? If fifty employees from the same company are customers, do all fifty receive mailings even though only two have bought anything in the last three years? And what do you do about the channels? Are online customers the same as catalog customers? What cards get updated when a customer buys online instead of from a catalog? It gets complicated, doesn't it?

Look at the numbers. Suppose you are mailing at the rate of twenty-six catalogs a year to one-year recency customers. If it is your policy to mail each customer—*contacts*—inside the business entity, and if you have twenty contacts for one entity, you will mail 520 catalogs into that single entity. If, in addition, you also mail the entity itself, you will add another twenty-six mailings for a total of 546 catalogs a year.

But what happens when only three of those twenty contacts in that single entity are in the one-year recency box? Maybe there is only justification for mailing twenty-six catalogs to those three contacts. This would bring the mailings down to seventy-eight catalogs plus twenty-six for the entity itself, or a total of 104. The difference in contact strategy is a reduction of 442 catalog mailings into that company. At $.80 each, this is a savings of $353.60 a year, savings that might be redeployed to web strategies, email contacts, other channel efforts, or to the always wise decision to invest in prospecting.

The answer, of course, is that customers are people first and last and you treat the individual as the customer. The individual person has to meet the recency standards to continue to be treated as a one-year recency customer. The individual contacts inside an entity are mailed based on recency performance. Whether the entity is mailed as well is a policy decision that is best made through testing. If the entity mailings produce acceptable sales, continue mailing the entities; if not, stop. It is not a simple matter of yes or no; it is a matter of tracking, testing and evaluating performance and return on investment, in each channel and in each segment of recency in each channel. Ultimately, a contact strategy will develop for each channel and each segment, and it will form into a hierarchy for spending advertising money in the optimal places.

A sufficiently beefy database is needed that can handle all of the necessary tracking and segmentation for all channels. At the same time, it must be capable of managing multiple contacts within entities while managing their individual and aggregate contact recency segmentation accurately. All of the reconciliation is done in the database; therefore, all of the analytic utility to be gained (read:

improved earnings) is dependent upon the database capability, capacity and infinite flexibility.

RECENCY AND MULTIPLE CUSTOMERS: PICKERING

There are few issues as vexing to business-to-business direct marketers as how to treat multiple customers (or a mix of customers and prospects) at the same site. There are some elementary steps that you can take to help guide decisions.

Title information captured at the time of purchase can provide a wealth of information about who is actually *ordering* your product. This may or may not be the person who actually specifies, chooses, or authorizes the purchase, but it does tell you something. If you find a high portion of your buyers say that they are the warehouse manager, those are the first customers to select for circulation.

There is no formula that I have seen that will yield the correct number of contacts per site to mail. Unless you are targeting very small companies (under twenty or even under ten) you should probably at least *test* the value of a second catalog.

Targeting which sites to mail multiple catalogs, therefore, is best accomplished initially segmenting by employee size, if it is available. If employee size is not available, you can count the number of contacts at a site and use that as an indicator of what sites are larger than others.

As a next filter, the more recent sites generally justify more contacts than less recent site—although there are other elements that will play into this as well. We will visit these issues in upcoming chapters.

With respect to my writing partner, more direct marketers have been under-mailing the number of contacts per site rather than over-mailing them. Often this is tied to corporate goals of acquiring X number of new sites. This is a poor substitute for a well-developed strategy based on profitability.

Many direct marketers send an additional catalog to the site title slugged to an appropriate title. The success of this is great for some mailers and does not cost justify itself for other mailers. The rewards are so great for a relatively low incremental cost that it is worth testing, at least to the larger, more recently active sites.

RECENCY AND ACQUISITIONS: LIBEY

In my firm's experience as advisors and investment bankers representing both sellers and buyers of multi-channel direct marketing companies, we often find knowledgeable buyers focusing closely on recency during the due diligence phase of acquisitions. The evaluation and, consequently, value attributed to the customer base depends on the growth of the recency segments over the most recent three- to five-year period. The scrutiny is almost always limited to the zero- to twelve-month buyers, thirteen- to twenty-four-month buyers and the twenty-five-month plus buyers. The changes in quantities between the recency segments are of primary interest, as the buyers are attempting to understand whether the customer base is regenerating or aging. A shift of weight from the one-year recency file to the three-year recency file over a two-year period is concerning, particularly if the one-year file has also become smaller. Savvy buyers of direct marketing businesses who are masters of recency can quickly understand a company's condition from the balance sheet, the income statement *and* the three-year history of recency in each channel.

Sellers of direct marketing companies who understand the importance of recency, will sometimes pump up prospecting in the two to three years prior to the sale in order to fatten the one- and two-year recency files. Others may choose to stop prospecting and shift to a reactivation strategy in order to refill the one-year file with lapsed customers at a lower cost, thereby saving on prospecting costs and increasing the earnings. It is the multiple of earnings, after all, that will determine the selling price of the business.

The point: Recency also is a partial determinant of the business valuation.

RECENCY AND ACQUISITIONS: PICKERING

Recency is a key component in determining the value of the company, and it may be the most important. It infrequently gets the rigorous analysis that it deserves during the acquisition process. More focus is paid to the overlap between files and other more superficial measures.

Most acquisitions are driven because the company for sale is doing exceptionally well or exceptionally poorly. There is little demand for a mediocre performing company unless the buyer is simply on an acquisition spree.

When a company is doing well, the focus is on how much profit is being driven to the bottom line. A critical question in determining future profitability: is the company able to continually acquire valuable customers? Examining the recency velocity, momentum, and attrition will show the company's recent success in customer acquisition. If growth is continuing, the value of the customer file (generally the most valuable part of a direct marketing business) is high. If the prospecting performance is decreasing, the value decreases. As always, it is important to drill down and separate the performance of the pure prospecting efforts from the house file circulation (including reactivation).

When a company is doing poorly (perhaps being purchased out of bankruptcy) the performance of the recent house file and prospecting efforts is more critical than anything else. After all, if they were acquiring profitable customers, the firm wouldn't be in dire straits. The purchaser either has a plan to deal with bringing profit to the business or is acquiring the company for other reasons. In either instance, the recency characteristics are the first indicator of the value of the company. Invest the money to do thorough research. It will pay enormous dividends.

RECENCY AND WHY IT IS NOT ENOUGH: LIBEY

For all of the supposed sophistication of North American, multi-channel direct marketing companies, there is an appalling lack of optimal recency, frequency and monetary value analyses as an integrated analytic tool. Many companies are competent with part of recency alone, but are unable to fully integrate recency, frequency and monetary value, let alone the advanced components of product, channel, position and market. For those companies existing in the incredibly competitive milieu of multi-channel commerce having only recency as their formulaic touchstone, they are courting disaster.

Recency alone does not a direct marketing titan make. Recency only gives a portion of the essential base information for managing a multi-channel direct marketing strategy and an effective multi-channel contact strategy. Companies operating only with recency are analogous to a professional golfer playing a PGA tournament with only a seven iron. It's great for about one shot out of twenty, but you can't compete against other golfers having full sets of clubs.

Knowing when a customer last bought is good for creating part of a contact strategy, but it does nothing to answer important questions like, "How often does a customer buy?" or "What channels do the best customers come from?" or "How much money do the best customers spend?" or "What products do the best customers buy?"

Recency allows you to choose which customers you will visit and how often you will visit them. Recency also tells you something about the individual customer purchasing trend and, collectively, the purchasing trend within the entire customer base over time. Through the reconciliation process, recency is an indicator of growth and shrinkage, of health and disease, the pulse of the formulaic, multi-channel, direct marketing company.

But you cannot go beyond recency without adequate resources, and these include capital, vision, talent, dedication, innovation, and systems. Companies that have not progressed beyond recency are generally lacking all of these resources. Given the speed of channel change today, the denial, tap-dancing, and constant excuses are irresponsible, even pathetic. These companies are disappearing because nobody knows what is happening. The owner or CEO is often hoping to just make it through another year. No, recency is not enough. But, it is a beginning and it remains the most fundamental component of direct marketing strategy across all channels; yet only a small percentage of companies—in any channel—have mastered its secrets, potential, and understanding.

RECENCY AND WHY IT IS NOT ENOUGH: PICKERING

There are many reasons why recency is not enough. My writing partner has highlighted the most important ones.

When recency is the prime focus, or the only focus, it is possible, even likely to create a vicious cycle, a veritable death spiral. It goes like this:

There is generally an inverse relationship between propensity to respond to an offer and the likelihood to spend a large amount of money or to make a second purchase. This is as true for consumer mailers as business-to-business mailers. If the focus is on keeping the largest amount of buyers in the most recent segments, response becomes the overwhelming concern. In short, you buy many customers that do not become profitable. As the mailer acquires more customers to fill the recent segments, they spend less money initially and spend less over time. They justify less investment or generate less revenue that can be spent on prospecting and house file circulation, so fewer catalogs are mailed, emails sent, calls made, or faxes faxed. As the number of contacts falls, so too will the customer file size decline. Thus, even though the goal was to keep as many buyers as possible in the recent segments, it has the exact opposite effect.

Not only is concentrating only on recency not enough, it is potentially fatal. When recency is used in conjunction with frequency and monetary analysis, direct marketers can survive. When RFM is optimized with other elements, the Master Marketer can—and will —thrive.

Chapter 2 Frequency

FREQUENCY CHARACTERISTICS: LIBEY

Frequency is how many times a customer buys. It is an indicator of usage and satisfaction. As an aggregate of all customers, by channel and collectively, it is a primary measurement of demand. By itself, it is the second in importance of the cardinal three—recency, frequency and monetary value.

Frequency describes a state of the customer's level of demand. Demand for products or services can be described as high, average and low. A customer who purchases twelve times a year could be considered to be a high demand, high frequency customer. Another customer who buys four times a year may be an average demand, average frequency customer. And a customer who buys only once a year may be a low demand, low frequency buyer. All three customers, however, are active, recent customers because they are reaffirming their loyalty by regenerating their one-year recency status.

When channel buying history is added, it is possible to be both a high demand, high frequency catalog customer and a low demand, low frequency online customer. Depending on levels of frequency in each channel, such a customer may be a high demand, high frequency multi-channel customer.

From purely a frequency point of view, a customer who buys twelve times a year is more valuable than a customer who buys only one time a year. Twelve opportunities to engage the customer are better than just one. Every interaction is, potentially, an opportunity to strengthen the loyalty, bond and reliance between the customer and the company, and to retain the customer, thereby lowering the attrition rate. Plus a customer who buys twelve times gives you twelve chances to sell them something additional. A high frequency customer is at least showing they care about your company by coming back time and time again.

If you think of frequency as the number of times a customer walks into your store, or the number of times a customer visits your website, you will understand the importance of frequent customer contact. But, there is a big difference between *visiting* and *buying something*. For direct marketers, in all channels, frequency requires a purchase. The more frequent the purchases occur, the higher on the frequency hierarchy the customer rises.

Frequency is influenced by product and usage rate. The frequency of an automobile purchase is much less than the frequency of toothpaste. An automobile dealer may have an average customer with four-year recency and a one-time frequency. The toothpaste seller may have a customer with one-year recency and ten-time frequency. At the extreme, a bridge building company may have customers with one hundred-year recency and one-time frequency.

Generally, consumable products produce higher frequency than durable products. The comparison of toothpaste and bridges illustrates this difference. The faster the usage or deterioration rate, the higher the frequency of purchases. Products having a short shelf life tend to drive a higher frequency of purchase; milk is an example.

Consumable products can be highly seasonal and frequency can be correspondingly seasonal. Consider ice melting products. Sidewalks, water and freezing temperatures are necessary to drive purchases of ice melting products. That implies a seasonality factor and it is logical to assume that a higher frequency of purchases occurs in the winter. The customer may be one-year recency, but frequency is compressed into the winter months.

Frequency can also be influenced by external forces. An abnormally severe and wet winter can increase frequency of ice melting product purchases. The hurricane season can drive a higher frequency of purchasing for plywood, pumps, generators, and hundreds of other products.

Most commodity products have a steady, fairly predictable rate of frequency. A wholesale distributor shipping large numbers of boxes purchases packing list envelopes 4.2 times a year, or every eighty-seven days, essentially a three-month supply. If that customer's rate of frequency changes it is a signal something has changed. Perhaps frequency is increasing indicating more shipments and, therefore, more demand for packing list envelopes. Perhaps frequency is decreasing indicating business is slowing and fewer packing list envelopes are being used.

Frequency is also influenced by fashion and fad. A line of stylish clothing can drive frequency and, overnight, can disappear. Millions of customers can go from one-year recency and five-time frequency to zero frequency. Fads die out. For a one-product company this is a problem. The same frequency behavior is seen with new restaurants. The first month or so, repeat customers may dine every week, then every other week, then every month. Soon, frequency drops to once every one or two years.

Frequency moves up or down with regulatory or legislative actions. A product that is suddenly restricted will drop in frequency; a product that is outlawed will cease frequency altogether. A restricted or banned product that is suddenly deregulated will experience an initial surge in both recency and frequency, moving toward equilibrium later.

And, of course, frequency is influenced, perhaps to the greatest degree, by satisfaction. If the customer is not satisfied, frequency diminishes or stops. Satisfaction comes in many shapes and guises; it is often impossible to know what constitutes satisfaction in the mind of the customer and it is often irrational. But, for the most part, satisfaction involves basic expectations like price, timeliness, courtesy, attention and quality. Marketers cannot control the irrational, but they can control the basic customer expectations and, thereby, some of the elements of frequency.

Frequency is not as cut and dried as recency. To some, frequency seems essentially the same thing as recency. But, it is not the same. Recency is all about *when* a purchase is made; frequency is all about *how many* purchases are made (**Figure L2.1**). The many complexities of frequency make it harder to understand the underlying motivations. My personal frequency rate at a hotel chain just went to zero based on an overpriced room that was dirty and a heating system that did not work. Nobody at that hotel or at that hotel's

Figure L2.1

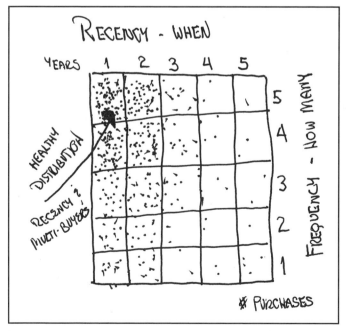

corporate headquarters knows that, but nonetheless, the chain lost thirty nights a year from this single customer. If 300 people a year stay in that room and half of them have the same reaction and are the same level of frequency of business travel, that hotel chain loses 4,500 room nights, and they don't know why.

The numerical counting of frequency is the easy part. Any good database will give you the number of purchases. The customer's hidden reasoning behind frequency—satisfaction—cannot be programmed and, unless you carefully analyze and research changes in frequency, remains forever a mystery.

At the outset, marketers must make a decision on how to define and track frequency. There is a choice and it can be done either of two ways. Multiple purchases can be counted on an annual basis or on a lifetime basis. On an annual basis, a one-time, one-year customer means that customer has purchased five times in the current year. On a lifetime basis, a five-time, one-year customer means the customer has purchased this year for the fifth time since becoming

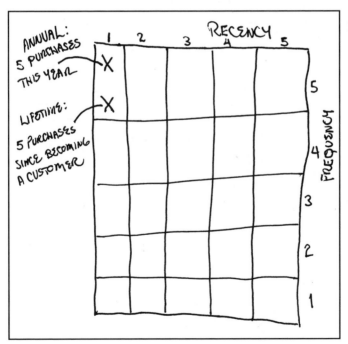

Figure L2.2

a customer (**Figure L2.2**). Either way works depending on how you want to track frequency, but one method must be chosen; you cannot mix apples and oranges. The structure of the database is very different in each of these methods.

To make frequency a bit more complicated, channels influence frequency rates. A customer who is a five-time a year catalog buyer suddenly drops to two catalog purchases. Are there three purchases in the online channel? Or three in the retail channel? Frequency has to be tracked in each channel and in total for all channels. Channel frequency can be an indicator of channel cannibalism. If the online channel is cannibalizing the telemarketing channel, it will show up in a higher online frequency and lower telemarketing frequency. If the total number of orders and the average order value remain the same, the cannibalism is benign. If, however, total orders and average order value drop, the channel cannibalism is cancerous.

Frequency can be measured in each segment of recency. If the four- and five-year recency boxes are loaded with customers who used to be five-time buyers, and the one- through three-year recency boxes contain only two-time buyers, something is wrong. Something changed four years ago that cut frequency of buying dramatically (**Figure L2.3**). This is information the Master Marketer gleans from frequency. A directional arrow can represent frequency for individual customers. The arrow can point up for increasing frequency, sideways for frequency that stays the same, or down for frequency that is dropping. As with recency arrows, only one direction is acceptable. For aggregate customers in channels, SICs, zip codes, employee sizes, or any other demographic or firmographic, the same arrows can indicate frequency condition (**Figure L2.4**).

Finally, if we think only of frequency, a customer with ten purchases is a better customer than a customer with only one purchase. The one-time buyer has not yet even demonstrated regeneration of recency. The Master Marketer, then, is skilled at moving all customers up in frequency, as well as up in recency. If all the customers are

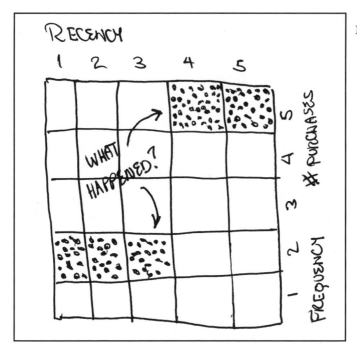

Figure L2.3

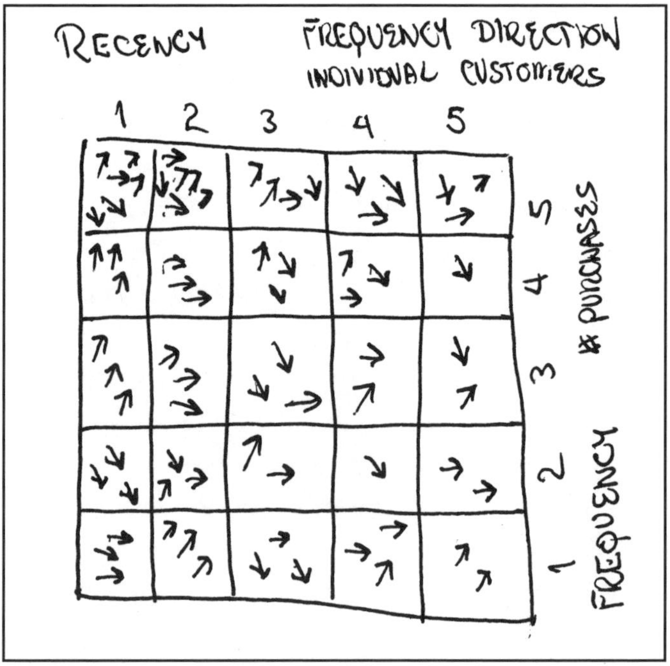

RECENCY
1 2 3 4 5

WHAT HAPPENED?

PURCHASES

5 4 3 2 1

FREQUENCY

RECENCY   FREQUENCY DIRECTION
               INDIVIDUAL CUSTOMERS

Figure L2.4

1 2 3 4 5

PURCHASES

5 4 3 2 1

FREQUENCY

jammed into the one-year box, and they are all ten-time buyers, life is large. Or, you're a drug dealer.

FREQUENCY CHARACTERISTICS: PICKERING

Frequency is the middle child. It is not as top-of-mind as recency, and viewed to be not as critical as monetary; frequency has traditionally been somewhat ignored. Ignore it at your peril; the Master Marketer does not.

Although there is no question that frequency is important, there is the question of whether to count frequency at a life-to-date (LTD) level or a rolling twelve months. This question is largely a philosophical one. Most systems used by multi-channel direct marketing companies carry *all* purchases. It is at the marketer's discretion to use all the data or just the recent, frequency information.

If you use only LTD frequency, you can run into a pitfall. Imagine that Don and I are both five-time purchasers and both have a recency of the last quarter. I made four purchases more than thirty-six months ago and one purchase recently. Don has made one purchase a month for the past five months. With this information alone, Don is the better customer. He should be treated as such in circulation and valued as such if the company is going through the valuation process.

Acceptable frequency can look very different to different marketers. A low margin, business-to-business company may have a business model that stresses repeat purchases to achieve profitability. A consumer company with a high margin product can survive with a lower level of repeat purchases.

Frequency can be triggered by innovation. When Microsoft releases a new version of Office, or Apple comes out with a new whiz-bang laptop, I am more likely than not going to make a purchase. If you can update your products with meaningful new features at reasonable and consistent intervals, you can increase frequency and make it more regular and predictable.

Frequency—ideal frequency—is a much more elusive definition than recency and monetary value. With recency, you want everyone in the most recent bucket if possible. With monetary value, you want everyone as high up as they can be. Frequency's ideal is not as easily defined, as we will see.

FREQUENCY AND PRODUCT USAGE: LIBEY

To explore frequency and product usage, we will use business envelopes as the product because envelopes tend to be almost entirely demand driven. If a business makes one sale and invoices for that sale, one envelope is used. If the same business makes fifty sales, then fifty envelopes are used to send invoices. Product usage varies in direct response to demand.

Product usage can be influenced by many things, internal and external. Internally, a company may expand and increase sales, thereby increasing demand for envelopes. Externally, an economic recession may be responsible for a decline in sales by fifty percent. As a result, fifty percent fewer invoices are mailed and the usage rate for envelopes and purchasing frequency drops accordingly. The economy can drive product usage in either direction.

Internally, cash flow can influence product usage rates and frequency of purchasing. If cash is plentiful, a company may purchase a year's worth of envelopes to take advantage of negotiated price breaks for large purchases. If cash flow is tight the same company may shift to monthly purchases of envelopes to conserve cash even though those envelopes will cost more in small quantities. Spending cash for a year's supply of envelopes may not be the best use of money for cash-strapped companies.

Internal purchasing authority can influence product usage and frequency. The person authorizing the purchase may be limited in authority to purchases of two hundred dollars or less. Rather than go through repetitive internal justification and requisition processes or competitive bidding, a quantity of envelopes costing under two hundred dollars is ordered more frequently, thereby driving up frequency while not necessarily increasing the annual usage rate.

External, uncontrolled events can influence usage and frequency. Weather-related events such as floods and hurricanes may drive envelope demand due to water damage. Relocation after major weather events, due to damage, can increase envelope ordering as addresses have to be changed. In these situations, increased frequency is being driven by replacements rather than actual increased usage. When forecasting customer usage, this subtlety must be understood. If weather causes increased demand by thirty percent and all of that increase was replacement rather than increased usage, demand and usage in following years will likely decrease.

Internal events such as technology adoption can influence demand, usage rates and, increasingly, product obsolescence. A company opting to shift from mailed invoicing to online invoicing and online receipt of payment will eliminate a sizeable portion of its envelope product usage and frequency may plummet. Technology tends to eliminate certain types of products, particularly products that are paper-based and hand-prepared.

Other factors influence product usage and frequency. Discounting can influence frequency, either by shifting market share away to discount competitors, or by buyers stocking up on large quantities while the discount is offered. Personal preference and changes in individuals who make buying decisions influence frequency. Acquisitions cause changes in frequency and usage rates. Moving to offshore operations generally takes the demand for products with the move. These are the considerations for only one product—envelopes. The complexities driving usage rates and frequency for the millions of products used globally are incomprehensible. As a result, few multichannel direct marketing companies have mastery over the ever-shifting foundations of product usage. For almost all, frequency marketing is a reaction. The opportunity lies in actually driving frequency intentionally. For the few marketers who recognize and understand that fact—and the fewer yet who have the ability to execute and innovate—*intentional frequency* is a direct marketing frontier.

FREQUENCY AND PRODUCT USAGE: PICKERING

There is an intimate linkage between frequency and product usage and this must be completely understood to make effective decisions. This applies to house file circulation plans, prospecting efforts, and even list rental decisions.

If you order eye protection and pay for it, that is one decision, one order, and the product is used until it is no longer needed, replaced, etc. End of story. If you order a set of cooking recipes from a continuity program and they are shipped every four to six weeks, how do you classify this? There is one initial purchase decision to send in the order form, dial the 800 number, or order via the web. This initial purchase decision is affirmed every time the customer pays the bill throughout the course of, say, eighteen shipments, when the series is completed.

When doing house file circulation for this continuity, do you regard the customer as having purchased once or eighteen times? If they opted for automatic debit, when they don't have to make that affirmation every month by writing a check, are they a more or less reliable customer from a frequency point of view? The continuity marketer generally treats this as one program purchase with seventeen affirmations and no bad debt. Even though the customer may use the recipe cards six or seven times a week, there is one purchase decision.

If you are renting a list of continuity buyers, or purchasers who order a product and pay over a period of time, there are nuances that you need to keep in mind. Any program that you pay over time changes recency and frequency considerations. A recent buyer may have only just ordered the product or may have ordered the product twelve months ago but made a regular purchase last month. Within the list rental area, there are not necessarily hard-and-fast rules. A good broker will know the nuances of ordering various lists on the market and this can make all the difference between a list with mediocre performance and one that is a consistent star of the continuations. The devil is in the details.

FREQUENCY AND PRODUCT PRICING: LIBEY

I believe price has become the dominant factor in business-to-business and consumer purchasing today. Four factors have contributed to the top-of-mind position price holds in the buyer's mind: 1) the Wal-Martization of America; 2) the economic slow-down of 1999-2005; 3) the Internet; and 4) online price comparison technologies. Each of these individually created a laser-like focus on price over the past decade, but collectively they have written the word large on the national commercial psyche. Also, I don't see this unprecedented American focus on price receding; it is likely here to stay and can only get worse. Yes, there will always be luxury buying, but for the vast majority of Americans, price is the everyday mantra, the defining aspect of competitive choice. And if you don't believe this is true, why are you buying so many of your products from China?

All things being equal, then, customers will buy on price. This inherently breeds customer disloyalty which results in a drop in frequency and recency unless you are the low-price leader. This is precisely the situation we never wanted to wake up and find ourselves to be in.

As a partial palliative to the pain, marketers who sell products with quantity-based pricing, generally commodity products like envelopes, can influence frequency by manipulating the price *multiple*.

If a single envelope costs $.01 to make, then 1,000 envelopes cost $10.00 total. If the manufacturer sells them on a three-time mark-up, the envelopes will sell for $30.00. If a customer buys 100,000 envelopes a year, the manufacturer could sell those envelopes for $3,000 ($.03 x 100,000). The sale would be a one-time sale, a one-time shipment and a one-time invoicing. Gross profit is $2,000.

If the customer wants to buy only a three-month supply of envelopes, or a quantity of 25,000, the manufacturer has to make four sales efforts, four shipments and four invoices; the cost of doing business increases. As a result, the manufacturer manipulates the price multiple from three-times to five-times and the price increases to $.05 each or $1,250 for 25,000 and, over four orders, $5,000 for 100,000 envelopes. Gross profit is $4,000.

If the customer conserves cash short-term and orders monthly, the unit purchase is about 8,000 envelopes a month. This could further push the price multiple to, say, eight-times, or $.08 apiece, or $8,000 a year over twelve orders. Gross profit is $7,000.

A frequency of one purchase a year drives a multiple of three-times cost; a frequency of four times a year drives a multiple of five-times; and a frequency of twelve times a year drives a price multiple of eight-times. Therefore, frequency drives quantity; quantity drives multiple; multiple drives margins; margins drive earnings. If you are selling 100,000 envelopes, do you want a one-time, three-time or twelve-time customer? And in the increasingly hostile, cut-throat and competitive environment created through the spawn of Wal-Martization, at what frequency level and price multiple can you competitively offer a discount to keep the business?

Discount pricing has become a dominant factor in Internet retailing, price comparison shopping, and retail membership outlets such as Costco and Sam's Club. But, discounting has emerged in the multi-channel, multi-position direct marketing companies in ways that are, as yet, unclear for the future direction. Discounting has never been as prevalent as it is at the present time. Because it is a war fought predominately across the supply chain logistics landscape, only the mammoth operators can win. There comes a point for others, including many multi-channel direct marketers, where they discount themselves out of business. In the final analysis, loyalty (recency) earned through discounting is a sham loyalty that ultimately and utterly fails the discounter.

I have been writing and speaking about margin erosion in direct marketing for over twenty-five years, predicting it would ultimately reach a crisis stage when cataloging, retail discounting and price comparison technologies converged. We are there. The answer is *not* discounting. We are nearing the end of that tactical error. The answer is found in both the expanding population and the expanding gulf between the wealthy and the poor. Marketers must straddle both; must make high margin sales as well as low margin sales; must capture share in both sides of the market. The next major frontier—as multi-channel marketing was a major frontier—will be *multi-position marketing*. A later chapter looks at this concept in some detail.

FREQUENCY AND PRODUCT PRICING: PICKERING

Test, test, test. That is what should be uppermost in the mind of a direct marketer. To that end, let's design a test that will show us the best pricing breaks on envelopes.

If we are selling this many envelopes, we are likely marketing to businesses. So, the rules are different. When we talk about our test and control populations, we cannot talk about these as individuals. Why? Let's imagine that Don and I are both purchasing agents sitting in adjoining cubicles. Don has to buy envelopes and we have a need for 25,000. He looks at his catalog and sees that the price is $0.05 each or $1,250. That seems steep to him, so he asks me if I have any catalogs for price comparisons.

I give Don a catalog with the same title, the same cover, and the same product, but different price breaks. I was selected to receive a price test catalog. My catalog shows a price of $0.03 each or $750. Having gotten my MBA, I can point out that paying $750 is better than paying $1,250 for the same product. Being a smart man, Don agrees and purchases from my catalog.

This type of scenario happens frequently for price testing on the house file and for testing the effectiveness of better pricing on prospect pieces mailed into existing buying locations (the testing strategy being that lower prices on prospecting increase response). Obviously the example of Don's purchase hurts the marketer on a number of levels:

1. True visibility to the test was lost. Absent any other information, would Don have ordered the envelopes at the higher price?

2. The marketer may have lost $500 if Don had ordered at the higher price.

3. The marketer has taught Don to mistrust that the catalog he receives has the best prices available. He may now actively shop your catalog against your web page and probably also against other marketers.

Although I do not completely share my writing partner's conviction on pricing being an overwhelming factor, it is as critical to your marketing mix as promotion and product. Therefore, we need to set up consistent, stable cells for pricing. It is easiest to set up a cell based on geography. One of the benefits of this is that it can be used for testing house file circulation pricing tests, or to test different pricing strategies on prospecting mailings versus house file circulation as follows:

1. Select a few well-populated geographies across the U.S. Make certain that they are in different regions to control for inclement weather adversely affecting deliverability.

2. Within each region select one or more Sectional Center Facilities (SCF) as designated by the first three positions of the ZIP code. You can find a map that will have these marked.

3. With each SCF, run counts on either the fourth or the fifth

position of the ZIP code. These counts will remain constant across time as ZIP codes rarely change.

4. Segment names by either the fourth or the fifth position of the ZIP to develop two numerically equal segments of customers. It may be evens versus odds, or 0-4 versus 5-9, or 1, 3, 4, 7, 9 versus 2, 5, 6, 8, 0, or whatever gives the most even split of customers and sites.

5. Telemarketers and fax marketers can set up cells with less precision but similar stability by using area codes.

Once you have identified the test cells, begin your promotion. You may wish to test only house file circulation to determine which price or price break yields the most revenue or frequency. This is a key driver of profit, but alas, more of the pricing decision is based on costs than on price sensitivity.

One of the best uses of this technique is to test cannibalization of the house file by the use of prospecting catalogs with lower prices. By cannibalization I mean stealing sales that would ordinarily have been placed via a house file catalog and pushing them to the prospecting catalog.

FREQUENCY AND PRODUCT SATISFACTION: LIBEY

You buy a product. You love that product. You buy more of that product or related products. Not a lot of magic there.

Loving a product does not mean that you buy it at the same place every time. Product satisfaction and frequency do not always go hand-in-hand.

As an example, you like the envelopes you bought from Company *A*. The next time you need envelopes, Company *B* has the same thing on sale for fifty percent less than you paid at Company *A*. You buy from Company *B*. You are now a one-year recency and one-time frequency customer at both companies. Your definition of satisfaction is price and as long as you remain satisfied by price alone

Company *A* is never going to get a repeat order from you unless they discount the price below Company *B*.

Six months go by and you are completely out of envelopes. Without envelopes, you can't invoice customers; in effect, you are temporarily out of business. Company *B*, the discounter, takes two weeks to fill your order. Company *A* has a rush order service and can deliver the envelopes to you in one day. You buy from Company *A*. Your definition of product satisfaction just changed from price to speed.

Company *B* contacts you and says they are sad you did not reorder. You tell them they are too slow. They tell you to plan ahead and can offer you a program where you will receive envelopes every six months without fail and they will guarantee you never run out, plus they will give you a thirty percent discount off Company *A*'s price. You sign up for Company *B*'s program. Your definition of product satisfaction is now price with service.

Satisfaction and frequency are moving targets. The customer can go along for five years, happy as a clam with Company *B*. One day the customer service representative is rude and the entire satisfaction history collapses in five seconds. Back you go to Company *A*.

It is impossible to define satisfaction for every customer. It changes constantly and is often irrational. But, existing within the customer base is an overall qualitative definition of satisfaction that you can understand provided someone is willing to look for it and devotes the time necessary to talk with customers, particularly one-time frequency customers. *This business is really very simple: your job is to get prospects to buy and once they have bought to keep them coming back. If they stop buying, your job is to find out why, fix it and bring them back as recent, frequent customers.* That's it. That is the secret to the money machine.

More often than not, product satisfaction has less to do with low frequency and lapsed recency than with the way customers are treated, which, coupled with price, determines whether they come back. When the customers become resigned to poor service, as we see in retail stores, they buy based on price because nothing else exists. Direct marketers have always had a high service standard and it is that standard that gave us the edge we enjoy. If we lose our service advantage, we not only lose to price, but we lose margin. At that point, we are just a form of retail.

FREQUENCY AND PRODUCT SATISFACTION: PICKERING

Most customers do not tell you that they aren't going to order from your company anymore. Some do, though. Despite your best efforts, from time-to-time some customers will return items, or try to return items. Although this is can be difficult to handle within some operational systems, this is a *tremendous opportunity*. Many items are small enough in cost that, if they are not correct or are only slightly damaged, customers will simply drop the issue. The perception of a high hassle factor drives this behavior. Some very important customers, however, will return products or make arrangements to return them. They are taking this opportunity to tell you that they want to continue to do business with you, but you missed the mark this time out. If you track the frequency of return items or orders—and you should—you will find that those customers buy more, buy more frequently and spend more money than the average customer. This issue should carry particular weight with the multi-channel direct marketers who sell online and by catalog.

The great lure of internet commerce is the ease of order placement. This drives many buyers to the channel. The difficulty of making returns trails only identity theft as a factor deterring people from ordering online. When you put in a painless, seamless returns system—and you can demonstrate it to the customer—you have helped to build strength around your offering and to build insulation against price pressure from your competitors.

FREQUENCY AND CUSTOMER SERVICE SATISFACTION: LIBEY

A happy customer is a frequent customer and a frequent customer is a happy customer. Ideally, customer service satisfaction is what *should* keep customers coming back, not price.

For marketers selling consumable, commodity-type products the best indication of customer satisfaction is likely to be the frequency percentage. If a high percentage of customers are in the one-year recency, multiple-frequency category, the business is probably well-run and the customers are probably satisfied. If, however, a high percentage of customers are one-time buyers and are found in the two- and three-year and older recency files, satisfaction may be a problem, particularly if product and price are not (**Figure L2.5**).

It is possible to determine when customer satisfaction deteriorated or improved from frequency analysis. If a large group of high-frequency customers suddenly stopped buying two years ago, they

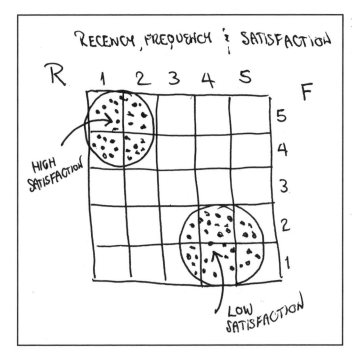

Figure L2.5

will be seen as a 'bubble' in the recency/frequency segmentation. When the bubble formed, satisfaction dropped **(Figure L2.6)**. The opposite is also true. When a large number of customers experience high satisfaction a bubble forms. A large number of one-time buyers become multiple buyers. When the bubble formed, satisfaction improved. By looking for these bubbles in frequency, it is fairly simple to isolate periods in a direct marketing company's history when high out-of-stock situations existed, when product quality was a problem, or when customer treatment was less than perfect.

If customers from the one-year frequency box who have a history of high-frequency purchasing over two, three or four years are isolated and examined, you will be looking at the best customers you have and, most likely, the customers with the highest customer service satisfaction levels. These are the heart and soul of the customer base and the people you must be talking to constantly. They can tell you what they like about doing business with your company, and that

Figure L2.6

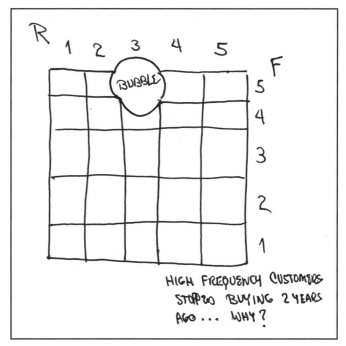

is some of the most important information you can ever obtain.

Flag each of those customers and when their frequency drops, find out why immediately. It is either price or service if the product has not changed. That is the moment when the customer can be saved. Using frequency is common sense. If a customer walks into your store every three days and buys something and that customer has been doing that for three years, something is wrong when the customer doesn't show up after three days. At that moment, your job is to find out why, fix it and bring the customer back.

As a direct marketer, you could have a million customers, but unless they are buying repeatedly they are not contributing to the profitability of the company. It is better to have one thousand customers buying four times a year for three years straight than to have twelve thousand customers who buy only once. The total number of orders is the same, but the costs to get those customers and the return on investment are vastly different.

The problem with customer satisfaction and frequency or recency is that rarely does a customer call and say, "Hey, this is my last order." They just get mad or go for the lower price and stop buying and there is no known reason for their disappearance. As a result, a year goes by and the customer is being mailed to every two weeks. At the end of the year, the customer is moved to the two-year box and is mailed every month for another year. At the end of the second year, the customer is shifted to the three-year box and mailed every two months. It is conceivable that this customer could be mailed for ten years and there isn't a prayer of ever getting a second order. If you knew that up front, you could either fix the problem or cut out a lot of expensive, unproductive mailings. But you don't know that up front. You never know when you have received the last order you will ever get from a customer.

Using recency and frequency information from the database, it is possible to set up a proactive protocol that attacks the problem of customer attrition. The database can deliver a daily report of all customers with three purchases or more who will age from one-year recency to two-year recency today. If that number is 232 customers today, it is time to get to work and contact those customers and find out why they have not purchased in the last 365 days. This uses frequency information and analysis for a positive and beneficial reason. It is no different from the mental process the peddler used when going over the customer histories from previous trips. When somebody stops buying, there is always a reason. The only way to bring that person back into recency and frequency is to know the reason and to solve the problem.

Frequency and satisfaction must be tracked, analyzed and managed on two levels: 1) overall across all customers; and 2) by channel across all of each channel's customers. Satisfaction-driven frequency will be different in all channels and requires different objectives, goals, measurement and solutions. Satisfaction is not one-size-fits-all. An online customer's satisfaction quotient is much different from that of a catalog or infomercial customer. Even the definition of *high frequency* or *low frequency* will change depending on the channel. An overall high frequency customer may be a low frequency online customer and a low frequency catalog customer; the channel driver for that customer may be infomercial response. Why? That customer watches a lot of television. Not a lot of analytic magic there. But, how do you know? How is the database set up to quantify frequency by channel (which is easy) and customer channel motivation (which is not so easy)? And how do you market to meet the motivation? Those are the differentiating skills of the Master Multi-Channel Marketer from those of the apprentice.

FREQUENCY AND CUSTOMER SERVICE SATISFACTION: PICKERING

Just as most customers won't tell you they have made their final purchase, most customers do not tell you at the time of their first purchase that they plan to purchase from you multiple times.

Many marketers have special services to treat high value customers in a 'high-touch' fashion. There are many different names for this type of program: strategic accounts; key accounts; large value accounts, or other variations. There is no consistent logic from company to company on how accounts are assigned to these special programs. Some of the methodologies include contract customers, Fortune 500 or 1000, employee size, or a minimum threshold of sales.

If you have a contract with a customer, it makes sense to assign a consistent account manager if you can. This will maximize your ability to keep this customer recent, ordering frequently, and to remain profitable. On the other hand, if a customer orders regularly, and is profitable, does it not make sense to let them qualify their way into getting an account manger? This is direct marketing Darwinism: if they prove themselves the fittest customers by buying recently, frequently, and profitably, they earn preferential treatment.

FREQUENCY AND THE MARKETING HIERARCHY: LIBEY

If, as above, the daily database output of aging customers for today is 232 customers with three purchases or more moving from the one-year to the two-year box, then within that unique mass of 232 customers is a hierarchy of frequency. At the very top of the list of 232, there might be three customers who have bought more than ten times in the last 365 days. They form the first tier in the hierarchy of retention. If you can only save three, these are the three given we know only recency and frequency at this point, not monetary value.

Below these three is another group of six who have bought exactly ten times; another group of twelve who have bought exactly nine times; another group of thirty who have bought eight times, and so on. The bottom group, the last in the hierarchy, of the 232 consists of sixty-three customers who have bought exactly three times. This hierarchical ranking represents a value ranking. The customers at the top have the highest value relative to the frequency of purchases; the customers at the bottom have the lowest value relative to the frequency of purchases. Note, however, that within *all* potentially aging customers today, these top 232 are the very best with three to more than ten purchases in a year. There may be another 645 customers aging today who have a one-time frequency and they rank even lower in the marketing hierarchy. *The point: You have to know who you are going to ask back first and who you are going to ask back last.*

The same hierarchy of value exists relative to frequency and customer mailings. If all two-year recency customers receive eight mailings a year, perhaps deviating and sending twelve mailings to two-year recency customers with ten or more frequency makes sense. Perhaps nine mailings to all two-year recency customers who have between three- and five-time frequency is a better tactic than just sending everybody the uniform eight mailings every year. On the other side, logic would indicate that a one-year customer with a four-time frequency spaced at three-month intervals is, perhaps, a candidate for no more than four mailings a year spaced at three-month intervals. Too often, direct marketers attempt to make the purchase fit the number and timing of the mailings rather than making the mailings fit the customer's frequency purchasing history and pattern. If you can obtain the same sales level with four mailings versus eight mailings, you are a rainmaker.

Obviously, these assumptions must be carefully conceived, tested and tracked over a sufficiently large sample and an adequate length of time and number of offers to be proven valid. In every direct marketing circulation plan, there is a *perfect* configuration of contacts based on recency and frequency. The skill lies in knowing how to find it. All too often, it is just easier to "mail eight catalogs to the people who buy most often."

The marketing hierarchy for an individual customer as well as groups of frequency customers, and all frequency customers, is further segmented into complex marketing hierarchies by channel. A single customer may have a marketing hierarchy for catalog mailings as well as another hierarchy for email contacts and a third for retail store promotions. The rationale for each channel and all channels combined must be based on individual and aggregate customer return on investment **(Figure L2.7)**.

Figure L2.7

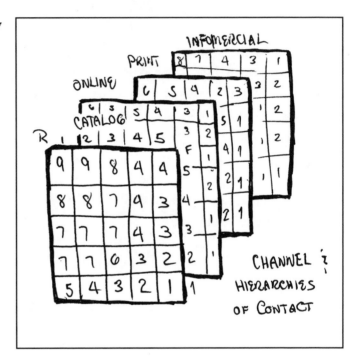

FREQUENCY AND THE MARKETING HIERARCHY: PICKERING

Do you incentivize frequency in one channel as opposed to another, thereby creating an inadvertent hierarchy? Possibly. Avoid the law of unintended consequences and find out.

Most large, multi-channel marketers who operate online and in at least one other channel grapple with the question: should we charge less for an item sold on the web versus any of our other channels?

My first question would be: could you charge different prices? Or, better: could you charge different prices without an inordinate expenditure of effort? Large organizations have many marketing and I.T. people, indeed, entire departments, devoted to maintaining different pricing on the web and in the catalog. That doesn't seem like the best use of five or six full-time employees.

In the recent past, the valuation of customers who were purchasing online was substantially higher than those customers who purchased via other channels *even though they did not spend as much.* In large part, the bubble has burst on that concept.

For many lines of business, the web offers a low cost way to capture orders. The web is especially adept at taking orders for commodity items. For items that require human intervention, such as imprinted products or items that have custom sizing requirements, the web cannot handle everything but you can create a 'web-enabled' channel and share much more information about the look, size or shape of the product.

There are some potential downsides to taking orders via the web. One of the most important is the loss of cross-sell and up-sell opportunities. Many of us have ordered from Amazon.com. When you find a book, even before you put the item in your shopping basket, it shows what similar books have been bought by other people. When I browse *Ogilvy on Advertising*, it says that others who purchased this book also have purchased books by John Caples, Claude Hopkins, and Robert Bly. Amazon does a good job at targeting cross-sell, because I own all of these books. It doesn't amaze me how well Amazon cross-sells, they have a market capitalization of $14.5 billion dollars and they bought an entire computer dating company to get the software to drive cross-selling. What does amaze me is how long it has taken other marketers to adopt and execute this strategy.

Although many marketers have deployed some sort of cross-sell on the web initiative, few have developed an effective means of up-selling. Cross-sell and up-sell can perhaps be better executed by a tele-sales agent, though only if they are well-trained and actually make the offer. The benefit of making these offers online is that you are assured (barring technical difficulties) that the offers will be made each time.

The ability of effectively and intelligently delivering cross-sell and up-sell offers will affect frequency. If a buyer orders a printer and it arrives, but without the correct cable, perhaps they will call you and order the cable. This would entail another shipping charge, additional time for delivery, but it would result in another order. Or, rather than increasing frequency, the buyer could go to the nearest computer accessories retailer and you could lose a sale, possibly also losing a customer.

You can use your hierarchy of channel to drive existing customers and prospects to different methods of orders. You then need to examine the effects of this on frequency to see if you are *actually* driving customers into a particular channel, or simply to a competitor.

FREQUENCY AND PRODUCT PROPENSITY: LIBEY

If the 80-20 Rule is alive and well (and it is), there will be a direct correlation between customer frequency and product propensity. If twenty percent of the customers are delivering eighty percent of the sales, it is likely twenty percent of the products are delivering eighty percent of the sales. If you know which customers and which products constitute the twenty percent, you are well on your way to The Big Money Machine.

The database you want allows 'give me' questions, such as, "Give me all of the one-year customers with three times or more frequency who have bought four or more products in each purchase; then give me a hierarchy of frequency and products with the most often purchased products listed in descending order."

In the same way, you can diagnose frequency problems by asking, "Give me all of the two-year customers with three times or more frequency who have not purchased in the past twelve months; then give me a hierarchy of frequency and products with the most often purchased products listed in descending order; then give me a hierarchy of products with the highest returns or replacement rates for the same period of time and correlate that hierarchy to those customers. Is there a valid correlation between product dissatisfaction and frequency drop-off?"

By going inside the shoebox and peering into the smaller boxes of recency, and then looking at the compartments of frequency in each one, specific questions can be asked and answered about the dynamics of products, pricing, delivery speed, shipping and handling charges, advertising changes and a host of other questions that assist in solving the prime directive: selling more of the products the best customers want.

Finally, by examining all of the above questions by channel, we can discover the unique product propensity by channel and understand how the channel drives the products or how the products drive the channel, and how products and channels drive frequency.

FREQUENCY AND PRODUCT PROPENSITY: PICKERING

The 80-20 Rule isn't wrong, but it may not always be right. First, let's stop calling it the 80-20 Rule. In the parts of the real world that I have been fortunate to see, it rarely gets as high as the eighty and as low as the twenty. Let's start calling it the Disproportionate Value Rule. Or we could call it Pickering's Law of Disproportionate Value. Your choice.

In almost any business you will be able to find a group of customers that is more valuable than another group. Usually that involves RFM*P* where *P* is product, actually some higher-level product group. When using this methodology, particularly with companies that market to consumers predominantly, you can find a minority group that spends the majority of the dollars. Find them and treat them as special customers. Then find more.

For companies that market mostly or entirely to other businesses, it has not been my experience that you can find a minority of the customers that account for the majority of the dollars. This may be heresy to some, but this is what my real world experience has shown. There seems to be some combination of reasons for this:

1. Many more SKUs and product groupings exponentially increase the difficulty of segmentation.

2. Most business-to-business marketers do not have tools in-house to perform the detailed RFMP analysis.

3. The two levels (individual and site) can make needs very different from one buyer to another within the same site.

Frequently, we find something that looks like the 'light half' instead of the 'heavy half' in the 80-20 Rule. This does take RFMX where X is something additional. Often this fourth element is a product class (a second or third level grouping of individual SKUs).

For the business-to-business marketer who sells into both the true business and more of a business/residential hybrid, you will find some products that start to segment value in your database. Frequently, those segments—when created using product segmentations—are put into even more sharp relief when using segmentations designed to separate true businesses with business-type demand from sites that are quasi-business, such as contractors working from home, that have much lower demand and lower frequency.

FREQUENCY AND PRICE CHANGES: LIBEY

A bubble of frequency drop-off in the month following an increase in prices may tell you something. Similarly, a bubble of frequency drop-off following an increase in shipping and handling charges may be saying something about what the customers think about that added expense. Frequency can give you a read on numerous changes in the multi-channel direct marketing program. If you will think about and list for yourself all of the possible things that frequency drop-off or frequency increase can signal, you will be amazed at what you can learn if you take the time to study this important diagnostic.

Products that are reduced in price or offered as a loss leader may drive bubbles of increased frequency for the life of the offer. The measure of the value of such offers is whether the frequency of purchases remains higher after the offer than before the offer. If a customer can be motivated by price and maintained at a higher frequency level thereafter, then the pricing strategy was successful. But if the loss leader only produces a momentary blip in frequency and the customers return to their former lethargy, then nothing has been accomplished except margin erosion.

Price tactics by channel can create differing responses in frequency. Where online prices are lowered periodically, bubbles in online frequency increase may be seen. If no offsetting bubble decrease in another channel is seen, then the online price strategy worked and new business was created. If there is a frequency decrease in, say, the catalog channel, then the online channel pricing tactic has simply cannibalized the catalog channel sales.

Predatory price strategies, such as those employed by Wal-Mart and other big-box retailers, are always based on intentionally changing frequency habits. If, through offering a festival of off-price attractions, frequency purchases are shifted from other channels of other competitors (usually Main Street merchants) to the predator big-box (usually built on the outskirts of town with tax abatements and other give-aways), then the first in a series of habit-forming purchases is created for some percentage of new customers. Over time, share is shifted, frequency is transferred and increased and the weaker local merchant succumbs, having paid the supreme sacrifice for spending thirty years helping to build a strong community with economic stability and civic responsibility. Remember how this works when Wal-Mart and its ilk come into your direct marketing channels as a dominant competitor. If a town of five hundred residents all have one hundred purchases a year each, the annual total town purchase frequency is fifty thousand purchasing events. If there are twenty-five stores in town, each store gets two thousand purchases, enough to stay in business, grow a bit, and add value to the community. Then the big-box arrives with twenty-five departments inside the insatiable maw of the concrete block monster. Those departments equal the twenty-five independent merchants, except the goods are all bought in China and retailed at prices less than the local merchant can buy them wholesale. Suddenly, frequency consolidates due to price. Year one, the big-box attracts twenty-five thousand frequency purchases; local business is off fifty percent. Year two, most of the locals are out of business and the big-box has all fifty thousand frequency purchases, nicely transferred over but leaving Main Street a ghost town. Of course, the money all goes back to Arkansas or wherever, but there are a lot of blue, plastic bags blowing around town and some part-time employees making minimum wage.

If you doubt the importance of frequency, stop and reflect on how it was intentionally manipulated to change the world in a very short period of time.

FREQUENCY AND PRICE CHANGES: PICKERING

Frequency can be increased or decreased by price changes. As discussed above, we need to consider the total cost, shipping and handling and all other fees, because the customer usually does.

Most consumer marketers charge shipping and handling based on the value of the order shipped. This encourages the customer to aggregate as much demand as possible; the larger the order value, the lower the shipping costs because of the sliding scale. Thus, the pricing can suppress frequency and increase average order value (AOV).

This sensitivity to shipping costs also makes free shipping above a certain dollar level a powerful offer. Beware, however, as—like other forms of discounting—many customers will be 'trained' to only order during free shipping times. Again, this affects frequency and AOV. That being said, for most consumer marketers shipping and handling costs are, to some degree, a profit center.

Business-to-business marketers operate differently on shipping and handling. There are fewer who have 'value-based' shipping costs and more who will actually charge *actual* shipping costs. For that reason, there is less power to the free shipping offers in the business-to-business arena than in consumer, but they do work in certain situations.

Business-to-business mailers make frequent use of premiums, particularly when selling commodity products. These can move frequency, but be careful how much you use them. The premium driven customer is not loyal; increasing their frequency will take great effort.

FREQUENCY AND QUANTITY PRICE BREAKS: LIBEY

Direct marketing companies that sell products in quantity often price the products attractively in the higher quantity levels. The multiple, or gross margin, for higher quantities is less than that for smaller quantities. There may be a four-time mark-up for quantities of one hundred and only a two-time mark-up for quantities of one thousand. Ideally, if every customer purchased lower quantities at higher mark-ups, the business would operate at a higher gross margin.

Some direct marketing companies make decisions on quantity price breaks and the merchandising of savings without fully understanding what happens to frequency and, ultimately, profitability. Advertising suddenly extols the virtue of buying larger quantities less often. Words like 'savings' and 'convenience' appear along with promises of 'never again run out.' Big red arrows on the page are pointed at the one thousand level prices and yellow bursts scream 'as little as two cents each!' Customers recognize the savings and buy in large quantities, but the usage rate has not changed and they are buying a year's supply in one purchase instead of four purchases. Suddenly, frequency drops from four purchases to one purchase a year. Margin drops sharply. Cash is scarce. The bottom falls out of profitability and the company asks, "Why?"

Experienced direct marketers understand the implications of decreasing frequency and margin without an increase in units sold. It is a prescription for disaster. Inexperienced direct marketers, however, see it as an opportunity for increasing top line sales fast, which it can do up front. The inevitable outcome, however, is that increased sales at lower margins without corresponding increases in total units sold is simply a form of accelerated margin erosion leading to financial collapse. The only benefit that results is a vacant position in the marketing or merchandising department.

As you would imagine, there may be channel differences in quantity price breaks. The catalog channel may have higher quantities and, therefore, deeper price breaks than the online channel. There may also be different price *sweet spots* for the price breaks. A sweet spot is a price break at a certain quantity that is particularly attractive to the customer. For example, if the average quantity sold is four hundred, and the price break from three hundred to four hundred is a normal three percent discount step, it might be very attractive to offer a sweet spot at the five hundred quantity level of a five percent discount step and do that in one channel over the others depending on how you want to allocate channel share for that product. By increasing the quantity by one hundred, the customer can save an additional two percent on the price, but they have to get the savings online as opposed to the catalog. When the known average quantity bought and the price break discount steps are skillfully manipulated, the result is a productive sweet spot strategy that increases sales and profitability.

FREQUENCY AND QUANTITY PRICE BREAKS: PICKERING

There are fewer and fewer pure business-to-business or consumer marketers in the marketplace. Fast growing are the marketers who sell into both the business-to-business and consumer markets. For them, the rules are different, especially about price breaks and frequency.

A careful balance must be achieved between the buyers who are highly responsive and lower in propensity to move up in frequency (look more like consumers) and those that are less responsive but more likely to move up in frequency and have higher average order values (look more like businesses).

The quantity that is ordered can be very predictive of frequency, though in ways that are not always intuitive. There are two orders for paper: one is for a box of paper which comes in at the highest price per unit around twenty-three dollars. The second order comes in for three boxes of paper at twenty dollars per box. Both orders came with four line addresses as the ship-to. If you know nothing else, you would imagine that the customer who will re-order more quickly is the customer who purchased one box. However, the customer that purchased a single box is from a home office and that order will very likely last a year or more. The customer who purchased three boxes is a small business that consumes this much paper every month.

A learned marketer will use all the tools available, such as list source, multi-buyer, postal information or business demographics to determine what potential a prospect or customer has. Those customers or prospects that look like businesses should be targeted with offers that include price breaks at business-type levels of consumption. Their propensity to move up along the frequency ladder is higher than that of a consumer.

Those prospects and customers that look like a consumer should be mailed less frequently and, if possible, offered no price breaks. Many predominantly business-to-business direct marketing companies have fallen to the siren song of somewhat higher response rates of consumer records only to be beaten on the shoals of low frequency.

FREQUENCY AND ADVERTISING SPACE: LIBEY

Frequency of product purchases can be influenced by the amount of advertising space devoted to the merchandising of products. If customers purchase blue wogglers 2.6 times a year when blue wogglers are displayed on a half-page of advertising, what happens when blue wogglers are squeezed into a one-quarter page advertisement? If price, quality and satisfaction are constant and demand measured by frequency drops, then the product and frequency are influenced by the amount of advertising space.

If a customer always bought two yards of blue cloth from the peddler, and on one trip the blue cloth was tucked away in the corner of the wagon instead of being in full view, the customer would not see the cloth and, as a result, not purchase it on that trip.

Frequency is at the heart of the shelf space wars in supermarkets. The more prominent the product, the more likely the customer will buy that product. The same common sense principle applies in direct marketing. If you want a customer to purchase a product repeatedly, then that product has to be displayed prominently and constantly merchandised.

If one product accounts for thirty-five percent of sales, it is logical to conclude that a lot of space should be devoted to selling that product. Frequency analysis is seldom linked to product propensity and, subsequently, to advertising space allocation; yet, perversely, every direct marketer recognizes the value of that logic. Getting it done is the problem.

Once again, frequency and advertising space relationships will vary based on the channel. For the catalog-assisted online marketer, the amount of space necessary to maintain frequency of purchases for a product in a paper catalog versus the online catalog likely will be different, but symbiotic.

FREQUENCY AND ADVERTISING SPACE: PICKERING

Advertising space is precious. It is scarce, and that is why it is so expensive. When investing valuable capital to advertise, best-selling products and products that attract the best customers should be featured on the covers and on the opening pages of the catalog. Conversely, products that are profitable, but not as profitable, are consigned to the middle pages. It is ignominy, but it is their lot.

Frequency of product purchases can be influenced by the amount of advertising space devoted to them. But that can become a self-fulfilling prophecy. If you want to attract good customers on your prospecting efforts, look at your best customers, those that purchased three times, four times, or more within the last twelve months. Look at the products that they purchased initially and move those further up into the 'hot spots' of the catalog, and perhaps feature them on cross-sell efforts by the tele-sales representatives or on the home page of the website.

FREQUENCY VELOCITY: LIBEY

Frequency velocity is the speed at which the number of purchases is increasing for both individual customers and for the entire customer base, in each and all channels, over time. For example, if the average customer moves from one purchase a year to five purchases a year, the frequency goes from one to five, a net increase of four purchases (+4). If the average customer goes from five purchases a year to one purchase a year, the frequency velocity is a decrease of four purchases (-4) **(Figures L2.8 & L2.9)**.

The assumption is that a positive increase in frequency velocity is also a positive increase in total quantities and dollar value of products bought. A customer buying envelopes or other commodity products who simply increases the number of purchases without increasing the total units, is only benefiting the direct marketer through higher margin on the price multiple for the smaller quantity bought. While that is a small improvement, it pales in comparison to the customer

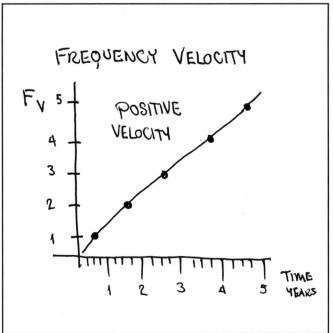

Figure L2.8

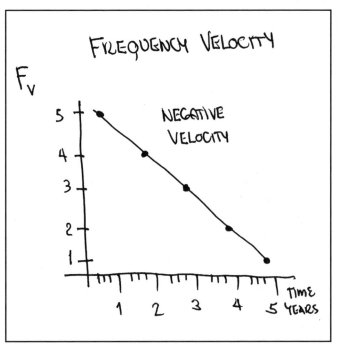

Figure L2.9

who buys more products, buys other products, spends more and, thereby, increases the average order value and lifetime net profit.

Segmenting customers into descending hierarchies from positive frequency velocity through negative frequency velocity can reveal frequency and product relationships. Studying all customers with a +3 frequency velocity and looking at the products they buy may reveal product propensity information that can be used to stimulate increases in purchases from similar customers with only +2 or +1 frequency velocity speeds. Better, such information may reverse negative frequency velocity and move failing customers to the plus side. In reverse, it may be very helpful to find product propensities among customers who move from a positive to a negative frequency velocity speed and take action to review those products for reasons why the customers are not buying, such as poor quality, product obsolescence or competitive price pressure.

Customer frequency velocity speed changes can also be studied to determine the effects of changes in pricing, shipping and handling charges, fulfillment policies, speed of delivery, number of mailings, reorder reminder initiatives, online special offers, package inserts, discounts, club offers, rush charges, premiums, and many other direct marketing variables. This is the stuff that moves needles. A positive increase in overall customer frequency velocity speed of 0.5 is an increase in total orders of fifty percent. Actually knowing what marketing or merchandising decisions move purchasing velocity up or down is important information. Most companies do these things with no measurements whatsoever. Six months later, the assessment is, "Hey, looks like we goofed."

Knowing as early as possible that fifteen percent of the +3 frequency velocity customers have dropped to a +1 velocity is critical knowledge. Frequency velocity is the heartbeat of the business. If the heart is slowing and pumping less blood, knowing that early and seeking treatment is far better than knowing it after the business has gone into cardiac failure.

These are subtle measurements. These are complex concepts. They are apparent only upon close, accurate examination over time. There must be standard reference points from which you plot the subtle movements and you must have the patience to develop the measurement system and to let it percolate until it becomes meaningful.

Keep the conceptual thinking simple. Go back to the peddler and the shoebox. If half the customers on the route suddenly stop buying on one of the two annual trips, the business has diminished by twenty-five percent (provided average order value remains constant). Something happened and you have to quickly find out what it is and fix it. So, you take the top frequency customers who had been adding purchases at the fastest rate and ask them, "Why have your purchases decreased?" It is simply amazing what your customers will tell you if you ask the question.

FREQUENCY VELOCITY: PICKERING

There are lies, damn lies, and statistics.
—attributed to Mark Twain

Most people use the above quote as justification to avoid numerical analysis. For me it is a reminder that there is an art in interpreting the science of direct marketing.

The dependent variable—the goal—of recency velocity is to move as many buyers as possible into the recent buckets. In general, increasing frequency velocity is a good thing. However, pulling on various levers to manipulate frequency velocity while eroding margins or increasing costs is folly.

That being said, in general, a high frequency velocity is good and a low one is bad. Unlike recency velocity, frequency velocity needs to be divided by the number of years (or portions of years) that the customer has been a customer. So, this is an implicit *vintage analysis* or analysis by year of client acquisition. This is always a good lens through which to view your house file.

Below is a basic frequency analysis (**Figure P2.1**). It isn't seg-mented by any additional data, which would be more useful. How-ever, it will serve to give you an idea of the mechanics. Customers are segmented by their year of first purchase, orders are Life-to-Date (LTD), and everything is based on individual level.

First Order Year	Customers	Orders	Years on file	Velocity
	(Orders/Customers)/Years on file=Velocity			
2005	5,341	6,394	1	1.20
2004	16,117	25,215	2	0.78
2003	13,882	32,984	3	0.79
2002	9,282	31,407	4	0.85
2001	8,195	32,691	5	0.80
2000	5,140	23,060	6	0.75

Figure P2.1

Even a cursory exam shows us that there are some things that bear discussion. First, the current year almost always looks better than the rest. This is because the time on the file is so short. This company began increasing prospecting efforts in 2000 and has been steadily increasing their efforts, and success, each year (the sales in-formation for year 2005 is incomplete).

Frequency velocity has been relatively stable. Even so, the veloc-ity of buyers acquired in 2002 is sufficiently better than the balance; it makes sense to investigate in more depth how those customers were acquired (using the same offer, same general mix of media) and how they were promoted once they were on the house file.

Frequency velocity will spark many questions and finding those answers will lead to actionable information that will strengthen your marketing efforts, or at least show you where improvement can be made.

FREQUENCY MOMENTUM: LIBEY

Frequency momentum is the aggregate force of change in frequency velocity of the entire customer base, in each and all channels. If the customers are, for the most part, all adding purchases and increasing their individual frequency velocity, then the customer base has a positive frequency momentum. In the reverse, if the majority of customers are decreasing their individual frequency velocity, then the aggregate frequency momentum is negative.

If you have one hundred customers buying one time a year in each of three years in a row, the frequency velocity is zero. It is neither positive nor negative. If ten customers increase their purchases to two a year, the aggregate frequency velocity is +0.1. If fifty customers increase to two purchases a year, the aggregate frequency velocity is +0.5. If all one hundred customers increase from one to two purchases a year, the aggregate frequency velocity is +1.0.

The rate of frequency momentum—the measurement of the force of frequency velocity change—would be ten percent for the +0.1 velocity above; fifty percent for the +0.5 velocity; and one hundred percent for the +1.0 velocity. In other words, if aggregate customer frequency momentum is increasing by ten, fifty or one hundred percent, the business is growing. If aggregate frequency momentum is decreasing by ten, fifty or one hundred percent, the overall business is slowing (**Figure L2.10**).

The value of these two measurements of frequency movement is more apparent when viewed over time. For example, a business may have a rapidly improving frequency velocity, but the overall frequency momentum has not turned from negative to positive (**Figure L2.11**). Turning a business is like turning an ocean liner. The speed of the ship is the velocity; the distance it takes to turn the ship is the momentum. You may be increasing the speed, but the ship has yet to make the turn and another three nautical miles have to be covered at an increasing speed before it is back on course. Distance is time; time is money. Positive frequency velocity and momentum are money.

Figure L2.10

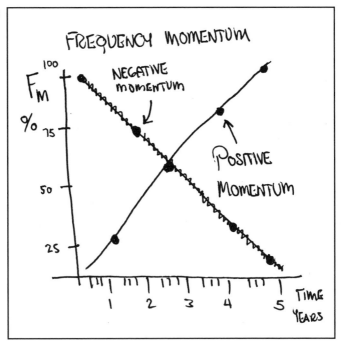

Figure L2.11

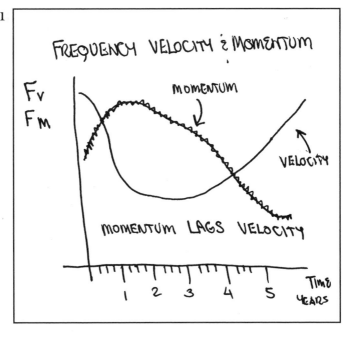

FREQUENCY MOMENTUM: PICKERING

Frequency momentum is full of layers and nuances. You can look at a figure and think that you are doing better than you really are. On the other side of the coin, you can look at a figure and feel good about the direction things are going when it is really not as good as you may think.

Here is an example for us to dissect (**Figure P2.2**):

		Q2 2005					Q3 2005		
First Order Year	Customers	Orders	Years on file	Velocity		Customers	Orders	Velocity	Momentum
(Orders/Customers)/Years on file=Velocity						Prior Veloc-Current Veloc=Momentum			
2005	5,341	6,394	1	1.20		8,760	9,847	1.12	(0.08)
2004	16,117	25,215	2	0.78		16,117	27,106	0.84	0.06
2003	13,882	32,984	3	0.79		13,882	34,633	0.83	0.04
2002	9,282	31,407	4	0.85		9,282	34,548	0.93	0.08
2001	8,195	32,691	5	0.80		8,195	35,633	0.87	0.07
2000	5,140	23,060	6	0.75		5,140	24,513	0.79	0.04

Figure P2.2

The momentum for the first order year 2005 is negative 0.08. On the face of it, this looks bad. It seems as though we are taking a step backwards. What happened in reality is that a large prospecting effort added many new buyers. As good as new buyers are, they can generally only order once in a short time, like a quarter. We added many buyers who had only one purchase and this created a velocity less than the prior velocity. That decrease in velocity, gave us negative momentum.

Momentum was up for all other years, but when we are measuring momentum only by year of first order, it is only possible to be positive because we aren't adding any more buyers who first purchased in 2003.

What we can see is that the momentum of 2003 seems lethargic compared to that of older years, even 2002. Therefore, it is time to roll-up the sleeves and see what happened to those 2002 buyers and what we can do to make them more active.

Recency momentum can be applied to many different segments, such as product category, employee size, etc. What is critical is to maintain the first order date on the database so that you can perform this analysis and, in fact, *to perform the analysis.*

FREQUENCY RECONCILIATION: LIBEY

All frequency reconciliation takes place in the one-year recency box since all purchases whether first-time or repeat, are accounted for there. Frequency reconciliation can be done on a daily, weekly, monthly, quarterly and annual basis. If done on a daily basis, more will be known about frequency performance faster; if done on an annual basis, information will be older and of minimum value. In a perfect analytic world, daily reconciliation leading to weekly, monthly, quarterly, annual and a twenty-quarter rolling reconciliation would provide ideal frequency information, understanding and knowledge.

Three numbers are required for accurate frequency reconciliation: 1) total number of orders; 2) total number of first-time orders; and 3) total number of repeat orders. If one thousand orders are received today and two hundred of those are first-time orders, then eight hundred are repeat orders. The first requirement for accuracy is the ability to separate first-time orders from repeat orders.

Once the two hundred first-time orders have been assigned to the first-year recency box, the eight hundred repeat orders can be classified. Of the eight hundred orders, some (say, 400) will come from customers already in the one-year recency box, some (200) from the two-year box, and some from each of the three-year (100), four-year (75) and the five-year and older (25) boxes. The total number of orders from all boxes is eight hundred and that reconciles with the number of repeat orders received; the reconciliation is accurate. For frequency reconciliation, count orders; for recency reconciliation, count customers.

With twenty quarters of accurate frequency reconciliation data plotted on *x* and *y* axis charts, it is possible to spot trends in customer reorder patterns. For example, knowing that you are getting a higher number of repeat orders from the four-year recency segment than the two-year recency segment tells you something is going on. It may be the two-year recency segment was left out of a mailing, or it may be that old customers are returning because of price increases by your competition. Many possibilities exist for variances in frequency performance; knowing who, what, where, when, why and how much, proven by solid analytics, is the difference between survival and extinction.

Frequency reconciliation is really the only information that tells you whether the frequency of individual and aggregate repeat purchases is increasing or decreasing. In short, unless you reconcile accurately and often, you will have no awareness of frequency velocity or momentum for individual customers or the customer base as a whole.

Frequency reconciliation must be accomplished not only across the entire customer base, but across entire channels and their seg-

Figure L2.12

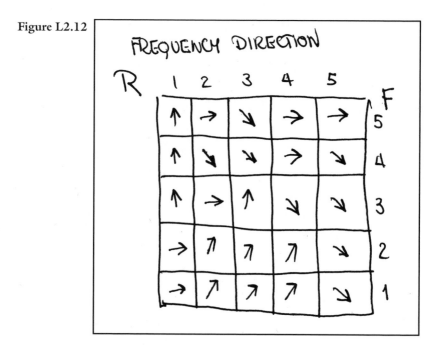

ments individually **(Figure L2.12)**. There will be channels where reconciliation points to an increasing frequency velocity and momentum and channels where the reconciliation points to a decreasing frequency velocity and momentum. There will be channels where the velocity and momentum are mixed. And there will be segments within channels where velocity varies from one segment to another. Again, arrows in each segment of each channel will point either up, sideways or down, and there is only one acceptable direction.

FREQUENCY RECONCILIATION: PICKERING

Frequency reconciliation would be simple if everyone placed orders from one location that served as both the bill-to and the ship-to address. Oh, it would also help if there were no cancels and no returns. And, no bad debt would help, too.

Obviously, in the real world we have to deal with all of these issues and more. One issue that is frequently overlooked by marketers is the issue of ship-to addresses. Almost all marketing efforts are geared to the purchaser who is generally reached at the bill-to address. What value is there in knowing something about the ship-to? Presumably, those who receive the product are fairly likely to use the product. And it isn't too large of a leap to think that they may have some input on the purchase decision.

Through many changes in purchasing agents, the ship-to address can remain the most constant way to reach the end user. Knowing that, why are marketers continually surprised when they promote to their ship-to addresses once a year and it does gangbuster response? How many marketers reconcile frequency to the ship-to address? Even smaller, how many segment and promote by it? Worth a try?

FREQUENCY SEGMENTATION: LIBEY

As with recency, a language exists to describe frequency. Customers are classified in one of two major segments: 1) one-time buyers; and 2) multiple buyers. A one-time frequency buyer has a history of only the initial purchase; a multiple buyer has a history of two or more purchases. The value of the multiple buyers is apparent and a premium is placed on these customers. In the world of not-for-profit and fundraising, the frequency terms are often one-time donor and multiple donor, or similar descriptive terms.

A one-time buyer can be found anywhere in the recency progression. Beginning with the first year, the one-time buyer can age through the second, third, fourth and fifth years of recency without ever becoming a multiple buyer. A multiple buyer can also be found in any of the recency boxes, preferably in the one-year box. Remember, multiple purchases can be defined in two ways and a decision has to be made: 1) multiple purchases this year; and 2) multiple purchases in the customer's lifetime history.

A customer who purchases once a year for five consecutive years is a one-year recency customer with a multiple purchase history of five separate purchases. A customer who purchases five times a year, however, is a one-year recency customer with multiple purchases in the same year. The first customer has one purchase and the second customer has five purchases in the same period of time. Both customers are multiple buyers and both customers are one-year recency customers, but they are very different. Plus, they may be customers from different channels, as well.

If both customers stop buying and age through the recency boxes, they will age as multiple buyers but of different values. The old five-times-a-year buyer is still more attractive than the once-a-year buyer (provided the average order value is the same). To order the value of the multiple buyers it is necessary to segment them in the database logically. Three frequency segmentations are called for at the minimum: 1) one purchase only; 2) one or more purchases in the aggregate; and 3) two or more purchases in one-year recency. The first describes all customers who have bought only once; the second describes all customers who have bought more than once during their lifetime as a customer; and the third describes all customers who have made two or more purchases during the current year. Clearly, a hierarchy of frequency value exists in these three segments.

The second and third segments can be further subdivided into actual numbers of purchases. For example, customers who have made two purchases in the aggregate, three purchases in the aggregate, or twelve purchases in the aggregate. In the same manner, the one-year frequency segments could be customers who have made two purchases this year, three purchases this year, or twelve purchases this year.

Unless purchases are accounted for individually, as with a continuity program, there may be little value in detailing individual numbers of purchases. Generally, frequency is subdivided into blocks of purchases, such as one, two to four, five to eight, nine to twelve and twelve plus. The blocks are entirely dependent on normal purchase patterns for the products, the needs of the company for analyses, and the flexibility of the database architecture. The important abilities are the differentiation and tracking between the one-time, multiple aggregate, and multiple one-year buyers. You cannot change analyses categories down the road and expect to wind up with oranges and oranges. Starting with a greater detail of frequency segments may not be a bad idea. You can always combine them, but you may not always be able to separate them. Nothing is more frustrating than having the data but not being able to attach accurate meaning to it because the yardsticks were changed.

Segmentation of frequency is essential for a fully furnished view of channel frequency. Everything that must be done for detailing frequency velocity, momentum, reconciliation and segmentation for the entire customer base must be replicated for each channel. And the individual channel reconciliations must collectively equal the overall customer frequency reconciliation. As we saw with recency where no single customer ever disappears without knowing where they went, no single purchase ever disappears or gets mislaid in frequency reconciliation.

When all of the segments of frequency have arrows pointing in one of the three directions, and each channel's segments are delineated, the arrows will show where the advertising dollars are being spent or where they should be spent, relative to frequency increase **(Figure L2.13)**. If big bucks are being spent on the online channel and frequency has increased by thirty-nine percent, it will show up in the segment analyses and the directions of the arrows.

FREQUENCY SEGMENTATION: PICKERING

Frequency segmentation is powerful in many ways and one frequently overlooked use is in prospecting.

It is an accepted rule of thumb for business-to-business marketers that a prospect (individual) at a buying site (where someone else is the buyer) will respond twenty to thirty percent higher than the average response rate for a prospecting effort. If all buying sites are treated the same, a prospect at a buying site that bought two times four years ago looks the same as a prospect at a site that has purchased twice within the last year.

Figure L2.13

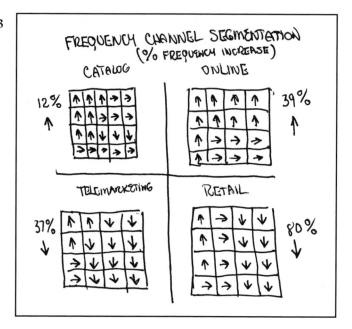

On the house file side, different frequency measures are used in different applications. As noted above, it is critical to be consistent in what type of frequency calculation is used.

LTD frequency is most appropriate for assessing overall health of the file, or when using frequency to drill down for product analysis. It gives the most complete picture and will allow analysis of trends over time.

When doing RFM to analyze or segment for house file circulation, it is much more appropriate to use frequency of a shorter interval, generally the same period of time that is used to define 'active' customer status. As with so many things in life, it is all about what you have done for me lately.

FREQUENCY AND LIST RENTALS: LIBEY

Many of the list rental considerations explored in the previous chapter on recency apply to frequency, the base premise being that if a one-year recency customer is a better customer then a three-year recency customer, then a one-year multiple buyer is a better customer than a three-year, one-time buyer. All things being equal, a multiple buyer is a better customer than a one-time buyer in every instance. After all, there is just something *unproven* about one-time buyers. It's a lot like fishing: you rarely go back to the lake where you caught one fish; you go back to the lake where you caught many fish. That one-time buyer might be just a nibbler, but two or more purchases qualify that buyer as a keeper, and a whole lot of purchases qualify that buyer as a wall-mount trophy.

When recency and frequency are combined, gradations of list rental quality and attractiveness become clear. A five-year and older, one-time buyer would have the least value as a rental; a one-year, twelve-time buyer would have the greatest value. And between these two recency/frequency extremes are the gradations of quality and response efficacy that determine the value of the segmented list.

A list renter may specify one-year customers with a frequency of four or more purchases. Because the quality of these names is better, the cost per name is higher, and rightfully so. If you want the best of any product, it costs more. As the level of frequency increases, from one time to two times, three times and progressively higher, the total number of names available decreases. At a frequency of twelve in the one-year box, the number of customer names will be very low. In order to obtain the necessary volume of names, a renter may work downward in frequency, or may simply specify all two-plus buyers in the one-year file from the start. Generally, multi-buyer names are rented at a premium, or up-charge, over one-time buyer names, and the justification for the increase is the proven quality of the multi-buyers.

Quality, however, is always worth testing. A four-time frequency, three-year recency customer may not necessarily have stopped buying through direct mail. That customer may have moved to a competitor or may be buying through another channel. By renting older recency customers with high frequency, it is possible to test the quality and, therefore, the potential value of the list at a lower rental cost. Remember, this is a business of pennies. One penny over one thousand names is ten dollars; over one million names it is ten thousand dollars. Plus, when everyone else is renting the first and second quarter hot names, try the older recency names. Chances are not nearly as many marketers are reaching those buyers.

In the world of multi-channel marketing, the opportunities for testing are far larger than in years past. Developing a recency/frequency test program that mixes high frequency buyers and channels is of interest. As an example, a head-to-head test of four-time, one-year customers from the catalog channel and from the online channel would be one test. A second would be to reverse channels for the same group. Instead of driving catalog buyers to the catalog, drive them to the web; and drive web buyers to the catalog. Look at the results and make conclusions for further testing. Just because a customer is frequent in one channel does not mean that same customer can't be frequent in other channels. In reality, the more channels you can convince a customer to buy from, the greater value that customer gains.

FREQUENCY AND LIST RENTALS: PICKERING

When contemplating list rental activity, most direct marketers don't think about frequency as much as recency of list rental segmentation. It is true that there are a few lists out there that will allow you to segment two-time buyers from one-time buyers (hint: two-time buyers generally work better, if recency is the same). The number of lists that allow you to select by frequency are few and far between. They are most often continuity lists of some type.

Instead let's consider frequency, as it pertains to list rentals, not as a sum of number of purchases, but a sum of the number of times we see that same individual's record in our prospecting pool. The common merge/purge term for this was *multi-buyer*.

In the language of merge/purge, a multi-buyer is an attribute that counts how many times a record with the same name and address occurs within a merge/purge. If there are four different records with the name Don Kessinger at the same address within a merge, the multi-buyer count is four. When we as an industry migrated to prospecting databases some twenty years ago, we took the terminology with us. So now, in databases, multi-buyers exist and you have great abilities to create many different sub-sets and super-sets of the traditional multi-buyer.

To the neophyte a multi-buyer is somewhat dreaded: you have to pay for two or more names (assuming they were provided by different list owners) but you only get one person to mail. To the Master Marketer multi-buyers are invaluable.

If the circulation decision-maker has done a credible job, there will be an overlap between prospecting lists from an interest point of view. There will be a common thread. If you are selling woodworking supplies you don't order lists of knitters, you order lists of people who read woodworking magazines, buy woodworking items, etc. Since these lists are generally owned by many different list owners and are coming from different sources, it is likely that the same individual is on multiple lists.

In our effort to identify good prospects for our woodworking offer we ordered several woodworking lists. And we decided to look at one person in-depth. That individual had come on two different woodworking magazine lists and one woodworking catalog list. Simply by the frequency that we have found this individual, we are convinced that they are an above average prospect.

For our woodworking offer we are getting ready for the upcoming season. We ordered all of our lists and have processed them. (It doesn't matter if we are doing a merge/purge or a database; the principle applies regardless of the processing environment.) We are going to use this pool of prospects for our fall efforts, and we will have four mailings, which will be spread out with about four weeks between drops.

The vast majority of our prospect pool will have a multi-buyer count of one because they won't match any other records (between sixty and eighty percent, in the average merge, are one time multi-buyers, though there are many qualifiers to that fact). We don't want to drop all of those records at one time as we would have to staff the phone operators for one large peak. We will stagger these between two mailings so that there is a more consistent flow of customers. Our contact strategy will look like this **(Figure P2.3)**:

	9/1 Mail Date	9/29 Mail Date	10/27 Mail Date	11/29 Mail Date
1X Multi Buyers	50%	50%		
2X Multi Buyers	X			X
3X Multi Buyers	X	X		X
4X Multi Buyers	X	X	X	X

Figure P2.3

This strategy helps us meet several objectives:

1. Stagger the largest amount so that we can manage call-center and order processing volume.

2. Rest the two-time and three-time multi-buyers between mailings.

3. Mail the four-time multi-buyers in each drop.

4. Avoid getting lost in events by pushing the last drop until just after the Thanksgiving holiday.

The strategy behind re-mailing multis is that, in addition to being better responding records, you are paying for them anyway in a traditional list rental arrangement. If you have net/net arrangements with your list providers (paying only for what you mail) or some other special terms, then you probably have to pay for each subsequent use of the name if you choose to mail it. You will want to assign separate key codes to each pool of multi-buyers to track the performance difference.

Within prospecting databases, you can create myriad types of multi-buyer counts. You can create them at the individual level, the site level, looking at only certain types of list, and so on. By teaming with a good circulation specialist and computer service bureau you can apply this meta-data to turbo-charge your new customer acquisition efforts.

FREQUENCY AND OFFER LIFE AND HALF-LIFE: LIBEY

Knowing how long it takes to get the orders is essential for forecasting all aspects of the direct marketing business, and particularly cash flow. As an example, if all prospect first-time buyers order within sixty days of the receipt of advertising, or the 'in-home' date, the full life of an offer can be fixed at sixty days in length. If fifty percent of the first-time buyer orders are received on the fifteenth day following the in-home date, the *half-life* of the offer is fifteen days (**Figure L2.14**). The half-life is always defined as the point at which half of the total orders have been received. If the prospect offer life is sixty days, and half the orders come in by the fifteenth day, then the remaining half of the total orders will come in over

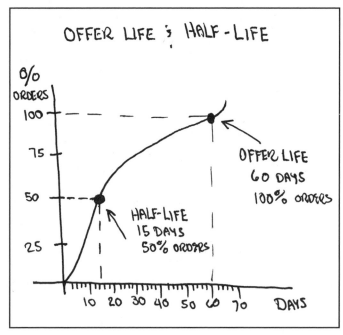

Figure L2.14

the final forty-five days of the prospect offer life. The shorter the half-life the better the cash flow, in most cases.

But what are the offer life and the half-life for one-year multiple buyers? Because they are already customers and know the company, it may be that the life of a customer offer is actually shorter and the half-life may be advanced. All orders from this customer segment may be received in thirty days instead of sixty and the customer half-life may be at ten days instead of fifteen. Not only is cash flow improved, but staffing patterns can be predicated on order life and half-life. If two-thirds of the orders are from customers and one-third from prospect first-time buyers, one can easily do the math and predict the *overall order life* and the *overall half-life*. I will purposely not do the calculation for you, but will reply on your professional curiosity to entice you to figure it out.

As frequency velocity and momentum improve, order life and half-life should also improve. Recognize also that customer order life and half-life will be different in each recency segment, generally extending out as the recency ages. A one-year recency segment order life may be forty days, but the five-year recency segment order life may take as long as eighty days. There will also be very different offer lives and half-lives in the multiple channels. The online offer life may be ten days and the half-life only three days. The infomercial offer life may be six hours and the half-life thirty minutes. The media channel and advertising mix, as well as the timing, will influence the offer life and half-life dramatically. Staffing and operating a multi-channel direct marketing business depends on accurate forecasting which begins with careful analyses of recency and frequency by channel by offer by segment. It's a formulaic business.

Order life and half-life can be used to confirm measurements of frequency velocity and frequency momentum. If the half-life is extending out, it may be an indication that frequency momentum is falling off (**Figure L2.15**). The customers who normally buy soon

Figure L2.15

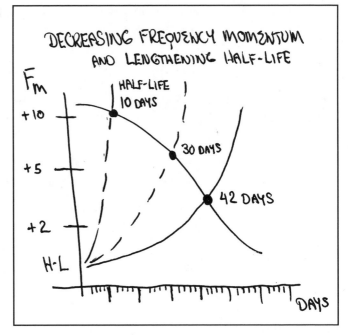

after the offer is received may not be performing to past standards. Knowing this is essential; not knowing is suicidal.

Order life and half-life are also critical to maintaining efficient inventory levels. If the lives shorten, out-of-stocks can occur. If the lives lengthen, too much cash is tied up in fewer inventory turns. Precision forecasting demands precision awareness of the order life and half-life measured in days and the dynamic changes taking place within those measurements. Additionally, awareness of the advertising pressure on each channel is needed in order to predict the future effect of order life and half-life and, thereby, inventory, staffing, cash flow and all other operational aspects of the business right down to the supply of shipping boxes.

This is very sophisticated stuff. Still—after all the years of writing and seminars—not often do you run across a good chart showing a twenty rolling quarter average of one-year, two plus multi-buyer half-life and order life compared to a twenty rolling quarter average of first-time buyer half-life and order life, displayed and overlaid on a classic *x* and *y* axis graph (**Figure L2.16**). Even less often do you find multi-channel direct marketing companies that, at the minimum, actually stock inventory and schedule employees as a result of this information. That is precisely why I will refute vehemently those who say recency, frequency and monetary value analysis is too simplistic for today's multi-channel industry. Any company that can perform the analytics that have been described thus far in this book is among the rarest of the rare. But, this is the stuff of which money is made. The direct marketing CEO who works through this infinitely detailed information regularly, looking for minute signs of changes and emerging trends in the prospect and customer bases, is the Direct Marketing Master who will remain competitive, cost-effective, profitable and relevant in an increasingly hostile economic and competitive environment.

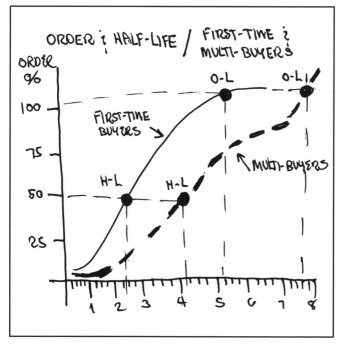

Figure L2.16

FREQUENCY AND OFFER LIFE AND HALF-LIFE: PICKERING

The concepts of order life and half-life assume perfect information. There is not much perfect information in the real world, but there are many degrees of better or worse information. We will examine how to get more complete information, closer to perfect. In this example we will focus on customer acquisition.

The conventional wisdom used to be that all programs (catalogs mostly, some solo mailings) were eighty percent complete at ten to twelve weeks, and complete fifteen to twenty weeks after the drop date. That was enough of a percentage of orders to have confidence that list results wouldn't change too much, so you could plan your next campaign. That was also at a time when many orders were received by mail with order forms having the key code pre-printed or ink-jetted, so you had very good information about what lists were generating the responses. This was shortly after man had descended from the trees and was beginning to walk erect.

The world of new customer acquisition today is much different. To begin, the overwhelming majority of orders generated from mailings are coming in to tele-sales representatives. The key code capture rate is much lower because not all representatives ask for it and not all customers give it.

The next important complicating factor is that most direct marketers do not have a single campaign per quarter. Some marketers have two campaigns per quarter, perhaps three or more in the busy season. There are even some marketers that prospect on regular weekly schedules. Online or email marketers can launch campaigns daily or even hourly. The increased number of campaigns is compounded by the fact that there are many more direct marketers out there making calls, sending catalogs, blasting emails, and broadcasting faxes. There is much more clutter.

Many marketers today discuss an eight to ten week offer life. This may be true or it may indicate a growing dependence upon projected response curves. The biggest challenge today is getting enough reliable information about where your orders are coming from, specifically your first-time orders.

A white mail rate of twenty percent is quite low in direct marketing and some mailers have a white mail rate as high as seventy percent. A range of forty to fifty percent is where most business-to-business marketers are today. Consumer mailers generally experience a somewhat lower level of white mail.

What this means is that, at best, you only know where four out of five new customers are coming from and, if you are average, one out of two. Generally speaking, this is not enough to make informed decisions on which lists to use for prospecting or even which channels are performing.

There are two good solutions to this. First, increase the training of your tele-sales group. They are your front door. It is not enough to train on this issue once, this needs to be stressed in each training session, which occurs usually during a change of buying season. This is especially true for those companies that have to hire seasonal tele-sales operators.

The second solution is to perform a match-back. This involves taking all the new to file buyers and splitting them into two sections: white mail (those without a key code or any other identifier that shows what promotion drove them in), and attribute mail (where you know what key code/promotion code they were mailed, etc.). These buyers are then matched to the promotion files, usually by various degrees of name and address matching logic. Sometimes this match can be done internally; often it is done at an external service bureau that specializes in this type of matching.

At the end of the process you will have a dataset that should be able to show what promotions generated seventy percent or more of new buyers. If you know the exact promotion, you know when it was mailed and when you received the order. When you plot that out on a chart, you get a much more accurate idea of the offer life and half-life.

Accurate knowledge of the order curve allows more accurate planning for ordering inventory, anticipating cash inflows and outflows and staffing for order taking and order fulfillment. A residual effect of equal importance is that you find out with a much higher degree of accuracy how your media (mailing lists, email lists, etc.) is performing. The Master Marketers are not necessarily smarter; they have just done the work to get the answers, the hard data. Perhaps that alone makes them smarter.

FREQUENCY AND THE LAPSED CUSTOMER: LIBEY

No analytic tool is worth anything unless it can be used to create and keep customers who buy. Information without sales is useless.

Multiple buyers, business or consumer, have buying patterns. The business envelope buyer often purchases on a quarterly basis based on normal usage patterns for that business. The consumer envelope buyer buys a box of one hundred every year based on a need for sending about eight letters a month. The ice melt chemical customer purchases in the fall of the year and may reorder after the first of the year if the ice season is particularly rough. Knowing these patterns of frequency is important if the marketer is to intervene when an expected purchase does not occur when it should. Frequency is often the first indication that something has gone wrong with a customer. When a lapsed customer finally shows up in recency, it may be too late to save the customer. Frequency tracking and the expectation of a customer's frequency pattern are early warning devices for optimal customer retention.

Direct marketers can overly complicate frequency pattern expectation. The method for determining when a customer may have lapsed becomes so cumbersome that it fails under its own weight. In reality, it is no more complicated than the peddler's simple and successful card system. If a customer buys every ninety days, note it on the card and check on that date to see if a purchase was made. If not, found out why.

Frequency pattern expectation is really a reorder reminder system. Every ninety days or whenever another purchase is expected, a reorder reminder is cranked out of the database and the customer is asked for another order. When the customer's frequency pattern changes the reorder reminder should also change, in effect learning and adjusting automatically. Few reorder reminder programs take this second step of automatically learning and adjusting. The Master Marketer is not satisfied with sending a reorder reminder and waiting for something to happen. It doesn't matter if the product is envelopes or gift fruit, when the expected order doesn't arrive, the Master Marketer finds out why. That is the point where customers can be saved, sold and retained and where the high cost of initially acquiring that customer is justified.

In its purest and simplest form, frequency pattern expectation should produce three lists at the conclusion of every business day: 1) customers who should reorder today; 2) customers who did reorder today; and 3) customers who did not reorder today. Any customer appearing on the third list is a candidate for immediate action.

Frequency pattern expectation requires some minimal amount of purchasing history, especially when the product is not a consumable. But even for first-time buyers, some generalization can be made about when another order should be expected. Start there and adapt to the individual customer patterns as they evolve over time. *Adaptive frequency patterning* can be a beneficial marketing and retention technique. By adapting to the customer's changing frequency pattern, the program learns. For example, consider the business envelope buyer who orders five thousand envelopes quarterly without fail for a three-year period. The reorder reminder is sent every seventy days after the last order was received, allowing a twenty day reorder window before the customer runs out of envelopes. Suddenly, the customer reorders in thirty days instead of the expected ninety days. The quantity of envelopes ordered is smaller, equaling a thirty-day supply. At this point an adaptive frequency pattern program would conclude that the customer has switched to a monthly reorder pattern for some reason. Two adaptive actions would then take place. First, the customer should be contacted to verify this change in pattern and the reason. Second, the reorder reminder schedule for that customer would be adjusted to a monthly pattern. If, later, the quarterly reorder pattern is resumed by the customer, the reorder reminder program readapts to that frequency and timing change and reverts to the every seventy day reminders. The customer's reason for the change in pattern has to be balanced with the importance of meeting the customer's changing frequency pattern and retaining the business.

Of course, as expected, these patterns are changing across all channels and are actually shifting back and forth from one channel to another. This is where the precision of frequency reconciliation will point up segments and channels where pattern shifts are out of the norm. The value comes from proactive steps that retain customers and increase channel and overall frequency momentum.

FREQUENCY AND THE LAPSED CUSTOMER: PICKERING

When looking at frequency in conjunction with recency to identify lapsed customers, the business-to-business marketer needs to make decisions based on multiple levels of data.

A buyer who has a frequency of three times but has decayed into the thirty-seven plus month shoebox may be a lapsed buyer. Or that person may have left the organization or moved into another job within the same organization.

If you segment your lapsed buyers by site level frequency for the last twelve months, you can get a different picture. Those lapsed buyers (based on individual recency) who are at buying sites that have one or more purchases in the most recent twelve months are likely buyers that have been replaced in that capacity by others within their organization. The smaller the organization, based on employee size, the more likely that this is true.

Lapsed buyers at sites where the twelve-month frequency is zero are truly lapsed buyers. The higher their frequency, the more contacts they likely merit to reactivate them. This can be confirmed, as we will see, in the next chapter.

For the consumer mailers, frequency offers an invaluable tool to identify top segment lapsed buyers. Many savvy consumer mailers begin making a retention effort as soon as a purchase has been made. Therefore, to make it to a lapsed status a customer has had to ignore a battery of regular house file promotions.

Reactivation is certainly valuable, and if your organization does not currently have a reactivation program, it must acquire this skill. If reactivation has been part of your promotion plan, then let cost and benefit drive your decisions. Your likelihood of reactivating a lapsed one-time buyer is not as good as reactivating a two-time plus, so after using recency to identify lapsed buyers use frequency to help drive the contact strategy decisions.

FREQUENCY AND ACQUISITIONS: LIBEY

Recency and frequency have been examined as indicative of a multi-channel direct marketing company's health or strength. The focus is always on improving customer retention and increasing the average order value. Both recency and frequency are important in the process of evaluating a multi-channel direct marketing business for acquisition.

Broadly, only two types of direct marketing companies exist relative to acquisitions: 1) successful businesses that sell at a premium; and 2) distressed companies that sell at a discount. There are numerous ways of valuing a business, but these are the opposite poles that determine the ultimate value for a company.

The first step for the buyer is to determine which of these two conditions exist. Among all of the indicators that will be looked at during the due diligence phase, an examination of the customer base for recency, frequency and monetary value is often revealing.

Ideally, an acquisition worthy of a premium purchase price will have positive recency velocity and recency momentum as well as positive frequency velocity and frequency momentum. All the arrows should be positively aligned in all segments of all channels. A distressed acquisition will have one or more of these key indicators trending negatively.

Profitability, or earnings before interest, taxes, depreciation and amortization, is the cardinal factor in the value of a multi-channel direct marketing company. But earnings alone don't get to the full understanding of the value of the business. If prospecting has been stopped or reduced, earnings can be increased but the business may not be growing. New customers are not coming in at the faucet. Recency velocity and momentum will deteriorate; frequency velocity and momentum will slow; in a short period of time the business will be in distress and the cost to reverse the trends will be greater than the artificial earnings found on the income statement.

The worth of any direct marketing business is in the proven satisfaction of the customer base and the future recency, frequency and monetary value that this satisfaction predicts. If recency and frequency are moving positively through time, the business is likely healthy; if not, the business is likely diseased. The difficulty in determining the health comes in assembling the necessary data. Good companies worthy of premium valuation have recency, frequency and monetary value information and can demonstrate performance across all channels and segments. Distressed companies not worthy of premium valuation are most likely distressed because they lack this critical navigation information.

FREQUENCY AND ACQUISITIONS: PICKERING

Potential. Perhaps this will be as important as 'plastics' when Mr. Robinson was imparting wisdom in *The Graduate*.

In today's business climate we don't talk much about mergers. There is rarely a union of two strong companies. That is why this section is called Acquisitions, not Mergers and Acquisitions. In an acquisition, by definition, there is a larger or stronger company. That is not to say that the acquired company is always small or inept. If it were inept, it most likely wouldn't be of interest, except to turn-around specialists or bottom feeders. And, in the real world, the acquiring company will generally absorb the smaller company. Often key personnel will change, attitudes will change, unique selling propositions will change, products will change, positions will change and cultures will change—sometimes for the better, sometimes not.

If the intangibles listed above change, it is more important than ever to have a clear-headed understanding about the strengths and weaknesses the acquisition will influence. One of the easiest to quantify is the customer base. How does the union of the two (or more) customer files make for one, single, wider, deeper pool of customers? You can determine this by asking and getting the answers to three simple questions:

1. How many of the acquiring company's one-time buyers are two-time plus buyers at the acquired company?

2. How many of the acquiring company's two-time plus buyers are one-time buyers at the acquired company?

3. How many buyers are two-time plus buyers on both customer databases?

If you can answer these questions it will become quite clear if there is a good strategic fit. Profit is addressed later. Without a good strategic fit the profit will evaporate. Here are a few tactical notes about the above questions.

First, you should be comparing active file to active file and a second analysis with inactive file to active file and vice versa. The business-to-business marketer should look at the above questions at both the individual level and the site level.

Recency, as previously discussed, is important also and should be analyzed. But often the ability to fill recency buckets, particularly with new customers, is a function of free capital. Often that is not found in the acquired company, so that should not be an automatic negative. Poor strategic fit is almost always a negative and, in most instances, should be a red flag signaling the need for careful consideration.

FREQUENCY AND WHY IT IS NOT ENOUGH: LIBEY

Frequency when combined with recency is more revealing and effective than recency alone. But it is still not enough because it does not quantify the money spent.

To illustrate the progression in the useful application of recency, frequency and monetary value, consider the following comparative case.

You own a paint store. Your customers buy paint and other related products. For the first ten years in business you track customer performance only by recency. If a customer does not show up every year and buy something, you send a postcard asking for that customer's business.

That seems to work okay, but you have a large number of customers who buy only once and never come back. You suspect that price has a lot to do with retention and decide to concentrate on getting more sales form your existing customers. So, you begin tracking frequency. For the next ten years, you use recency and frequency and are able to isolate the twenty percent of the customers who make eighty percent of the purchases. You work hard, but you are not making a lot of money.

One day you take out the shoebox and go over the customer cards. You find out that you have basically three types of customers: 1) one-time only buyers; 2) one-year recency and one-time frequency customers; 3) one-year recency and multiple purchase customers. The one-time buyers bought only once and have not been back for twenty years. The one-year recency, one-time buyers come in once a year and buy something. The one-year recency, multiple purchase customers come in twelve times a year and buy something.

You decide to concentrate on the one-year recency, multiple purchase customers and spend a lot of money on advertising to them with special offers and VIP customer plans. Your rationale is logical: a twelve-time multiple buyer is a better customer than a one-time customer. You have divided the customers into segments of value after twenty years in business.

Unfortunately, reality shows a very different picture. The twelve-time multiple buyers come in every month and spend about $20 each time for a total of $240 a year. These are small, do-it-yourself customers. The annual buyer spends $360 every year on one purchase. These are regular maintenance paint customers. But some of the one-time buyers spend $3,500 every five years. These are customers who own horse farms and factories and have to paint sixteen miles of fence or 800,000 square feet of warehouse space every five years. Now which customers are you going to wine and dine?

The multiple buyers spend a total of $1,200 over five years and require sixty individual sales. The annual buyers spend $1,800 over five years and require twelve individual sales. The one-time buyers spend $3,500 over five years and require one sale.

And that is why recency and frequency are not enough.

FREQUENCY AND WHY IT IS NOT ENOUGH: PICKERING

Frequency is so powerful because it helps us discriminate between those customers we really want—the profitable ones—and the other customers that just limp along.

As we have seen in so many examples in this chapter, the peril in looking at frequency alone is twofold: 1) you can miss some good customers who are of lower frequency (or who have a longer interval between purchases); and 2) you can do things to move customers to higher frequency segments that add little or nothing to the bottom line. Like many powerful things, frequency can work for good ends or for bad. But, it should never be allowed to work alone.

Chapter 3 Monetary Value

MONETARY VALUE CHARACTERISTICS: LIBEY

Monetary value is how much a customer spends. It is an indicator of value. As an aggregate of all customers, it is expressed as average order value and sales. By itself, it is arguably the most forceful indicator of the cardinal three—recency, frequency and monetary value (RFM). Monetary value, however, is quite different from recency and frequency. Monetary value is where the rubber meets the road. We are talking about money, here.

Monetary value describes a state of a customer's worth. There are only two states of worth that describe customers: profitable and unprofitable. A customer either spends enough to be profitable or does not. Monetary value measures that spending. As with frequency, monetary value can be measured one of two ways and the choice is yours to make. Monetary value can be expressed as the total amount spent this year, or monetary value can be expressed as the total amount spent in the lifetime of the customer. Neither is right; neither is wrong. But pick one and stick with it.

From our paint store example, it is clear that wrong conclusions can be drawn from recency and frequency analyses when monetary value is not included in the analysis. Only monetary value can validate the hierarchy of customer value described by recency and frequency. To rely on recency and frequency without monetary value as the measurement of performance is dangerous. It is like a checkbook. You may know when and to whom you wrote checks and how many checks you wrote, but if you don't know the dollar amount of the checks you can have big problems.

As a rule, monetary value (expressed as average order value for this example) rises in tandem with inflation. If inflation has been five percent in each of the last three years, and the business has matched inflation through price increases each year, then the average order value will have increased by 15.76 percent just to remain even with inflation. But if average order value has increased by thirty percent over the same three years, and if price increases were limited to the 15.76 percent inflation factor, then real monetary value growth has been 14.24 percent, a strong indication that customers are, indeed, purchasing more. Determining the real monetary value increase or decrease is essential to an understanding of performance.

Monetary value, adjusted for inflation or deflation, can increase, decrease or remain static; no other choices exist. Only a real increase in monetary value over inflation over time is a symptom of robust business health. Static or declining monetary value is a symptom of disease and must be aggressively treated. If monetary value is static, the business is experiencing margin erosion as a result of inflation. If monetary value is declining, the business is experiencing margin erosion due to both inflation and decreasing customer purchases. The first is critical; the second is terminal.

Monetary value relative to total sales must also be evaluated. If monetary value is increasing and sales are increasing, the symptoms are positive. If monetary value is decreasing and sales are decreasing, the symptoms are negative. And, there are nuances. Monetary value may be static and sales may be declining, or monetary value may be declining and sales are static; both indicate negative outcomes for the business. Other combinations are possible, as well.

As with recency and frequency, the historical trend over time must be understood. The classic *x* and *y* axis chart of twenty rolling quarters displaying both monetary value and sales is, minimally, necessary for this understanding (**Figure L3.1**).

To illustrate the basics of monetary value, work through this example. Monetary value (average order value) is $10.00. Sales are $10,000. Therefore, the total number of orders is 1,000. If customers order twice a year, the customer count is 500. If the customer count and the number of orders remain the same, but sales increase to $20,000, then the average order value increased to $20.00, an indication that customers are either buying more or that prices doubled. Of course, it is always possible that one customer ordered $10,000 worth of product. Diabolical, isn't it?

What this conundrum shows is the absolute necessity of knowing *exactly* what is going on with monetary value. Actually, you cannot understand monetary value alone; it must be evaluated along

Figure L3.1

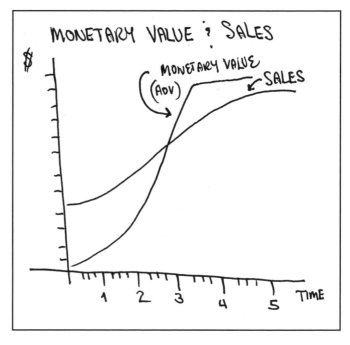

with recency and frequency and, most often, frequency is the active comparative component.

Everything covered on basic monetary value thus far also applies to each channel of the multi-channel direct marketing company. The monetary value characteristics in the catalog channel will be quite different from those of the online channel. Retail monetary value characteristics will be different from email, infomercial or telemarketing. The overall company monetary value performance consists of the combined monetary value performances of the individual channels. Of course, overall company recency and frequency performance also consists of the combined performances of the individual channels. There can be no more compelling reason for managing multi-channel direct marketing businesses on an integrated basis. Where individual channel management is separate and non-integrated, analyses are disparate, non-uniform and usually contentious. *The point: Multi-channel direct marketing companies absolutely must be managed on an integrated basis across all marketing, merchandising, operations and financial components.*

MONETARY VALUE CHARACTERISTICS: PICKERING

Money is a standard of measurement or measure of value. Therefore, it follows that monetary value is a convenient way of making measurements and comparisons between customers, across time, and between two industries. That is the fifty thousand foot view, and the high-level, strategic lesson. Let's get to the blocking and the tackling.

As with recency and frequency, monetary value can be used in two ways: 1) as a critical component in the analysis of the house file (or the entire company); or 2) as part of a segmentation process for promotion.

When segmenting customers by monetary value for mailing purposes, ranges are set up, as will be discussed in the next section. Customers fall into a segment that will drive whether they are selected for promotion.

175

Monetary value for analyzing the health of the house file, the validation of selection standards, or other analyses, requires aggregating all the dollars spent and then doing something with that information. Knowing only the dollars spent is of little value.

Here are some (not all) common measurements used in direct marketing:

Lifetime Dollars (LTD). This is the sum of all dollars for a customer (individual or site) from the beginning of time. This is infrequently used on its own. It most often represents the gross demand, the value of the order when placed, but frequently doesn't subtract out returns and other adjustments.

Twelve-month or Twenty-four Month Dollars. As the name implies, this is the sum of gross demand over a period of time. The time period often corresponds to the period established to define an active buyer.

Lifetime Value (LTV). LTV is one of the most complex monetary measurements. LTV measures gross revenue, less cost of goods sold, less cost of promotion and adjusts for the time value of money. This is a complex calculation to deploy, if for no other reason than establishing—in a timely and accurate fashion—the actual cost of goods sold and agreeing on the rate of interest used in adjusting for the time value of money. Projecting lifetime value at the time of acquisition is something that is generally the domain of organizations that are predominantly or entirely direct marketing focused.

Average Order Value (AOV). As the name implies, it measures the average monetary value of each order without making any deductions for things like cost of goods sold or the time value of money. AOV is useful in new customer acquisition analysis and is an important measurement to track over time. It is generally not used in selection processes.

As my writing partner has pointed out, for segmentation it is critical to choose one measure, either lifetime dollars or a measure that tracks revenue over some specified period of time. The dollar breaks between the groups, and the number of groups, should be changed very infrequently as it makes historical comparisons difficult.

In measuring the value of customers, most direct marketers simply look at gross demand. A few of the more industrious marketers back out costs (using a company average for the margin) and also divide dollars by the number of years on the file. This is an eighty percent solution. It is not the most complete picture of the profitability of customers, only eighty percent of that view. Paradoxically, doing eighty percent of the job of figuring out the true profitability of a customer puts you ahead of about ninety-nine percent of the direct marketers today.

Customers can be divided into two sections: profitable and unprofitable. Look at the unprofitable customers as Michelangelo looked at a large piece of marble. He didn't consider that he was making a statue. He felt that he was 'freeing' the statue that existed inside. He saw the idea in the large piece of marble and carefully removed those parts that obscured the David. Within your unprofitable customers are a group of profitable ones and it is up to you to 'free' them to move into profitability. Michelangelo would have been a great direct marketer.

MONETARY VALUE AND SEGMENTATION: LIBEY

Once again, return to the days of the peddler and the shoebox database with the handwritten customer comment cards. They are all ordered by recency and frequency in preparation for a trip. You can pick out the most recent buyers and the most frequent multiple buyers. Wouldn't it be nice if you could identify the cream of those good customers who have spent the most money?

First, determine what dollar levels of spending are realistic segments of monetary value for your business. Choose a range of monetary value that reflects your company's experience being sure that the range chosen is logical, useful and constant.

Begin with your average order value and work upwards and downwards in value. For example, if the average order value is $150, you will most likely be interested in $25 or $50 increments or segments of value. You could establish the following monetary value increments for tracking: $0-$25; $26-$50; $51-$75; $76-$100; $101-$125; $126-$150; $151-$175; $176-$200; $201-$225; $226-$250; $251-$275; $276-$300; and $300 plus. This places the average order value in the middle of a range of increments that extend from a low of $0 to a high of $300. Remember, establishing the overall range of monetary value to track and the smaller increments of value within that range is a long-term decision; changing the monetary value increments down the road can cause massive conversion problems with the data. The future effect of strategic and tactical decisions on the average order value must also be included in the planning. As no catalog company specifically attempts to lower average order value, the artificial shift in the incremental design of the monetary value range to compensate for future revenue enhancement should be made in favor of raising the upper range.

By distributing each order into its increment of dollar value, you will segment all orders by monetary value, just as you segmented recency and frequency (**Figure L3.2**). The greatest number of orders will fall into increments on either side of the average order value; lesser numbers of orders will fall into increments in an ascending and descending pattern. A bell curve will form with the bulk of the orders peaking in the area around the average order value. When you make strategic or tactical decisions designed to shift the average order value, the bell curve should shift over time with the outcomes of those decisions.

With proper segmentation and relational database technology, you now have the ability to say, "Give me all of the orders and

Figure L3.2

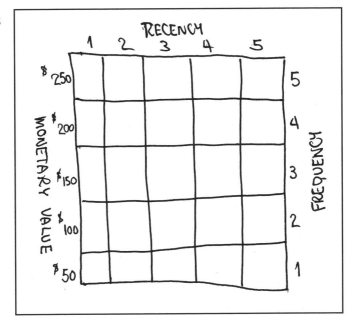

customers between $251 and $275 in monetary value." That list of transactions is a unique segment of the customer base and tells you something unique about those customers: they spend $100 to $125 more than the average customer.

All customers can be ranked in a descending hierarchy of monetary value. At the top will be the one customer who has spent the most money (either this year or over the lifetime); at the bottom will be the one customer who has spent the least amount of money; and in between will be all the rest.

Once you have the hierarchical ranking by small monetary increments, it is usual to lump increments together into larger segments and to look at monetary value in performance groups. Generally, these performance groups are: 1) very profitable; 2) profitable; and 3) unprofitable. For example, if the AOV is $150, set up three monetary value groups at $0-$100, $101-$200, and $201-$300 plus. If you must have a minimum order of $101 to break even, the first monetary value performance group at $0-$100 is unprofitable; the second monetary value performance group at $101-$200 is profitable; and the third monetary value performance group at $201-$300 is very profitable. Some marketers refer to these groups as Dogs, Cows and Stars **(Figure L3.3)**. Logically, you want to market aggressively to Stars, steadily to Cows and carefully to Dogs. The intent is to find new Stars while keeping existing Stars and Cows and shedding Dogs.

Caution must be urged at this point. There are many ways monetary value can be segmented and analyzed. Assuring continuity from measurement to measurement, from hierarchy to hierarchy, from analysis to analysis is crucial if the information is to have any validity whatsoever. One way to segment monetary value and generate the hierarchy may be to look only at the last or most recent purchase across the entire customer base. Whether that purchase was today or five years ago, only one purchase per customer will be included in the hierarchical ranking. A second way to construct segmentation may be to look at an aggregate of all purchases for all customers across the entire customer base. This is the aggregate lifetime monetary value hierarchy and it provides information of a

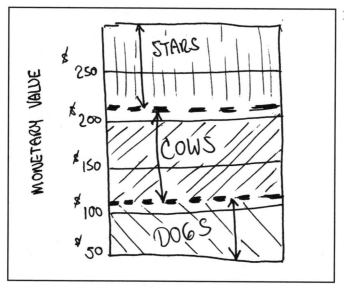

Figure L3.3

different kind. A third way to segment may be to look at the year of recency. For instance, a hierarchical ranking of all segments of monetary value in only the one-year recency classification can be done. Similarly, a monetary value hierarchy for all two-, three- or four-year recency customers could be done and would produce information unique to those segments **(Figure L3.4)**. Obviously, each of the recency segments could be analyzed for either last purchase only or aggregate lifetime purchases.

Before the complexity of monetary value becomes overwhelming, remember that there are only a few questions that are really important:

1. Is the average order value increasing relative to sales?
2. Is the ratio of Stars to Cows improving?
3. Is the ratio of Cows to Dogs improving?
4. Is the monetary value performance in each year of recency as good as, better than, worse than, last year (or some other time period)?

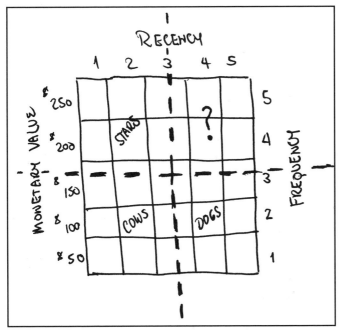

Figure L3.4

5. Is the monetary value for the most recent orders higher than the monetary value for historical orders (average lifetime aggregate monetary value), or is there a surprise in the making?

If you know the precise answers to those five questions, you will be ahead of ninety percent of the competition, maybe ninety-nine percent.

As you may have come to expect, this last paragraph reminds that the foregoing discussion about monetary value segmentation applies to all channels as well as overall. A full understanding of monetary value can only be had when the individual channel monetary value performance is known. Each channel and segment of recency and frequency within those channels will show monetary value as increasing, remaining the same or decreasing. As always, increasing is the only acceptable direction. The complexity of the database and the analytics becomes quite significant with large numbers of combinations of recency, frequency, monetary value, segments, channels, incremental values and performance groups to be considered.

MONETARY VALUE SEGMENTATION: PICKERING

David Ogilvy, the advertising legend, wrote that direct marketing was his secret weapon. In some ways, it is more secret now than ever because there are fewer masters. The most important aspect of direct marketing is that it can be *measured*. And, the single most important way that you can measure success is using monetary value in some way.

Monetary value segmentation is an immeasurably valuable addition to the decision-making process. Consider the peddler, traveling his route, with an idea of the value of his customers. If one of the particularly valuable customers isn't home, he may try to hit them again on his way out of town (using monetary value segmentation to drive contact strategy). When at the home of a particularly valuable customer, the peddler may spend more time and show more wares than to a customer of average value (using monetary value segmentation to drive allocation of advertising space). In your application, this may mean sending out a 'big book' instead of a flyer to the best customers.

To expedite quick and accurate decision-making, many direct marketers use indexes to compare across segments. **Figure P3.1** is a simple example that segments customers by their lifetime dollars and their average order values.

TOTALS	Customers	Orders	Total Dollars	AOV	AOV Index
$1-50	70,533	85,347	$1,891,036	$22.26	16
$51-100	48,113	76,565	$3,525,579	$46.05	34
$101-250	63,764	149,940	$10,304,632	$68.73	50
$251-500	36,764	142,440	$12,955,850	$90.96	66
$501+	58,273	715,850	$131,904,353	$184.26	134
Total	277,447	1,170,141	$160,581,449	$137.23	100

Figure P3.1

The data creation for this is straightforward. For each of the five segments of total lifetime dollars we summed the number of customers, number of orders, and dollars. We then calculated the average order value for each segment as well as for the whole. We then took the average for each segment, divided it by the overall average and multiplied by one hundred.

When using indexes, 100 is average. When we look at the $1-$50 segment, we see that the AOV is only sixteen percent of the average. The AOV for the $501 + segment is thirty-four percent above average. This is an easy and accurate way to make comparisons and it starts to show us where the center of gravity is for our most valuable customers. For example, if a customer is in the $251-$500 segment, but they have an AOV of $155 (which is above average) it seems like they are customers waiting to make the move into the most valuable segment. They may be worth an additional email, catalog, or perhaps assigning them an account manager.

It is important to have this information accessible (and checked for accuracy) for each channel and for the enterprise as a whole. As with any analysis, be careful to check for *outliers*. Outliers, while there isn't a specific definition, are observations that are far different in magnitude from others.

As an example, suppose that a General Motors plant between five hundred and one thousand employees had a need for shelving for their warehouse. The order came in via an assigned account manager and was worth nearly six figures. To include this with orders generated via a catalog would dramatically change the AOV and other key statistics and render them much less useful. Since the General Motors purchase is an extraordinary event and came in via a direct sales channel rather than catalog, it is best to exclude this outlier order from analysis of the catalog channel.

MONETARY VALUE VELOCITY: LIBEY

Monetary value velocity is the speed at which individual channel and aggregate customers increase their level of purchases over time. If the average customer moves from an average order value of $150 to an average order value of $200 in one year, the monetary value velocity increases by +50. If the average order value drops from $150 to $100, the monetary value velocity is a net decrease of -50. Any increase in monetary value velocity is positive; any decrease is negative; and the greater the positive velocity, the greater the level of spending.

Dividing the customers into descending hierarchies of positive and negative monetary value velocity, by channel and in the aggregate, over twenty rolling quarters, provides important information relative to performance of the business. By studying all customers with, for instance, a +100 monetary value velocity relative to products purchased may reveal product propensity information that can be used to stimulate similar increases in velocity in other customer segments àt the +25, +50 or static levels. In the same manner of analysis, it may be instructive to isolate product commonalities among customers who move from a positive to a negative monetary value velocity.

Individual positive monetary value velocity represents customers who suddenly are spending more money than they have historically spent over some period of time. Something has motivated these customers to purchase more; knowing what that motivation is, when it occurred and how much it creates in additional monetary value are essential pieces of information.

Equally important is the ability to use monetary value velocity to measure the effect of pricing changes, shipping and handling charges, product mix alterations, shifts in marketing emphasis, channel concentrations and mix, contact frequency and other strategic and tactical factors. As an example, if you raise prices ten percent across all products and the monetary value velocity on an average order value of $150 only increases by $7.50, you have a -7.5 decrease in monetary value velocity. This is a five percent decrease in adjusted average order value, most likely due to price resistance.

In the examples, monetary value velocity has been expressed simply as a number equaling the dollar difference. It can be expressed several ways—as a percentage, as a dollar amount, as a score—as long as the calculation remains consistent over time. The end product of monetary value velocity measurement and analysis is to be able to state, "This customer (individual, SIC, segment, channel, or overall) has improved by (unit of measurement) over the last (period of time)" or, "This customer has deteriorated by (unit of measurement) over the last (period of time)." These are kernels of knowledge that lead to wisdom which justify the analyses.

Once a clear understanding is gained about the health of the monetary value velocity direction, which can only be increasing, remaining the same or decreasing, the information can be examined relative to recency velocity and momentum and frequency velocity and momentum. From those examinations, precise performance of customers in precise segments will be seen and optimal performance in optimal segments will be revealed, as will sub-optimal performance in sub-optimal segments. From there, strategies can be adjusted to maximize the optimal performance segments and to improve the sub-optimal segments **(Figure L3.5)**.

All velocity analyses of monetary value are carried out on two levels: 1) by individual channel; and 2) by the aggregate of all channels. Each channel will have differing measurements. Knowing the directional trend of the individual channel velocity is essential to an effective understanding of this nuance of the overall business performance.

Figure L3.5

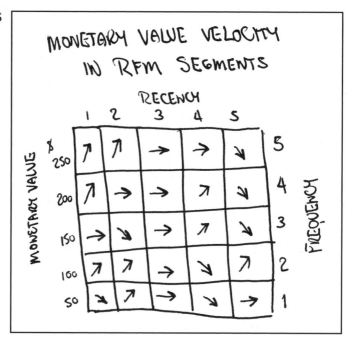

MONETARY VALUE VELOCITY: PICKERING

Monetary value velocity—now we are really getting somewhere! Your non-direct marketing co-workers probably don't understand things like recency or frequency or propensity to repurchase. But if you tell them where and how we are making more money for the company, then you have their undivided attention.

The mechanics of velocity are rather straightforward. Here is an example **(Figure P3.2)** comparing one-time buyers on the active file (last purchase within the last eighteen months) versus multi-buyers (two or more purchases) also on the active file.

	Q1 AOV	Q2 AOV	Velocity
1 x Buyers	$ 146	$ 135	$ (11)
2 x + Buyers	$ 225	$ 232	$ 7

Figure P3.2

Simple analysis shows us some mixed news. On the downside, the velocity of one-time buyers is decreasing, they are spending on average $11 less per order in Q2 (second quarter) than in Q1 (first quarter). This is not a good thing, but points to the need for additional analysis. Perhaps the featured product(s) on the prospecting piece has been lowered in price or perhaps there are new featured products at lower prices. Changes like this are often done to boost response, so careful comparisons to recent response rates and recency velocity are warranted.

On the positive side, the monetary value velocity for multi-buyers is improving. This is especially good news for those marketers who rely on multi-buyers to provide the profit. Again, this news should be drilled down into further. Monetary velocity increase of AOV with a decrease in frequency velocity may not necessarily be such a good thing, especially when it results in lower lifetime dollars. Also, changes in price breaks and offers may be driving some of this change. An example: if the hurdle for free shipping goes from $50 an order to $60 an order, this could account for the change. As happens so frequently, the answer to one question spurs several other questions.

For marketers who do not charge for their offer, like trade show attendee offers, electronic newsletters or controlled-circulation publications, monetary value analysis needs to be adapted. What is the worth of acquiring a controlled circulation subscriber today and how much advertising revenue will that generate over the next twelve months? This is straddling the line into lifetime value analysis, and will require more work.

Special note to those working with solo offers, seminars, and other offers with a single product or service and a single unit of sale: monetary value velocity is still an important analytical tool. Although a seminar may be the same price from year to year, the monetary velocity will change based on the number of attendees sent.

MONETARY VALUE MOMENTUM: LIBEY

Monetary value momentum is a measurement of the force being exerted on the individual customer, the customer base as a whole and by channel as a result of changes in monetary value velocity. If the velocity is increasing at an increasingly faster rate, the momentum is positive. If the velocity is decreasing at an accelerating rate, the momentum is negative. For example, if, over the last three mailings, the $150 average order value increased by $4, $6 and $8 successively, the average order value stands at $168, a monetary value velocity of +18 and a momentum of +6 (18 divided by 3). If the AOV increases by $12 on the fourth mailing, the velocity will be +30 and the momentum +7.5 (30 divided by 4). The momentum increases by +1.5. The business is moving in the right direction. Plotted over twenty rolling quarters on the classic x and y axis, the monetary velocity momentum trend will be visually apparent (**Figure L3.6**).

It is possible to have a positive, slowing momentum and also a negative, increasing momentum—increasing but starting to slow; decreasing but slowing or improving faster; or staying the same. Knowledge of the trend allows you to say with certainty, "We are recovering our loss of monetary value at an accelerating rate."

With the addition of the monetary value velocity and momentum component, in the aggregate and by channel, it is clear that the

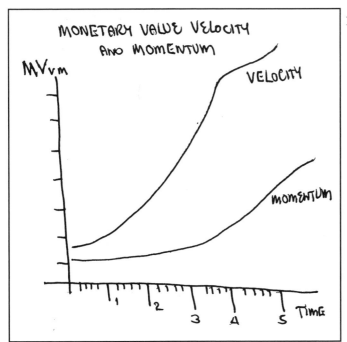

best customer you can have is the customer with a universal accelerating momentum and increasing velocities in recency, frequency and monetary value. If the trends in each component are positive and gaining in velocity and momentum, the customer is a top-of-the-hierarchy buyer and one that must be focused on for retention with obsessive concentration.

Of course, all monetary value momentum analyses are conducted across the aggregate and channel segments. As with velocity, similar momentum differences should be seen in each channel. Separate twenty rolling quarter charts by channel will be helpful in comparing channel performance relative to advertising expense and comparing individual channels to the overall momentum.

MONETARY VALUE MOMENTUM: PICKERING

Monetary value momentum is tracking the effect of velocity over time. This is one of the most telling of all measurements. It is so straightforward it can even be safely shown to members of the board of directors.

Monetary value momentum can be defined as the sum of monetary velocities divided by the number of measurement periods. **Figure P3.3** continues the example we used in velocity where we are measuring the velocity of average order value (AOV). We will examine the last five quarters, although twenty rolling quarters is the ideal.

	1X Buyers AOV	1X Velocity	2X+ Buyers AOV	2X+ Velocity
Current Qtr	$135	$ (11)	$232	$ 7
Q4	$146	$ 34	$225	$ (22)
Q3	$112	$ (41)	$247	$ 38
Q2	$153	$ 19	$209	$ 10
Q1	$134	$ (9)	$199	$ 5
Momentum		$ (2)		$ 8

Figure P3.3

Plotting the AOV and velocity on a chart yields the following (**Figure P3.4**):

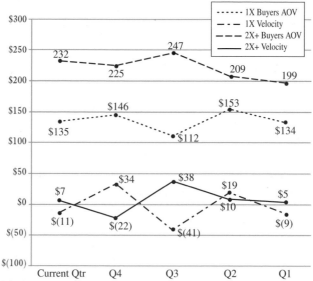

Figure P3.4

190

Although the above makes a nice picture, it is difficult to explain. The concept of monetary value gives you the vocabulary to distill this to a concise statement:

The velocity of AOV over the last five quarters has been volatile. The one-time buyers have been particularly erratic, with an overall force pushing the AOV monetary momentum to negative two for the last five quarters. The multi-buyers have been much more stable with four out of the last five quarters having positive velocity and an overall momentum of positive eight.

In addition to helping give a historical context for momentum, the other benefit of keeping at least twenty rolling quarters is that it will allow you to track and make allowance for seasonal changes.

MONETARY VALUE RECONCILIATION: LIBEY

Monetary value reconciliation is a process of counting customers rather than orders and assigning them a value classification. Each customer has a monetary value classification determined from either the last purchase or the aggregate of all purchases in that customer's lifetime buying history with the company. The classifications are the segments of value you have chosen for your business. The segments can be small dollar increments, such as $51-$75, or in larger monetary value groups, such as Stars, Cows and Dogs, as previously discussed.

At the end of any business day, the shuffling and arranging of individual customers in the monetary value segments will change based on that day's purchases. A certain number of customers will be in the highest monetary value classification; a certain number will be in the lowest; and the balance will be spread across the rest on a bell curve. New customers will be assigned a monetary value classification based on their first purchase spending level; repeat customers will either remain in their existing monetary value classification or move up or down depending on their purchases. But every customer can be accounted for and assigned a monetary value level.

Tomorrow that reconciliation will change. Customers will move to other monetary value classifications. New customers will be classified for the first time. The total number in each box will be different from the total number today or yesterday. Movement of customer monetary value—like movement of customer recency—is a dynamic phenomenon.

Monetary value classifications—measured in dollars—each have a total number of customers residing in each classification or box. The changing totals over time are the fruit of the analyses. Are customers flowing in the direction of increased monetary value or are they flowing toward a diminished monetary value? Taken together with recency and frequency, the question becomes, "Are customers flowing in the direction of increased monetary value, increased frequency and increased recency?"

Obviously, the average of all customer monetary value is the average order value, but it is only a single, moving point in the monetary value landscape. The gain or loss in each category of monetary value is the revealing information. Cows may be improving, but Stars may be declining. Or, lower segments of Stars may be improving rapidly while top segments of Stars are static. *The point: The relationship between categorical monetary value information and advertising, product, service, time and price—by channel and overall—is the knowledge and wisdom to be gained from monetary value analysis.*

Precise reconciliation must provide total customer number counts in all dollar level monetary value categories. The numbers of customers added to or moved between all categories must reconcile with the total number of customers found in the recency reconciliation counts. Knowing the counts in each segment today is useless unless you can replicate the reconciliation tomorrow and be able to examine and draw conclusions about the changes at will. The ebb and flow of customer movement among categories of monetary value is meaningful only when examined over time. Therefore, the discipline of tracking and reconciling monetary value on a regular schedule is necessary. Reconciliations can be performed on a daily, weekly, monthly, quarterly or annual basis. For most multi-channel direct marketers, a quarterly reconciliation is the minimum time period that can be expected to produce meaningful information; monthly is better. Visualized over twenty rolling quarters, the display and charting of monetary flow and the trends in direction develops a unique perspective of the performance of any multi-channel direct marketing business.

MONETARY VALUE RECONCILIATION: PICKERING

Monetary value reconciliation is about counting people who transit into and out of various RFM cells. There are few direct marketing companies who rigorously do this; those who do, however, have a great view into their profitability.

In addition to counting how many people are in the various segments, a marketer looking to get an even more granular view will total the dollars that those people represent (either lifetime dollars or most recent twelve months, whichever is the consistent measurement). The reason is clear: most direct marketing companies have four to six different monetary ranges. More than that is too difficult to manage. Within each range there can be fluctuations of fairly large proportion. Much of this fluctuation can be seen by performing velocity and momentum analysis; they will show which way things are trending. But to get the full impact, reconciliation is the final piece.

Examine the reconciliation below (**Figure P3.5**). The overall change is anemic, somewhat benign. The business doesn't appear to be skyrocketing nor falling into a death-spiral.

Active Customers by AOV			
	1st Quarter	2nd Quarter	Inc/Dec
$1-50	23,347	22,917	-2%
$51-100	13,437	14,212	6%
$101-250	9,871	9,413	-5%
$251-500	3,476	3,297	-5%
$501+	2,112	2,347	11%
Total	52,243	52,186	0%

Figure P3.5

Now let's look at the same breakout but count dollars instead of counting people (**Figure P3.6**):

Active Customers by AOV			
	1st Quarter	2nd Quarter	Inc/Dec
$1-50	$1,009,991	$1,084,891	7%
$51-100	$ 770,209	$ 961,726	25%
$101-250	$2,222,653	$1,656,594	-25%
$251-500	$1,240,932	$1,430,898	15%
$501+	$1,645,248	$2,044,237	24%
Total	$6,889,033	$7,178,346	4%

Figure P3.6

The story seems much more dramatic. Overall, the AOV seems quite positive, increasing four percent. The large increase in the upper tier is quite promising, but the change in the middle tier is distressing. Analysis may show that a change in product mix or price breaks could be driving this change. Without carefully performing and reviewing the reconciliation, there could be surprises having profound effects on the business.

MONETARY VALUE AND LIST RENTALS: LIBEY

Segmentation by monetary value is a valuable list enhancement. Companies renting your customer list will frequently specify dollar levels of monetary value when placing their list order. As an example, a list renter may ask for all customers whose last purchase was $200 or more. If you classify monetary value in $25 increments beginning at $150 and ending at $300 plus, you will collapse the four highest segments ($201-$225, $226-$250, $251-$275 and $276-$300+) into one monetary value segment ($200+; one purchase only) and rent all the customer names that fall into that category.

Your own list rentals doubtless request monetary value ranges. If your average order value is $250, it is logical to rent names of buyers who have spent $200 or more. You would not want names of buyers who spent only $25 on their last purchase. To demonstrate the value of proper monetary value segmentation, consider the following request: "Give me all customers who have spent $200 or more on only one line item." A segmentation request such as this may isolate customers with a high dollar level purchasing authority. The problem often encountered is that an adequate number of customer names must exist at the $200+, one item specification, or whatever the specification may be. If only five such customers exist, there is little utility for the renter.

Monetary value segmentation for list rentals is universal. Being able to segment and micro-segment customers by monetary value requires the ability to manipulate transaction and line-item data. The database must allow for capture and output of dollar value, line-item count, line-item value and line-item product identification, at the minimum. It is not enough to know how much money was spent. Knowing what was bought, the value of each item, the number of items, and the value of the whole transaction is essential. Plus, you have to know all of these micro-segmentations by channel since the list renter may specify, "Give me all customers who have spent $200 or more on only one item from the email and online channels." And, of course, by offering segments, micro-segments and channel segments of monetary value, you can increase the rental charges for your list.

MONETARY VALUE AND LIST RENTALS: PICKERING

Although the ability to do list rental segmentation by monetary value is universal, few list owners choose to make it available. Monetary segmentation is more prevalent for list rentals on the consumer side of direct marketing than on the business-to-business side. List owners most often provide an AOV for their entire file in the synopsis of their list on the datacard. In general, it is easier to make a list work where the AOV is higher than yours, than for a list whose AOV is lower than yours.

Another way of segmentation of list for prospecting purposes is by demographic or firmographic information. Many list owners choose to overlay their file with estimated household income (for consumer files) or annual sales volume (for business-to-business files). It should be well noted here: these dollar values in almost every instance are modeled values. Thus, on a consumer file the estimated household income is generated from sources like census information. On a business-to-business file the values are generally based on averages developed for different SIC and employee size combinations.

The approximation necessary to develop monetary overlay information requires that selections using those elements be done carefully. If you have a product that seems to be in demand only by companies that have annual sales volumes between $2,500,000 and $4,999,999, be certain to test the adjacent segments. It may not be that your assumption is incorrect; it may be that many of the companies that you are targeting are falling into the wrong ranges.

Many other types of monetary segmentations are useful in prospecting. The education market is one that is increasingly attractive, as enrollments are increasing and school expenditures are less affected by economic fluctuations than those seen in other markets. However, simply segmenting by spending per student may not be enough. Understanding the various linkages, like percentage of per-student-funding provided through property taxes, and other factors, will be critical in correctly understanding the file and making good selections. For vertical markets like education, government, healthcare, and religious organizations, it makes sense to consider using a consultant or becoming very familiar with the various specialty files and selects available.

MONETARY VALUE AND ADVERTISING FREQUENCY: LIBEY

How often you mail, telephone, email, insert or otherwise contact customers is, in part, determined by how much money those customers spend with you. If they spend a lot, you contact them a lot; if they spend little, you contact them less. Contacting customers often who spend little is a problem; contacting customers infrequently who spend a lot is also a problem. Getting the mix right is the general idea.

Previously, with the paint store example, it was concluded that the most recent customers deserve more frequent contact. Also, it was concluded that the most frequent buyers deserve an increased number of contacts. And it was demonstrated that only by knowing the monetary value can those conclusions be valid.

The customer who spends the most money should be contacted the most. If that customer is also the most frequent and the most recent buyer, then you have isolated the *best* customer (**Figure L3.7**). If you can increase every customer's recency, frequency and monetary value, you are turning all customers into best customers. If that is true, you can stop reading right here because you already have the ultimate money machine. If that isn't true, you may want to continue reading.

It is possible that the customer who has spent the most money is not a recent customer or a frequent customer. In fact, it is possible that the customer who heads the monetary value hierarchy bought only once five years ago. Should you send that customer a catalog a week for years? The answer to that question depends on the size of the customer's order value. If the monetary value of the one order is

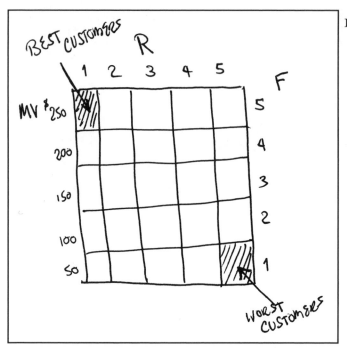

Figure L3.7

big enough, it may be worth spending the advertising dollars to assure you get the next order in five years. If the cost of the advertising
exceeds the profit of the purchase, there is little sense in sending five
year's worth of catalogs. The decision is formulaic.

Describing a customer in RFM terms can help. For instance,
consider the following description of the top one-year customer:

One-year recency; 12-time frequency; $300 average order;
60 total orders aggregate; $18,000 total aggregate purchases.

Numerically, this customer can be described as:

1 – 12 – 300 – 60 – 18,000

Narratively, this customer is described as:

A one-year recent customer who buys monthly and spends
an average of $300 per purchase who has 60 previous orders
and has spent a total of $18,000 over the past five years.

If you simply add the numeric description together, the product or score is:

$$1 + 12 + 300 + 60 + 18,000 = 18,373$$

Divide the product by 1,000 and you arrive at a descriptive customer RFM score of 18.373. Array the RFM scores of all one-year customers in a descending hierarchical listing and you have a simple but useful method for determining the relative comparative values of all one-year individual customers. Total the individual RFM scores for all one-year customers and divide by the number of one-year customers and you have the average RFM score for the one-year customer base. Compare that score month-to-month and you will be able to determine which direction the business is going.

Based on the range of RFM scores, you can segment the hierarchical rankings in each year of recency and assign contact or mailing frequency accordingly. For example, all customers with RFM scores between 17.400 and 18.373 and above will be contacted or mailed fifty-two times a year; customer groups scoring between 16.400 and 17.399 will be contacted or mailed thirty-six times a year, and so forth.

The actual number of advertising contacts—and the channels employed—are only relevant to the business doing the advertising. Whether the number is fifty-two or four is driven by the individual business and makes little difference in this discussion. *The point: Recognize that some experiential hierarchy of advertising allocation is essential to multi-channel direct marketing success, and RFM is one way to determine that empiric hierarchy; without it you are forced to guess at how many times to contact or mail a customer.*

Now, I realize my RFM scoring formula is simplistic; indeed, unscientific. Over the years, however, I have found that almost *any* method works as long as you *always* use it. Many years ago, when I was a gold, silver, platinum and foreign currency trader on the Chicago Board of Trade, I used a method of buying and selling gold on the phases of the moon. It worked. It had nothing to do with the moon; it had to do with absolute *discipline* of method. It's the same here. Over the years following the first book on RFM, hundreds of people have contacted me with their correct or improved method of RFM scoring. I have replied to all of them exactly the same: "Wonderful." You must use whatever you must use; weight each component as you must weight them; develop, tweak and twist your RFM scoring method as you must. The only thing that matters is you must use *something*, it must work for you and you must be disciplined about using whatever you develop. So, there is no need for you to send along your RFM scoring method and model to me. I can go ahead and give you my personal "Wonderful" now and extend my congratulations on discovering a better way of doing it for your business.

Oh, yes, by the way—you have to do RFM scoring and contact allocation in each segment in each channel. But you already know that.

MONETARY VALUE AND ADVERTISING FREQUENCY: PICKERING

Monetary value is the critically important measure in determining the success or failure of an advertising frequency strategy. The question is more nuanced than just simply how many times a customer is mailed, or emailed, or faxed. To be certain, customers will respond better to one advertising vehicle than another. Some customers absolutely require a catalog as a reference, some customers will respond very well to an email telling them that they may want to order more paper and perhaps check the toner.

There will be instances when there are two types of customers who both prefer a particular channel. One has higher monetary potential and one has lesser potential. Use monetary value to drive frequency and vehicle decisions.

High scoring customers may rate the large (customer) catalog. The lower value customers may not produce enough revenue to justify this more expensive catalog, which often can cost forty percent or more than the prospecting catalog. Letting the value drive the mailing decisions can yield a solution that looks like this:

High value customers:
12 'big book' catalogs per year at $1.10 each = $13.20

Low value customers:
4 'big book' catalogs per year at $1.10 each   = $ 4.40
8 'prospect' catalogs per year at $0.40 each   = $ 3.20
12 total combined catalogs per year   = $ 7.60

The thirty-nine percent lower cost of the combination of big books and prospect books allows the mailer to keep up frequent contacts but at a cost of promotion that makes sense.

Comparing these different strategies, assuming identical response rates of two percent per monthly campaign and lower AOVs we see the following results (**Figure P3.6**):

Customers	Annual Cost of Catalogs	Total Mailings	Total Orders	AOV	Total Revenue	Adv as a % of Revenue
1,000	$13,200	12	240	$300	$72,000	18.33%
1,000	$13,200	12	240	$200	$48,000	27.50%
1,000	$8,000	12	240	$200	$48,000	16.67%

Figure P3.6

As we see, in the first cell the larger AOV justifies the increased cost of advertising. In the lower AOV segments we see that the twelve big books a year strategy at a $13,200 per year advertising cost leads to an unacceptably high advertising percentage of revenue of 27.50 percent. By mixing lower cost prospect books or flyers with a less frequent schedule of big books, we can achieve acceptable advertising costs as a percentage of revenue. The correct strategy is fairly simple: spend more on better customers. This strategy and the advantages aren't apparent until you have the facts and you are able to make measurements to the penny.

MONETARY VALUE AND CUSTOMER ATTRITION: LIBEY

The one customer you don't want to lose is the one who is spending the most money and delivering the most profit. Obviously, knowing who that customer actually is gives you an advantage in developing customer retention strategies targeted to keeping that customer happy, loyal, recent, frequent and profitable.

Any one-year recency customer with high frequency and high monetary value who ages into the two-year recency box should be identified for immediate customer retention efforts. Even better—more proactive—any one-year recency customer with a high RFM score who drops in scoring should be identified for immediate fore-stalling customer retention efforts *before* slipping into the two-year recency box. Remember, you never know when you have received the last order from a customer.

Highly advanced customer retention strategies have one level of effort for slippage of recency alone, a second level for slippage of recency with frequency, and a third level of effort for slippage of recency, frequency and monetary value. In other words, you work hard to keep one-year recency customers; *really* hard to keep one-year recency customers with multiple purchases; and *frantically* to keep one-year, multiple buyers who spend big dollars.

Unless the monetary value component is known, the customer retention effort is limited to recency and frequency and, as has been shown, that is not enough. The high-dollar customer can fall through the crack.

One way to guard against high value customer attrition is to isolate high-scoring RFM customers and pinpoint them as a part of the RFM reconciliation process. When high RFM scorers move down by some number of points or, at the least, when they move to the two-year box without buying, flag them for retention investigation, tracking and regular and specific follow-up. This is done overall and by channel.

MONETARY VALUE AND CUSTOMER ATTRITION: PICKERING

It is an unpleasant task, but as part of our jobs many of us have had to fire someone. Sometimes you have to fire 'bad' (read: 'unprofitable') customers.

As you become intimately familiar with your customer database and perform time-series analyses, you will find certain markers that indicate that this person or site is very unlikely ever to become profitable. They only order from the loss-leader product categories; they only order from sales fliers; or perhaps they are a consumer purchasing a product from a business-to-business marketer. You will be able to see where these trends are and, armed with this knowledge, you need to do something about it.

A fully developed and deployed contact strategy can put these 'suspect' customers on a lower frequency schedule. This is a good strategy, but it requires fairly complete information, strong historical analysis of profitability and product category information. It demands a great amount of work, but the dividends are significant.

Increasingly, there are direct marketers whose product lines appeal to both consumers and businesses. These can be as diverse as office products, outerwear, and technology. The thing that they have in common is that they attract buyers with much different rates of attrition.

It is not uncommon to find that true consumers have about one-third to one-half the propensity to re-order as a business customer. This is in addition to the fact that they will have a lower lifetime dollars monetary value even if they do re-order. Simply put: *most of these consumer buyers will spend less and marketers will spend more to get those dollars.*

The resolution to this is simple: find what defines these customers as consumers. It may be as simple as records that have a company name or are identified as a business address by the USPS, although it usually is not this straightforward. When these lower potential consumers are identified, understand that they will attrit more quickly and in higher percentages. Your own study will reveal this. So the answer is clear: you must 'fire' these customers and deploy the resources where they will yield better results.

MONETARY VALUE AND PRODUCT PROPENSITY: LIBEY

Certain products create a higher monetary value than others. In fact, in hundreds of direct marketing companies I have worked with, business-to-business and consumer, the 80-20 Rule is almost always alive and well. Twenty percent of the products are responsible for eighty percent of the monetary value.

Product commonalities are found in the higher regions of RFM scoring as well as the nether regions. By this, I mean that certain products are associated over and over in the purchasing patterns and in the upper regions of frequency and monetary value, individually and combined. The degree of association, or the combinations of products that can be identified, becomes larger as the total number of SKUs increases. Companies with a limited number of products have a smaller number of associated products in RFM scoring analysis. A good example is pet supplies. A niche catalog of dog blankets, sweaters and other apparel will produce much smaller combinations of product propensity than a full-line catalog with thousands of SKUs running the gamut from canary treats to aquarium heaters. The same is true with retail stores. A smaller association of products in high monetary value shoppers will be found in a gift shop than will be found in a big-box discounter. The opportunities to associate product purchases because of availability are greater.

At the high end of monetary value the associated products tend to be better products, that is, higher priced, non-commodity, personalized, high margin, unique, and other attributes of good products. At the lower end of monetary value the associated products tend to be lesser products, that is, lower priced, commodity, low margin, commonly available, and so on. Good products make good customers; bad products make bad customers.

High monetary value is good provided that enough products are sold at that value to make it worth offering the products to customers. It does no good whatsoever to sell four items a year with high monetary value if the costs exceed the profitability on those products. The mark of an inexperienced marketer is falling in love with a product that doesn't sell.

The hierarchy of monetary value previously described by RFM scoring overlaid by the products bought is a most valuable comparison worth the time to establish and regularly evaluate. Knowing which products drive monetary value is so basic as to be elementary; yet most direct marketing companies do not have a clear and precise understanding of this relationship. A dispassionate divorcing of the number of orders, the number of units and the monetary value of those orders and units must be accomplished if this analysis is to have any utility for strategic purposes. Separate the orders, units and value in the mind in order to achieve objectivity. It is not enough to know only which products produce high monetary value. Knowing the units and number of orders relative to that value is the essential knowledge to be learned. Together, these individual knowledge components produce a wise understanding of the marketing dynamic.

A secondary understanding of product propensity is gained when high monetary value product sales are examined alongside associated product purchases. As an example, only one product *A* is sold but it produces multiple unit sales of associated product *B* in every case, thereby increasing monetary value. An expensive laptop always spurs sales of multiple new and upgraded software programs, as an example. Once associated sales are added to the marketing mix—a tactic known as *bundling*—monetary values increase significantly.

The monetary value hierarchy and product propensity overlay will be different for each channel. Therefore, each channel must receive its own separate analysis of monetary value and product propensity. One great benefit of the multi-channel analyses is being able to shift unprofitable product sales from one channel to another channel where costs are lower and the product sale becomes profitable. There will also be product similarities among the high and low monetary value products across all channels. Quite often, product dogs are discovered that are simply not worth selling in *any* channel. And, of course, all products identified for add-on sales, cross-sells and daily specials are determined from the monetary value product propensity hierarchy. If ninety percent of customers who buy product *E* also can also be enticed to buy product *H*, that is something you should know about.

MONETARY VALUE AND PRODUCT PROPENSITY: PICKERING

High value customers, and low value customers, frequently have characteristics that separate them from each other. Some of these are external data, like the number of employees or SIC code. However, since these are usually available when selecting prospecting lists, the experienced marketer generally avoids recruiting these customers in the first place. Product purchase information can segment high value customers from low value customers; all that you have to do is look for it.

As we have discussed, most marketers group their items (SKUs) into one or two or more higher-level groupings. The blue sweater I order may be SKU 01234, one of 34,000 SKUs in the catalog. Obviously, this is too many items to use effectively to predict monetary value, but the blue sweater rolls up to the sweaters product category and that rolls up into the menswear product group. And because most marketers have about a dozen or two of these higher level groups, you can now do some meaningful analysis about which product groups are indicative of high value customers.

Looking at a dozen or two product groups will yield some easy answers. If a customer buys from a product category that has higher than average prices, it isn't surprising to see that these customers will be of high monetary value. What is under the surface? Some further analysis may show the customers who buy from a particular product category on their first purchase, even if it is a low price point category, go on to produce higher than average monetary value. This is a little more off the beaten track, but a well designed database keeps track of things like first purchase product or product category. This is why good database design is essential.

Another method to find high monetary value customers, using product information at a higher and even more simplistic level, is to query from how many different product categories has the customer purchased? If you do the math, you will be absolutely stunned at how strongly this is correlated to high monetary value.

There are many other types of analyses, each generally specific to a particular business. Part of the success of a good analytic program is knowing what unique, custom analyses are demanded by the market space in which the business operates.

MONETARY VALUE AND PRICING: LIBEY

While pricing is a topic for another book, several points can be made regarding monetary value and pricing. First, the concept of *price thresholds* should be explored. One of the most frequently asked questions concerns the level of price relative to product. Every direct marketing company has what is known as a *product price threshold*. This is the price below which no products will be offered in a channel. After calculating the marketing costs, fulfillment costs, and factoring in cost of goods, contribution to overhead and an acceptable profit, a minimum threshold product selling price may be $34 for a business-to-business cataloger and no products selling for less than $34 will be included in the catalog except those that may be add-on components of other products meeting the threshold and above. The minimum threshold product price in the catalog channel will, perhaps, be different from that of the online channel. Recalculations of the channel threshold prices are accomplished regularly and the thresholds adjusted as necessary.

A second point concerns *gross margin*. To be perfectly clear, gross margin is defined very simply as product selling price less cost of goods; it does not include shipping and handling revenue, freight or any other elements. Direct marketing companies tend to have average gross margins of 54.3 percent for all catalogs taken together. Separately, consumer catalogs average 54.3 percent; business-to-business catalogs average 51.7 percent; and hybrids of consumer and business-to-business average 53.2. The opposite side of these numbers is the cost of goods which, for all catalogs is 45.7 percent. Separately, the cost of goods for consumer catalogs is 45.7 percent; for business-to-business catalogs 48.3 percent; and for hybrids 46.8 percent. These are not specific or fixed average gross margins and cost of goods; rather, they are the gross margins and cost of goods generally found if you take all business-to-business or consumer or hybrid catalogs, put them in a blender, whir them up and pour out the results. These average numbers were current as of 2004-2005 but will continue to fluctuate and be influenced by external factors including product sourcing from China and other low-cost producers, the value of the U.S. Dollar, competitive influences of big-box retailers, and others.

What these numbers tell us is that most multi-channel direct marketers are paying about $.46 for a product that sells for $1.00. They have about $.54 left to work with. This is essentially how things have been for a very long time. The *Keystone Mark-up*, a term used for hundreds of years, describes the doubling effect of buying something for $.50 and selling it for $1.00. In an earlier book from 1981, *On Gold*, I researched the relationship between gold and rice prices in the markets of China going back to 800 A.D.

Suffice it to say, from production to end-buyer, the various mark-ups throughout history tend to be Keystone Mark-ups. Not a lot has changed.

Combining the realities of gross margin and threshold product price can offer the direct marketer leverage for increasing not only monetary value, but net profits as well. The Master Marketer understands *product margin mix*. For every three products with a 54 percent gross margin, you need one product with an 81 percent gross margin that sells comparably. That mix increases overall gross margin by 12.5 percent. Moving a business from 54 percent gross margin to 66.5 percent gross margin is the stuff of rainmakers. A good product person who understands product margin mix is an artist, a poet, a maker of music. Few marketers have the talent or the intimate knowledge of their products, customers, sources and the pricing sensitivity to master this artisanal skill. But, where these masters do exist and ply their craft, the businesses are robust and very profitable. By way of encouragement for those who have this innate love of products, mastering the product-price-source-mix relationship and learning how to manipulate those elements to increase gross margin and, thereby, net earnings and, by extension, business valuation, is the essence of business management. And, if you are already a master of this art, practice it in your own business because almost no company in my experience will ever leave you alone long enough or give you the independent latitude to practice your art to its fullest extent and benefit. There is just too much politics and turf. You possess the elusive 'entrepreneur gene' and you are rare; go build something of your own.

To reach mastery of the product-price-source-mix relationship, every product must have its own individual history of cost, number of orders, number of units, individual order and aggregate dollar sales and mark-up performance. This information must be examined for shifts in trend on a regular and replicable basis. To make it more complex, the information must be examined relative to recency and frequency and evaluations made about the trends in one-time buyers, multiple buyers, one-year repeat customers, two-year repeat customers, three-year repeat customers and the host of RFM analytic combinations concerning product propensity.

Another aspect of monetary value and pricing is the ability to examine the effects of price changes. Knowing what happens to overall monetary value momentum when a five percent across-the-board price increase is taken is an important bit of information; equally important is what happens when a five percent price decrease is made.

With a five percent across-the-board price increase, monetary value can be expected to increase by five percent. If it increases only two percent, then three percent of the dollars are being withheld due to price resistance or customer attrition to lower-priced competitors. That three percent shortfall will have to be made up by additional orders, product cost savings or increased operating efficiencies. The ability to compare price effects on an individual and aggregate product basis is necessary to manage the mix and the threshold for maximum profitability. And the ability to conduct all of the product-price-source-mix analyses discussed by channel as well as overall is required.

MONETARY VALUE AND PRICING: PICKERING

Simply stated, evaluating monetary value and pricing is beyond most direct marketers. The reason it is beyond most marketers isn't because pricing and pricing analysis are too complex, though they are challenging analyses. It is because the data doesn't reside in an easily used environment.

The standard marketing or fulfillment database is developed to look at customers, either at the individual or site level. It looks at those customers and the orders, dollars, products, and dates of activity associated with them. Some systems also track promotional history. The database to do pricing analysis needs to be oriented toward the product. When drilling into a specific product the database needs to return answers to questions like:

1. How many different people or sites order this product?
2. How many orders included this product?
3. What was the gross revenue generated by this product?
4. What is the average gross margin of the product?
5. How has this product's change in margin, over time, affected the gross revenue?

There are more questions than these, but if you have access to data that can easily answer these questions you are in good shape to do this type of price and product analysis.

Many marketers find that a separate view of the database, or indeed, a separate database altogether, is necessary to do price and product analysis. This is generally an effective way of accessing this information and can greatly increase the efficiency of doing this analysis, as well as provide valuable insights into the profitability of the business.

MONETARY VALUE AND ADVERTISING: LIBEY

In a perfect world, it would make sense that some logical relationship should exist between monetary value and advertising. Products producing the greatest revenues and the greatest gross margin should receive the greatest amount of advertising space and dollars. In fact, some allocation of advertising should be made on a descending hierarchy of monetary value performance. The products delivering the greatest value get the largest allocation; those delivering the least value get the smallest allocation. Of course, it is not a perfect world and this almost never happens.

Returning once again to our Star, Cow and Dog classifications, there is sound reasoning for assigning advertising expenditures based on performance, not only at the customer level but the product level as well. Products should be advertised in a manner that optimizes space, costs, customers and revenues. Within Stars there is a gradation of contact strategy. Top-ranked Stars may get fifty-two catalogs or contacts; middle-ranked Stars may get fifty; and bottom-ranked Stars may get forty-eight. Such a gradation plan may be better than simply sending all Stars fifty-two catalogs. The same gradation patterns are applied to the Cows and the Dogs. The promise of RFM-based advertising allocation comes in the Rule of Thumb I have used for many years: *through proper RFM analyses, you can reduce advertising costs by twenty-five percent without reducing revenues.* Think about that. Now think about that combined with product margin mix. What could you do with twelve-and-a-half points of additional gross margin and twenty-five percent lower advertising costs?

The number of catalogs or other channel contacts to be allocated to customer segments is driven, in part, by monetary value. Remember our paint store example? Perhaps in the final analysis the customer who spends the greatest amount of money is the customer who gets the greatest amount of advertising. But basing strategic contact decisions on monetary value alone is dangerous and can produce enormous waste.

Square-inch analysis, another topic for another book, is a formulaic allocation of total square inches of advertising space based on product monetary performance. Another space allocation method is revenues received per dollar spent, and there are others. Regardless of the method used, you must have complete and accurate monetary value information on each product over an adequate period of time, preferably twenty rolling quarters. *The point: The value relationships among products, advertising space allocation, advertising space cost, profitability and return on investment must be accurately measured and replicated over time in each channel.*

MONETARY VALUE AND ADVERTISING: PICKERING

In the section on monetary value and frequency we saw how changing the mix of big book and prospect book can bring the advertising cost in line for less productive customers. Let's look at the other side of the coin—investing more advertising dollars in the best prospects.

Even for the direct marketer who invests money on prospecting (loses money acquiring new customers), there will be segments of new customers that are profitable or break-even on the first order. This more profitable group merits more advertising expenditure. However, these greater expenditures must yield an even higher level of performance or there is no justification for the practice.

Sending a big book or a house file book to best prospects will generally yield two positive results: higher response rate and higher average order. This won't pay out for all prospecting segments, but it will for best segments whether those are defined as prospects at buying sites, large employee sizes, or even simply as prospects from the best continuation lists. For telemarketers, the increased advertising strategy could prescribe several different tactics: assigning best telemarketer agents to the best prospects; making additional attempts to contact the prospect if they aren't available for the first call; and the like.

This strategy requires that the marketer has complete, accurate information about the performance of the prospecting effort. To meet that requirement, customer service representatives need to capture key codes or finder numbers as frequently as possible, and consistent match-backs must be accomplished to drive the white-mail rates as low as possible.

MONETARY VALUE AND WHY IT IS NOT ENOUGH: LIBEY

Having only knowledge about the dollars spent is like knowing the balance in your checkbook but having no idea to whom you wrote the checks or when. Monetary value has to be examined with recency and frequency—as well as some other elements—in order to successfully manage direct marketing performance.

If you have a listing of all customers hierarchically ranked by dollars spent, it means little unless it is augmented with a cross-listing of recency and frequency. Otherwise, you have no idea whether those customers are still active or whether they are multiple buyers.

As the three components—recency, frequency and monetary value—have evolved in the first three chapters, it should be clear that recency must be optimized with frequency and both recency and frequency together must be further optimized by monetary value. The customers that rise to the top of the three-dimensional hierarchy are the very best customers that you have. And, for all the complexity, all that you are really doing is shuffling the cards in the shoebox and pulling up the best customers to be called on during the next trip.

MONETARY VALUE AND WHY IT IS NOT ENOUGH: PICKERING

Monetary value is the measure that tells direct marketers who is the most valuable customer *thus far* and how much gross and net profit has been made. It is only when used in conjunction with recency and frequency that we begin to be able to determine things like the cost of new customer acquisition, the propensity to move into profitable RFM segments, and to project the lifetime value of a customer into the future. That data drives the investment decisions that must be made today and what value the firm has, both today and in the future.

Monetary value alone is not enough because, for direct marketers, it is not only about what have you done for me lately, but what might you do for me next.

Chapter 4 Optimized RFM

OPTIMIZED RECENCY, FREQUENCY AND MONETARY VALUE: LIBEY

In the preceding chapters we have examined recency, frequency and monetary value in some detail and have demonstrated the necessity for combining all three into an optimized hierarchy that isolates the most recent customers who buy most often and spend the most money. Equally important, we have described how to use the hierarchies to isolate the least recent, least frequent and least valuable customers. With that knowledge as a baseline, overlaying other optimizing elements on the hierarchies of customers produces an even greater benefit for multi-channel direct marketers: *Optimized RFM*.

In this chapter, we will assume that the three-way RFM optimized hierarchical listing of customers has been created. At the top are the very best performing customers and at the bottom are the worst performing customers. If your company can create this simple hierarchy of recency, frequency and monetary value for all customers, it ranks among the ten percent of companies in the direct marketing milieu that have this ability. If your company can add the additional optimizations described in this chapter, you will be among only the top one percent or so of all direct marketing companies able to perform these optimization analyses. And if your company actually applies the knowledge for strategic enhancement, you are among a handful of direct marketing superstars.

RFM, while valuable, is not enough. It only takes you half way to the full benefits. Optimized RFM causes you to do something with the knowledge to improve earnings. The various overlays to RFM hierarchies are the money makers. From them you pinpoint tactical applications that refine the performance of individual customers, individual segments of customers, and individual groupings of customers—by channel and overall.

OPTIMIZED RECENCY, FREQUENCY AND MONETARY VALUE: PICKERING

Here begins our post-graduate studies of RFM. There are two things for certain: 1) RFM is the basis for all meaningful segmentation and analysis of the house file; and 2) it can be improved by adding an additional factor. RFMX will be the key and while we can give you some guideposts for what X may be, it will require some iterative work on your part.

Whether the X is employee size, gender, or the number of divisions purchased from within a multi-division organization, there are two vital keys that must be present in order to do optimized RFM segmentation: the data must be accurately appended to a reasonable portion of the file (at least fifty percent), and the data must be accessible. Appending of outside data is another of these 'nuts and bolts' issues that aren't flashy, but are crucial to executing the strategy correctly.

Consider a piece of appended firmographic data like employee size. There are many providers of this data and there are differences in the accuracy and coverage from these providers. Using one provider may yield coverage of forty percent, maybe as high as sixty percent of the buyer file. Using two files (or more) in tandem can frequently raise coverage another twenty percent. This requires a bit more legwork to find a service bureau, or other provider, who has more than one source. Using an outside service bureau may also yield the additional benefit of having better or more customized matching logic.

The second point is having good access to the data. The number of direct marketers with sub-standard access to their house file data is staggering. This is especially the case with more 'old economy' catalogers or catalog-assisted companies.

There has been a trend toward more consolidation among direct marketing companies today. There are two keys to consolidation or acquisition: 1) the ability to reduce costs by eliminating redundant functions; and 2) the ability to leverage the best abilities and assets from one division across the entire organization. Among direct marketers, almost without fail, the best asset of any division is the house file. The inability to create an enterprise level database that gives a clear and accurate picture of the health of the entire company and enables information sharing among divisions condemns most acquisitions to mediocrity or, at best, unrealized potential.

OPTIMIZED RFM PLUS NORTH AMERICAN INDUSTRIAL CLASSIFICATION SYSTEM (NAICS): LIBEY

The North American Industry Classification System (NAICS) has replaced the U.S. Standard Industrial Classification (SIC) system. NAICS was developed jointly by the U.S., Canada, and Mexico to provide new comparability in statistics about business activity across North America. The official US NAICS Manual, *North American Industry Classification System–United States, 2002,* includes definitions for each industry and a comprehensive index. Updates to the codes are published about every five years. The NAICS codes can also be accessed online at www.census.gov/epcd/www/naics.

Business-to-business marketers are very familiar with the codes, which assign every industry and sub-industry a unique code number so that all businesses are classified in an orderly manner. When business-to-business direct marketers target specific industries for contacts, compiled lists are rented by NAICS groupings. As you would imagine, over time, business-to-business marketers build response histories by NAICS codes and rely, in part, on those histories for prospecting strategies. By matching top performing customers against their NAICS codes, marketers can see which industries offer better prospecting performance and can purchase compiled or response lists based on those NAICS codes. It is possible to append customer lists of businesses with their NAICS codes. Approximately a seventy percent match is attainable by having the list tagged by a service bureau. Periodic updating of the NAICS codes on the customer list will assist in maintaining beneficial performance history by industry. With each update, additional businesses will be matched and the initial seventy percent tagged businesses will increase to, perhaps, eighty to eighty-five percent. Of all the enhancements for business-to-business marketers, the NAICS code is among the most important.

OPTIMIZED RFM PLUS NORTH AMERICAN INDUSTRIAL CLASSIFICATION SYSTEM (NAICS): PICKERING

The NAICS codes feel like the metric system: it is simply easier to use than the incumbent SIC (Standard Industrial Classification) system and there is tremendous resistance to it.

The fact is that most major providers of business-to-business information offer SIC codes—not necessarily because they feel that it is a better system (it certainly is not), but in response to demands of the market. Most business-to-business marketers have SIC codes embedded in their systems and it is easier to keep in a BAU (Business As Usual) mode. That being said, using either NAICS or SIC is the most logical place for business-to-business marketers to look for the X factor to add to their RFM segmentation. The power is strong, perhaps only equaled by employee size.

Both codes, NAICS and SIC, go to at least four digits (NAICS actually goes to six and there are proprietary SIC classifications that go to eight digits). For all but the very largest business-to-business marketers this is not practical because it creates too many segments of too small a size. Paralysis by analysis will inevitably set in. To avoid this, use the codes at their two-digit level or even at a super-two-digit level—there are some industry standard groupings that collapse eighty plus two-digit groups to about twenty groups.

When you have the level of segmentation you can easily use, pockets of much higher than average and much lower than average value (defined by lifetime value, lifetime dollars, monetary momentum, etc.) will appear. Rather than allowing this simply to become 'gee whiz' information, ask the following questions:

1. If my best segments defined by RFM + NAICS accounts for forty percent of my value and twenty percent of my customers, am I targeting an appropriate and corresponding percentage of my house file circulation to these segments?

2. Am I looking at these high value RFM + NAICS segments and targeting them in my new customer acquisition, even suffering a lower response rate because of the higher payoff?

3. Am I looking at these low value RFM + NAICS segments and avoiding them in my new customer acquisition, even foregoing a higher response rate because of the lower payoff?

The Master Marketer has asked and answered these questions and continually revisits the question to see how the customer base has changed. It is all about making a closed loop system: use the intelligence gained through analysis to drive better decisions.

OPTIMIZED RFM PLUS GEOGRAPHY: LIBEY

Both business-to-business and consumer direct marketers benefit from overlaying geographic information on the hierarchies of RFM analyses. Knowing where the best customers come from is instructive and can be used in the targeting for new customer prospecting. Geography also plays a large role in seasonal product purchases. For example, if all of your customers live in the south, you will not sell a lot of ice melting products in the winter.

Geographic overlays can be done on a broad basis, such as regions or individual states. They are most effective, however, when they are done on a specific basis with a rationale that benefits performance. Overlays of ZIP codes or carrier routes, augmented by high disposable income, can pinpoint specific pockets of affluence and enhance the performance of, for example, a luxury goods catalog. List rentals can then be structured to saturate these optimal geographic locations.

Sophisticated 'cluster' mapping programs pair RFM hierarchies with block maps and display individual 'hot cells' and even individual homes with histories of purchases that meet pre-determined criteria. Those addresses are subsequently used in building cluster-focused mailings on a local, regional or national basis. A similar approach is to overlay RFM data on geographic mapping data to pinpoint address locations of top customers. Then, households immediately surrounding those customers are targeted for offers under the 'birds of a feather flock together' assumption.

To understand the frontier that geography represents, it is necessary to understand how the big-box discounters, such as Wal-Mart and Home Depot, approach geography. They use a saturation strategy that seems to place stores in slightly overlapping circles of geography covering about twelve miles. Most people will travel twelve miles or less to get what they want. Cover all of the twelve mile circles and you own the market. Add predatory pricing and you eliminate all the independent competitors within the twelve mile radius. Then drive the saturation strategy with lowest cost supply-chain efficiencies. This is an expensive strategy; it is a bricks and mortar and supply-chain strategy; but so far it has been a single channel strategy. The only way to beat it is to target the twelve mile circles, but do it through effective use of the online channel coupled with the catalog channel. *The point: Direct marketers have to learn geography not at the national level, as they have always done, but at the twelve mile circle level, as they have never done.*

OPTIMIZED RFM PLUS GEOGRAPHY: PICKERING

Geography may be the most under-utilized X factor in RFM segmentation. It is also one of the easiest variables to identify and deploy. For direct mail marketers or telemarketers it is an immensely powerful tool because it is present, in some form, on every record. State, ZIP code, area code must be present to send the mail piece or package or to make the telephone call.

Geography can be used to make appropriate media decisions, either for prospecting or house file circulation. Multi-channel marketers use direct marketing for a variety of reasons: to drive catalog sales, internet sales, store traffic, etc. When planning an integrated campaign, the business rules can be put in place that specify: 1) within four miles of the retail location send a store-traffic mail piece with an in-store coupon; 2) from four miles to twenty miles send a catalog that offers free next day delivery from the retail location for orders over fifty dollars; and 3) for prospects over twenty miles from a retail location offer free two-day shipping from a regional warehouse distribution center.

Geography can also be used in counter-marketing. If a competitor opens a retail location you can saturate that area with special offers to try to retain your customer base within the competitor's newly established trade area. Obviously, this requires a diligent study of your competitors, but this is frequently a matter of public record in their annual report or on their website location finder section.

OPTIMIZED RFM PLUS FINANCIAL INFORMATION: LIBEY

Financial information is a particularly instructive overlay for RFM. Annual income, disposable income, annual sales, net earnings, EBITDA or other financial indicators can be matched to the hierarchy of customers, whether businesses or consumers, and examined for patterns and commonalities.

Once optimal financial indicators are related to the top customers, and to the worst customers, tailoring of prospect lists can be enhanced to target those prospects that are financially most like the best customers and to eliminate from prospecting lists those prospects that are most like the worst customers.

Other financial information for overlay and matching can include related indicators such as home ownership, investments, 401(K), luxury car owners, second home owners, luxury hotels, foreign travel, and other high net worth attributes.

Too often, financial overlays are accomplished only to isolate top prospects. By appropriate segmentation overlay work, reduction of low value prospects and customers can be equally beneficial. The primary enhancement resulting from financial optimization is a migration of customer value upwards in RFM as well as in retention.

OPTIMIZED RFM PLUS FINANCIAL INFORMATION: PICKERING

A prospect, in order to become a customer, must have need, willingness, and ability. They must need (real or perceived) your product or service, have the willingness to buy it from you, and have the ability to pay for it. Without all three they won't become a customer. Financial information can help you find those with the ability to pay and it can, in some instances, help determine if there may be a need.

On the business-to-business side, the financial information generally available is annual sales volume. This is almost always a modeled variable that looks at NAICS or SIC and employee size. Sales volume is often useful, but is rarely as powerful as NAICS/SIC or employee size.

On the consumer side, financial information can be particularly powerful, even though it is almost one hundred percent inferred from census data or other modeled efforts. This is because the modeled data is generally applied down to a ZIP + four level, which in the real world generally means a block face (only one side of the block), or a floor in a high-rise. If you look at your neighbors, in financial terms, they probably aren't all that much different than you.

Financial information can help determine who are likely prospects to respond and who can be profitable. These results may not always be what you expect. Consider a credit card offer. Credit card issuers generally make their money from two places: 1) charges to the merchants taking the charges; and 2) fees (interest and other associated fees) the consumers pay. Wealthy households are less likely to respond to credit card offers, especially those that tout low interest rates, because they are more likely not to carry a balance than the average credit card user. That also makes them less profitable to have in the portfolio. Having this information about the prospects ahead of time may lead to reduced circulation to these higher income levels.

Middle-income consumers may be receptive to low interest offers because they may carry a balance from time-to-time. They are also easier to get approved because of their financial track record. Given their propensity to carry a balance occasionally and their low likelihood to go into bankruptcy, they are likely to become good and profitable customers. This is a good, core audience for a card issuer.

Lower-income consumers have a different set of drivers, based on their income. Because of their lower income they are more likely to carry balances and produce profit. But there are hurdles to getting them approved. Knowing the income level can help manage risk and target the appropriate product to the audience, like a secured credit card.

There are analogs of this example for most every direct response marketer. The rub is that many have not explored it, or look at it infrequently.

OPTIMIZED RFM PLUS GENDER: LIBEY

While gender is predominately a consumer attribute for direct marketing, it does have business-to-business applications, as well. By appending gender to the RFM hierarchies, percentages of customer segments can be compared. As an example, if the top two hundred customers in the RFM hierarchy are ninety percent female, but the next two hundred are only sixty percent, what does that mean? Has the business migrated more to female buyers? Have the male buyers stopped buying? Was there a product shift? Did the creative become more feminine in design characteristics? Has the target industry changed, such as veterinary medicine, which was once mostly male and is now a majority female?

Within the optimization potentiality of gender, there exist other important optimization elements. The gay and lesbian populations may be important differentiators to be matched to the RFM hierarchy. The primary classification of female and male can be further defined as single, married or divorced. In combination with age, they can be appended as senior, middle, young adult, teen, etc.

Once gender is understood—at more than one level—it is helpful to match that knowledge against the creative work used on websites, in catalogs, on infomercials, and all other channel advertising. If the top RFM segment is senior women and the catalog creative is designed for middle-age males, there is a serious disconnect. Actually, it is interesting how often this occurs. Even creative directors should take optimized RFM analyses into account when executing their portion of the direct marketing mix.

OPTIMIZED RFM PLUS GENDER: PICKERING

Women rule. That isn't just a pithy saying, it is a fact. In the home, women are the primary decision makers or have influence in purchases that make up between sixty and eighty percent of the expenditures. Frequently women place more orders and more *valuable* orders for a majority of direct mail marketers. Great. What do we do with this?

Several things. First, if we find that women are placing orders with higher value than men, and/or are more responsive, we can target them. On both the prospecting and house file circulation side we can prioritize the selection of women over men with the most competent query and output tools. Gender is almost a universal select, even on list rentals.

Second, as my writing partner has mentioned, we can use this to drive creative decisions: how the website looks, what types of products are featured on the cover, etc. Some sophisticated marketers even have several versions of their catalogs available and target based on female, male, or unknown/unspecified (this includes Pat of Saturday Night Live fame, as well as other names like Blair, Chris, Lee, etc.)

Even the lack of gender can be indicative of value. For many business-to-business direct marketers, the number of purchasers that come in with no name (hence no gender) can be quite high. Frequently these are the most valuable purchases, usually because they come through a purchasing department at a larger organization. This can be a compelling argument for title slugged mail pieces to be sent into larger business sites.

OPTIMIZED RFM PLUS SIZE: LIBEY

Once the business-to-business customer base has been hierarchically ranked by RFM, it is essential to overlay the ranking with company size, measured by number of employees. Correlations generally exist between the top performing RFM customers and employee size of companies. Employee size can be appended to the customer list by service bureaus by passing the customer list against lists of all known businesses and their various characteristics.

Generally, employee size is captured in segment sizes listed below:

20,000 +	500-999	5-9
15,000-19,999	250-499	2-4
10,000-14,999	100-249	1
5,000-9,999	50-99	unknown
2,500-4,999	25-49	
1,000-2,499	10-24	

In some cases, employee size segments are collapsed and simplified:

20,000+	500-999	50-99
10,000-19,999	250-499	20-49
1,000-9,999	100-250	1-19

It makes little difference what level of detail is captured as long as it is consistent and fits the needs of your business. If the top RFM customers have 20 employees or less, that is the useful information that must be applied to selecting lists that target businesses with less than 20 employees. The opposite end of the employee size and RFM hierarchy is equally as important. If the Dogs all come from businesses with 250 employees or more, it makes a great deal of sense to exclude businesses with 250 employees or more from prospecting lists. The last thing you need is more Dogs.

While it can be expected that a bell curve will form when RFM performance and employee size is overlaid, it is not uncommon to find pockets of excellence and pockets of poor performance throughout the employee size range. One business-to-business marketer will do very well in the 1-19 employees segment, again at 100-250 employees, and again at 1,000-9,999. The same company will have poor performance, however, in the 20-49 employee segment, the 50-99 employee segment, and the 500-999 employee segment. While often logical reasons for these optimization patterns can be found, sometimes there is no explanation other than, "That's just the way it is."

Size can also apply to consumer direct marketing. Total family members is one calculation; total number of children is another; total adults living in the household is yet another.

The specialized marketers to schools tend to measure size as number of students in the various school units such as pre-schools, K-6, middle school, high school, colleges, universities and graduate schools.

Medical marketers define size as number of doctors in a practice, number of dental chairs, number of beds in a hospital, number of x-ray machines, and numerous other size elements that help optimize the performance information.

Of course, it bears mentioning that channels and optimal RFM plus size will vary. Where a catalog may work well in businesses with 20 employees and less, the online channel may work best in businesses with 100-125 employees and again in businesses with 1-19 employees. In fact, *all* optimization characteristics have to be tracked, analyzed and optimized by channel and aggregated to arrive at the overall optimization.

OPTIMIZED RFM PLUS SIZE: PICKERING

Employee size can be quite powerful, in segmenting house file as well as prospecting universes. The key is how to use it.

It is quite true that in terms of response there is generally a bell curve that develops when plotting employee size. There is a floor level of employee size under which a direct marketing offer doesn't work, as there is also a ceiling over which it is less profitable. This will vary from offer to offer, but once established, it is generally quite consistent and predictable.

One of the nuances to consider, and one of the keys to finding those pockets that work within the large group that doesn't work, is the interplay between employee size and either SIC or NAICS. This is because size is a powerful variable, but it needs to have *context.* That context is usually the primary business classification.

Most marketers view a business location with one hundred employees at a site as a large location. But if you know what kind of work they perform, you are better equipped to make the determination. A manufacturing site with one hundred employees isn't particularly large at all. Compared to other manufacturing sites they may have a rather low demand for things like safety products, labor law posters, etc.

On the other side of the coin, a law office that employs one hundred individuals is rather large. They likely have a much larger than average demand for things like office supplies, legal publications, office furniture, technology products like servers, PCs, software, copying machines, and a raft of other items.

This type of RFM + employee size + SIC/NAICS becomes more important when looking at prospecting. Large employee sizes, wherever that line is drawn for the business, frequently suffer from exceedingly poor response rates. Often, the rates are so low as to warrant foregoing the larger employee sizes.

The complicating factor is when an order is obtained and it is considerably higher in average order value, sometimes as much as three hundred percent, or more, than average. So, these long shots, when they come in, are quite valuable. Using employee size coupled with the SIC or NAICS code can help shorten those odds and make it a better opportunity for the direct marketer.

OPTIMIZED RFM PLUS LIST SOURCE: LIBEY

From what response lists, email lists, subscriber lists, compiled lists or co-op lists do the very best customers come from? By overlaying and segmenting the optimized customer hierarchy with the list source, a picture should emerge that reveals high-grade list sources.

Within list source optimization analyses will be found specific segments of RFM performance that further define the lists from the best sources. For example, if the best customers come from list *A*, what segments of RFM produced those top customers? Was it the one-year recency, three-time frequency, $250 monetary value segment or was it the two-year recency, one-time frequency, $500 monetary value segment that was optimal?

Another tactic for list source optimization using RFM analysis involves finding the optimal combination of response, compiled, subscriber and co-op list segments *within* a single top performing RFM segment. Another way of saying this is: find the best combination of the largest mix of lists that produces the best customers. By doing so, marketers can expand the prospecting universe and reduce the list fatigue that comes from repeatedly relying on one list or list type.

To adequately optimize list source with RFM, several additional pieces of knowledge are required. First, the exact cost to acquire a customer, to the penny, over twenty rolling quarters is essential. Second, the lifetime net profit of that customer must be calculated and projected. *The point: Only when the cost to acquire and the lifetime net profit are combined with RFM performance and list source will you have the definitive answer regarding list source.*

OPTIMIZED RFM PLUS LIST SOURCE: PICKERING

RFM analysis by list source is crucial to keeping acquisition strategies aligned with house file profitability. It is a wonder why so many companies do not diligently perform it.

List source information, to be most useful, is best kept in two fashions: generic and specific. In the generic form, list source refers to the type of list: direct response, subscriber, controlled circulation, compiled, registration, etc. This is very useful in determining what is the ideal mix of list types. Like a well thought out invest-ment portfolio, a wise marketer doesn't overload with too much of one list type.

At the more granular level, keeping the actual list the buyer was acquired from gives the best view of the *true* list performance. If the decision to continue or not on a list is based solely on one variable, like initial response, there are several shortcomings. One problem is that looking solely at response rates treats all lists as though they have the same list cost. It is not uncommon to have a wide range of list costs from the forty or fifty-dollar range of compiled lists to one hundred-twenty dollars or more for catalog buyers. Frequently the higher priced lists justify their cost by better performance, but not always. Cost to acquire should be measured, including the actual list cost, not an average.

Second, there is the quality of the customer that is acquired. A given list may have average or even below average response rate, but generates customers who are twice as likely to make a second pur-chase. Conversely, some lists can have astonishingly high response rates but customers generated have such a low propensity to repur-chase that the acquisition efforts are better directed elsewhere.

In final analysis, it is about the quality of the customer, not just the quantity of new customers. Tracking initial list source is one of the most important tools available to direct marketers to help find those quality customers. Joseph Stalin has been credited with say-ing that there is a certain quality to quantity. That may be true, but look what happened to the Soviet Union.

OPTIMIZED RFM PLUS TITLE: LIBEY

Business-to-business customers have titles. By capturing or ap-pending titles, some relationship can be identified between title and customer RFM performance. If a large percentage of the top per-forming RFM customers have the title Warehouse Manager, it is a safe bet you should be looking for more warehouse managers as prospects; you may also benefit by contacting the warehouse managers of existing customers in the hopes of adding a second—and even better—customer inside a company that is already buying from you.

Title is often a function of company size. Small companies with few employees seldom have Vice Presidents or HR Directors. These companies usually have Owners and Others and that's about it. Still, after optimizing by employee size, optimizing by title can be beneficial. If you market to large companies, title can be very important to the prospecting performance. In fact, if you are fortunate enough to have many differing titles, a separate study of which hierarchy of titles produce the best performance may be instructive.

The primary reason, however, for title optimization is to learn which titles produce the highest RFM performance. With that information, *title slugging*, that is, basing a contact strategy on the title rather than an individual, becomes a more viable strategy.

OPTIMIZED RFM PLUS TITLE: PICKERING

Title is so powerful that every direct marketer should be using it in analysis. The problem is, titles are hard data to come by, and once acquired, not easily used.

The first issue is coverage. The average business-to-business buyer file has captured titles on less than fifty percent of buyers, most often in the twenty to thirty percent range. It's hard to use data if it isn't present. This can be improved with more training of the tele-sales staff, but often this falls low on the priority list.

The second issue is classification of the data. Titles are very free form and not only vary from company to company, but even within companies. It is difficult for most direct marketers to develop their own classification and hierarchy system. Some external service bureaus can classify titles based on tables. This is a great solution, especially since service bureaus can use variations of the title to increase codification.

One final suggestion: use the old Mark 1 eyeball on what is populating the title field on your house file. By doing this exercise periodically you can see that there may be new titles (new people) using your products. This can help target new media as well as come up with good new ideas for title slugging.

OPTIMIZED RFM PLUS AGE: LIBEY

In some sectors of direct marketing; indeed, in some channels, age is an important optimization element. Insurance marketers use age as a primary prospect differentiator, as do beauty marketers, sports marketers, and many others. An optimization with customer age may reveal productive information. If the very best customers tend to be between forty-five and fifty-five years of age, that is strategically vital information as it tells you to focus on prospects who fall into that age range.

Knowing the influence of age on profitability is also essential for determining which non-profitable customers are too old or too young for intense marketing efforts. Channel differences are likely to be very important when examining age. A catalog buyer and an online buyer may have very different age profiles and the reality may surprise you.

Consumer marketers are constantly attempting to move their customer average age lower. The reason is the inevitable aging of the customer base. If your average customer is fifty-five, that customer will be sixty-five in ten years unless you are recruiting customers who are forty-five. By dropping the average customer age by a year each successive year, consumer marketers stay ahead of the 'gray curve.' Only when you are able to study optimal RFM plus age over twenty rolling quarters, will you be able to see the effects of age on optimal performance.

Business-to-business marketers may find correlations between RFM customer performance hierarchies and the number of years a customer has been in business, its age. Further optimizations of top performing customers showing years in business plus employee size and annual sales can be definitive as to prospecting criteria.

OPTIMIZED RFM PLUS AGE: PICKERING

There is a small industry in direct marketing that does nothing but produce clusters. Clusters are ways of segmenting a file based on a combination of other data. These segmentation and cluster data are more prevalent on the consumer side, though they also exist for business-to-business. They are, in almost every instance, proprietary. What makes up the algorithms may be proprietary, but most data providers will talk in broad terms about what types of data are used.

There is no hard and fast rule about what segmentation products, or what types of products, work and which do not. The best way to determine if a cluster or segmentation data works is to try it out on a portion of the house file. Most providers will prove the concept on real data without charge.

Some of these tools can be quite powerful. As an example, here **(Figure P4.1)** is a typical segmentation of a house file using a proprietary segmentation tool developed by MeritDirect's analytic department:

	LTD $ Index	12 mo Repurchase
Segment 1	125	71%
Segment 2	111	74%
Segment 3	101	67%
Segment 4	82	62%
Segment 5	80	54%
Segment 6	51	38%

Figure P4.1

This example shows very good distribution of life-to-date dollars from segment one to segment six. And on the propensity to repurchase within twelve months, with the exception of a flip-flop on the top two segments, there is also good distribution.

Although it is tempting to simply use this segmentation tool by itself for house file promotion decisions, it is simply one tool and is a great compliment to RFM, not a substitution.

OPTIMAL ANALYSES: LIBEY

As you can see, numerous possibilities and opportunities exist for optimizing the recency, frequency and monetary value hierarchical information. By adding optimization upon optimization, a smaller and smaller slice of the customer base is isolated. For some companies, multiple optimizations are unnecessary and would add little benefit. For others, the ever-sharper definition of optimal customer performance is essential to survival.

So much depends upon size. A fully furnished RFM optimization program is beneficial only if sufficient customers exist in the database to produce statistically valid results. An optimized hierarchy of the best customers that produces only eight top performers is of little practical value. But where sufficient numbers of active customers exist to produce meaningful and actionable slices of performance excellence, optimal RFM is useful.

Of all the information available to multi-channel direct marketers in the ever-increasing aggregation of information, recency, frequency and monetary value remain as the cornerstones of a well-constructed direct marketing house. Yet, RFM alone is no longer enough. We have moved from a one-channel to a multi-channel world with all of its many implications in a very short period of time. It is now necessary to augment RFM with more, to take this classic and exquisite analytic tool beyond . . . .

OPTIMAL ANALYSES: PICKERING

The great strength of direct marketing is that it is measurable. We can employ formulas and measures to determine if a given effort or strategy was successful.

Using formulas and measures does not preclude creativity. Developing the optimal RFMX formula takes creativity to look at myriad different choices and combinations of different choices to find the right one. Marketers with this type of passion and proclivity need to be sought, encouraged, and provided with the data and analytic tools to find the optimal strategy.

Art teachers are taught that art is about the process, not the product. For direct marketers finding optimal RFM is about the process *and* about the product.

Chapter 5 Product

PRODUCT LIFE CYCLE: LIBEY

The *product life cycle* is a fascinating phenomenon. It consists of at least seven sub-cycles including *ideation,* or the conceiving of a product, and extends through *research and development, testing, introduction, growth, maturity* and *obsolescence.* The life cycle can also include sub-cycles of *redevelopment* and *reintroduction.* Product lives can be short or long; chip technology and baking soda being good examples of life cycle extremes. Within the life cycle of any product are an infinite number of strategies and tactics employed to create only one outcome: maximum possible profits. Keep that point in mind; it is the Product Prime Directive.

Measuring the product life cycle can be done in time, sales, units, price, gross margin, contribution, net profitability, investment, return on investment, or any other measurement of relevance that is desired. The life cycle is almost always shown on the classic x and y axis chart with the horizontal line representing time and the vertical line representing the variable (**Figure L5.1**). In this example, the life cycle is portrayed relative to time and sales.

236

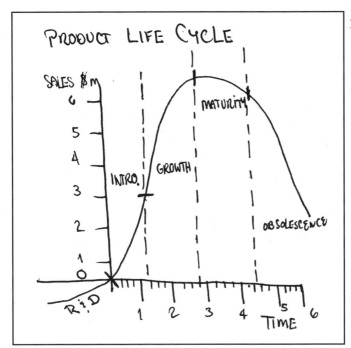

Figure L5.1

Prior to the introductory phase of the product life cycle (the portion of the curve below $0 sales and to the left of the vertical axis), the product required investment to carry it through the ideation, research and development and the testing phases. While investment may continue to be needed during the early portion of the life cycle after introduction, the curve above the $0 dollar line represents product sales dollars. Often, this is the critical period for a new product. If there is insufficient investment for adequate research and development, or for proper testing, the product may be doomed at the outset. The initial pre-introductory phase investment is as important, or possibly more important, as the investment in advertising or inventory.

During the introductory phase, sales can be rapid or slow depending on the type of product and the normal 'go to market' approach. For instance, products for the internal computer memory market must be quickly introduced and rapidly grown in the introductory phase because of the exceptionally short technological life expected for memory products. Rosewood knitting needles, however, would have a long, slow introductory phase because their growth will depend primarily on word of mouth among knitting enthusiasts. The slope of the curve—and the resultant financial implications—depends on the type of product and its inherent marketing approach. Products with broad usage will generally have a steeper curve than products with limited usage. A new inexpensive ballpoint pen will have a steeper curve than a new expensive fountain pen, for instance. However, sales of one million ballpoint pen units may only produce the same net profit as sales of ten thousand fountain pens. Whether the introductory phase is short or long, steep or slow rising is determined by the product and market characteristics.

At some point, the introductory phase ends. The end point is a function of the attainment of performance objectives for that product. If the introductory objective is to reach eight percent market share during the introductory phase, then share is the active determinant. If the introductory objective is to reach a sales level of $14 million, then sales is the determinant. If the introductory objective is to earn twenty-five percent return on investment prior to moving out of the introductory phase, then ROI is the measurement. *The point: The strategic plan and its objectives determine the parameters for product life cycle performance and definition.* Products are *not* simply dreamed up and offered to the world. Products go through the product life cycle in an *intentional* manner. At each step of each phase, product performance accountability is measured and optimized.

Continuing to look only at the introductory phase of the product life cycle, pricing will influence the length and slope of the curve. Some products are introduced at a low price and the price is increased during the introductory phase; other products are introduced at a high price and the price reduced as introductory momentum builds. Other products are introduced and maintained at one price with little increase or decrease other than as an adjustment to inflation.

Introductory phase pricing strategy may dictate a low introductory price that creates demand as a result of the buyer's recognition that the product price will increase soon **(Figure L5.2)**. Certain products, such as specialty foods, beauty products, and products relying on repeat buying—like wine—benefit from this strategy. Low introductory pricing is used to create demand. Over time and demand, gross margin is increased through stepped price increases so that, at the end of the introductory phase, the product is producing margin as well as demand as it moves into the growth phase.

The opposite strategy is to introduce a product at a high price and lower the price as the product matures and demand slows **(Figure L5.3)**. Luxury products, high tech products, and fad-driven products fall into this format. With these often short-lived prod-

Figure L5.2

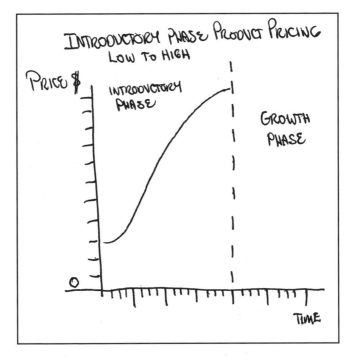

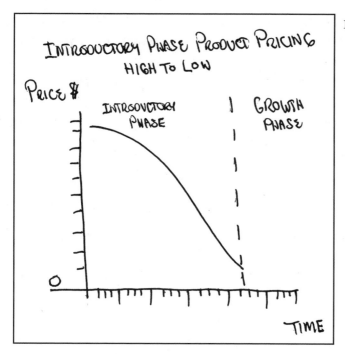

ucts, maximum profits can be created in the early phases of the life cycle; the late phases can produce a smaller profit per unit, but greater overall profitability based on demand.

As the life cycle moves from the introductory phase to the growth phase, strategic decisions must be made. Has the product performance during the introductory phase met expectations? Are growth projections adequate for the cost of rolling out the product in the growth phase? Are product redesigns and tweaks necessary? Is the market properly identified and targeted? Is the product positioning correct? Once these—and numerous other strategic questions—are answered, the product enters the growth phase.

The chief driver of a product's growth phase in multi-channel direct marketing is advertising breadth and depth by channel. If the catalog channel, the product is featured through increased space allocation, prime pagination location, and circulation exposure. If the online channel, the product is featured not only in space allocation, but also in landing page strategy, pop-ups, shopping cart add-ons, search emphases and other online drivers. If direct response television, the product may go into long form infomercial format and expansion of both broadcast schedule increases and time-slot enhancements. *The point: The product growth phase requires profitably selling more of the product to more buyers by whatever channels and drivers are appropriate.*

Growth phase product management can be done rapidly or slowly. Again, the life expectation of a product determines how that growth is managed. Short-lived products are managed on a fast-track growth plan; long-lived products are managed on a slower pace. The previous examples of computer memory and rosewood knitting needles point up the differences in growth phase management. Computer memory products will be rapidly accelerated across all channels and drivers to produce the greatest and fastest growth possible before the product is obsolete. Pricing will likely be slowly decreased as the growth phase extends. The growth phase may be as short as six months. The knitting needles will be grown through additional channel exposure and space allocation. Pricing will be steady or increasing as demand for the product grows. The growth phase may be as long as ten years or more.

Many products undergo product expansion tactics during the growth phase. Red ones and green ones are added to the basic blue product; jumbo size versions are added to the regular size; leather accents define the upscale version; stain bleaching properties may be included or the 'rainforest' scent option is featured; speed increases or the larger capacity model is added to the line; all products tend to get better, improved and bigger during the growth phase of the product life cycle. These are the product's salad days when time in the sun is sweet.

Then—at a mystical, ethereal moment in time that cannot be precisely identified—the product becomes mature; growth is over. The slope of the curve lowers and the product begins to flatten out over time. Like most things that become mature, the product slows down in velocity and momentum. Sales may still be good, but the velocity of increase has slowed. The product has had its run and now is settling in for the maturity period. Again, depending on the product, this portion of the life cycle may be as short as a few months or as long as thirty, forty or fifty years. Two cleaning products—Bon ami and Barkeeper's Friend—have been mature for a *very* long time, but are still great products with good sales. There are mature adhesive mailing labels in the NEBS catalog that have been shown unchanged in size or design for over twenty years, and they keep selling and continue to earn their space. Mature products are not bad; in fact, they are often lovely cash cows.

The maturity phase of the product life cycle presents several strategic options for a product. The first option is to leave it alone. The product may keep selling for years and will produce a steady profit for the space or channel exposure it receives. Sales of a mature product can generally be forecasted very accurately; inventory management becomes formulaic; and merchandising shifts to maintenance mode. A second option is to add features, such as colors, sizes, attachments, enhancements, anything to give the buyers product options while not abandoning the core product itself. A third option is to take the mature product through a 'New and Improved' initiative that will create a new growth spurt and extend the life cycle.

Pricing reflects the strategic option that is chosen for a mature product. If the decision is to leave the product alone, that is a milking tactic and the price is usually kept stable with increases only for inflation. If the strategy is to expand the product options, the expansion options will normally have beneficial price increases. If the strategy is to reintroduce a new and improved product and to revitalize the mature product, prices will almost always be higher.

Advertising space, channel allocation and channel mix will also vary depending on the mature product strategy chosen. The 'leave it alone' strategy often results in a decrease in space allocation but not necessarily a decrease in channel exposure. Mature product buyers know how to find the product and giving it less advertising space is not a high risk decision. The 'options and expansion' strategy requires an increase in space and channel mix. And the 'new and improved' strategy is, essentially, a return to the introductory phase tactics and requires advertising and channel exposure that will drive the newly-formatted product's velocity.

The final phase of the product life cycle—*obsolescence* or *decline*—is a very interesting phase. There are really only two questions to be answered: 1) will the product be continued or eliminated; and 2) will the price be increased or lowered? The point at which a product slips into decline is clear from the life cycle curve. Sales are declining at a steeper rate. The product has moved from mature to obsolete. The time for 'new and improved' has passed; reintroductions and enhancements take place only in the mature phase. Once decline has set in, the focus is on how to manage the profitability of the obsolete product.

If the decision is to eliminate the product, the tactic is self-evident. If, however, the decision is to continue the product, three choices exist: 1) pricing can be lowered and the product can go through a phase-out period; 2) prices can be maintained as sales dwindle over time to zero; or 3) prices can be raised. An obsolete product may continue to have demand, albeit dwindling, over time. Where adequate demand exists, raising the price and creating exclusivity or scarcity is an excellent tactic to improve that product's profitability. A good example is the one company that still produces and sells—direct—tires for Model T Fords. You want a Model T tire? You have to pay—a lot. *The point: Obsolete products can be turned into distressed inventory or gold; the choice is yours.*

Product life cycle management is an art. The ability to understand any one product's life cycle phase and comparative profit position, out of hundreds or thousands of products that may be in the lines, requires an intellectual juggling act of world-class proportion. The ability to modify product mix to concentrate products in the introductory and growth phases, or in the growth and maturity phases, but not in the maturity and obsolete phases is equally Herculean. Few possess either the understanding or the talent. Few possess the analytic systems to accurately track and project individual product progressions through the phases of the life cycle. Those that do, however, have one of the most powerful profit drivers in multi-channel direct marketing. To make it all even more complex, products will often be in different life cycle phases in different channels. A mature online channel product may be a growth product in the catalog channel or an introductory product in the infomercial channel.

Perhaps the highest expression of the art and science of the Product Masters is the ability to overlay the product life cycle on recency, frequency and monetary value segmentations and hierarchies in order to understand what products in what stages of the life cycle are being bought by specific customer segments. If eighty percent of the net profit is driven by twenty percent of the products to twenty percent of the customer base, and if those products are all in the introductory product phase of the product life cycle, the company clearly is, or should be, new product driven. Stated another way, product strategy and positioning can be a reflection of the product life cycle reality. One of the great catalogs, Vermont Country Store, is driven by obsolete products; in fact, a new product in the catalog was probably discontinued by the original manufacturer twenty, thirty, fifty years ago or more.

Product life cycle and RFM segmentation correlation can produce interesting revelations. In some instances, the top performing RFM segment may be purchasing mature products with decreasing gross margins; in others, the bottom RFM segment may purchase primarily obsolete products for which closeout pricing has been assigned; yet another may show that RFM cash cows mostly buy long-lived growth products having stable prices. The truth about the interplay of product life cycle and RFM segments is almost never understood, much less actively managed and optimized for profitability. Few direct marketing companies can produce a lifecycle chart of all products showing the exact percentages of products in each life cycle phase, perhaps one of the most revealing visual indications of corporate health you will ever see (**Figure L 5.4**). *The point: Do you know? How is the profile changing? What does it mean for the future of the business?*

Figure L5.4

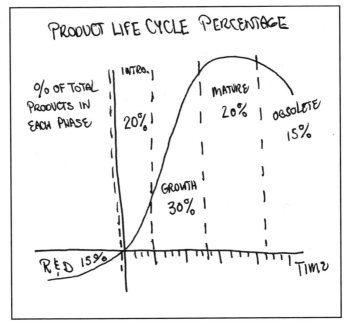

MECHANICS OF RFM PLUS PRODUCT SEGMENTATION: PICKERING

Product is powerful, not only in the intangible ability to create excitement and stimulate demand, but also in the qualitative sense. Segmenting by product can give enormous power to your RFM segmentation.

The question becomes, *how* do you segment by product? The answer, the standard answer taught at business colleges across the land is this: it depends.

Most direct marketing companies have between a few hundred and a few thousand products or SKUs. Using hundreds or thousands of variables to create different RFM segments would generate a set of data impossible to work with effectively. Additionally, the cells would be too small to produce meaningful, repeatable results.

At the highest product level, usually referred to as product category, there are generally a reasonable number of categories, a dozen or two. Initial analysis should be done on all available product categories, though with some analyses these can be collapsed further into *ad-hoc* groups that have similar predictive abilities.

There are nuances to using product categories for RFM segmentation. Some very powerful historical analysis can be done using the *first* product category purchased. Alternatively, ongoing RFMP segmentation frequently develops from the first product category purchased to *if ever purchased* from a given product category.

As an example, computer peripherals manufacturers and retailers frequently sell printers at or near cost. The paradigm is set up to make money from the ink cartridge sales, not the printer. If you would fill the average automobile gas tank with printer ink, it would take nearly $100,000 worth of ink to fill it up! As you can see, that is a lot of margin.

Thus, a customer who consistently buys a printer but not ink will not be a very valuable customer. This may not show when looking at RFM only, unless monetary value also includes some gross margin or profitability measure. Looking at the RFM + product category and being able to use an average margin can help separate the truly profitable customers (printer and ink buyers) from the pretenders (printer only buyers). The printer and ink example provides a good reason to assign margin or profitability on as micro a level as possible, at the product category at least and preferably at the individual product level.

The quickest way to include product in the RFM segmentation is to simply set up a counter of how many different product categories have been purchased. Although not perfect, segmenting RFM cells by one product category purchased versus two, three or more product categories purchased will rank-order profitability in almost every instance.

PRODUCT CATEGORY HIERARCHIES: LIBEY

The extent to which we categorize products may seem to be an unimportant element of the overall product strategy; however, as with so much of the product discipline, this also is a science.

Have you ever gone through a catalog and marveled at the logic and precision of the product presentations? There are catalogs that just exude perfection as you thumb your way through interesting categories of products. Not only is the product mix well conceived, but also the order in which the various categories of products are presented is compelling and engaging. You want to buy more than one product. That is the point.

Grouping products into categories and categories into paginations—and doing the same thing on the website—is seldom accomplished based on analytics. The logic of influencing additional items on orders is seldom quantified and reduced to metrics. It should be.

Mastering product categories is a science beyond square inch analysis. In fact, product categorization is as much an art as a science; there has to be an innate feel for the work. The guiding principle is that proper categorization of products and proper pagination order produces sales of more line items. To say it another way, good product categorization and discipline increase average order value.

Consider a catalog for, say, general residential contractors. Logic dictates that product categories reflect the order in which homes are built: site survey; excavation; footings; foundation; utility supply; cement floors or floor structures; framing; roofing; siding; masonry; electrical; plumbing; HVAC; drywall; trim carpentry; lighting; kitchen and appliances; poured driveway/sidewalks; interior painting; flooring, tiling and carpet; quality control; and clean-up. Within each of those categories is another logical progression of product presentation that reflects the steps used in the actual category work. The tiling category, for example, would begin with floor preparation and leveling compound and progress to chalk lines, mastic, trowels, tile cutters and saws, spacers, grouting tools, grout, grout tints, grout additives, clean up supplies, acid etching products, grout sealer, and tile sealer. With the entire catalog organized properly, the pagination is a systematic guide to the construction of a house.

Now, each customer and prospect can be expected to purchase a variety of categorical products based on their Standard Industrial Classifications. A ceramic tile contractor would be expected to pursue some or all of the products in the tiling category; an electrical contractor would be expected to purchase some or all of the products and parts in the electrical category; a plumbing contractor would be expected to purchase a variety of plumbing products and parts; and so on. There may be some customers who are general contractors and who will buy multiple products across multiple categories. We are now ready for the magic.

With hierarchical recency, frequency and monetary value segmentation *by Standard Industrial Classification*, an overlay of product category penetration can be done and the breadth and depth of actual product purchasing can be evaluated relative to potential product purchasing. Customers can be scored for both their existing purchase penetration and their potential purchase penetration. If the total expected category purchase penetration is eighty percent and the customer has purchased only twenty percent of the potential, another sixty percent is waiting to be developed. If the customer is also a high RFM customer, the potential for accomplishing that sixty percent increase is high and should likely be pursued. Finally, each SIC can be hierarchically ranked so that marketing efforts are aimed at those SICs with the greatest potential sales benefit to be harvested. Here, we have a hierarchy inside a hierarchy inside a hierarchy, and it is all based on simple analytics.

From here, it is only a simple step to developing an integrated, multi-channel marketing and merchandising plan that targets customers and prospects in the high-ranking SICs and seeks to both acquire new customers and to penetrate product breadth and depth of existing customers.

For the truly sophisticated, one additional overlay would segment all of the products that are high penetration potentials and rank them hierarchically by either gross margin or return on investment. At that point of product mastery: 1) the most profitable products are selected; 2) to be optimally promoted by channel; 3) to increase the purchasing penetration of the highest RFM scoring customers; 4) of the most productive hierarchy of SICs. And that means the money machine is cranked up to full power.

PRODUCT CATEGORY HIERARCHIES: PICKERING

If you understand product category hierarchies, you understand what makes your catalog tick. It is that simple.

Product category A may bring in more customers than product category B. However, those customers generated by product category A have a significantly below average propensity to repurchase, and there is not much margin to category A. Product category B customers are much more likely than average to repurchase and there is good margin in category B. Which customers do you want to acquire and invest in on a prospect and house file circulation basis; those generated from product category A or those generated from category B? I thought so.

Here is a real world application: catalog covers. Most experienced direct marketers know that you sell in a catalog starting with the cover. What products do you feature on the cover? The answer is simple: look at RFMP analysis to see what product categories produce the best customers.

A further extension of this analysis and application is the prospect catalog. Many direct marketers have so many products that to feature them all requires a catalog that costs $1.00 or more each to produce. Spending a $1.00 per catalog may very well be a worthwhile investment on proven customers. In order to prospect widely and cost effectively, direct marketers frequently develop smaller prospecting catalogs. These prospecting catalogs cost one-half or less the amount of a full, customer book allowing more of the prospecting budget to be spent on more catalogs, more names, and more postage.

Without a fully furnished RFMP analysis, any marketer lacking perfect intuition will be hard pressed to develop the proper balance between products that drive interest and response and product categories that attract profitable customers who will make a second and third and multiple future purchases.

NEW PRODUCT INTRODUCTION AND RETIREMENT: LIBEY

Without exception, new products are the lifeblood of direct marketing. Product remains king. Product will always be king. The customer attitudes about product and channel are interesting.

In the catalog channel, the customer's attitude is summed up in the three questions that are asked when a catalog arrives: 1) I wonder what's new; 2) Where is it; and 3) How much does it cost? Those are product-driven questions.

The online customer most likely already knows what product is new or what product they want and their attitude is summed up in the three questions that are asked when shopping online: 1) Where can I get the product; 2) Who has the best price; 3) Who can get it to me fast, free, and easy? Those are search or source-driven questions.

The attitude of the catalog shopper/browser is one that welcomes new ideas and enticements. This customer might be interested in buying something someday. The attitude of the online shopper/searcher is one that I call 'intentional immediacy.' This customer is going to buy right now. Both of these very different attitudes begin and end with product, however. The online attitude drives product, search and price perhaps more 'intentionally,' a characteristic of the channel that encourages price comparison.

In both channels, one question is constant: "What's new?" In the catalog channel, the question is implied; in the online channel, the question is explicit. The catalog channel customer muses about there possibly being new products of interest in the catalog; the online channel customer has moved beyond musing and explicitly wants a particular product. Therefore, the multi-channel direct marketer has a primary responsibility to satisfy the demand for new products.

I am frequently asked what percentage of all products offered should be new products. Much depends on the sector. Women's clothing will require nearly one hundred percent new products every season. Office products will require less, perhaps fifteen percent new products annually. Within sectors, the rate of new product introduction will vary among product categories. Dog flea collars may need only ten percent new products each summer, but dog toys may require fifty percent new products each Christmas season. *The point: Both consumer and business-to-business marketers should have new product threshold rates for each product category and overall.*

If all business-to-business catalog companies were tossed into a blender, the ideal minimum new product introduction rate—in my experience—would be thirty-five percent per year. Similarly, the blender rate for consumer catalog companies would be minimally sixty percent per year. These 'common size' percentages will vary dramatically across sectors, but these seem to be the general, minimum percentage rates that *satisfy* the question, "I wonder what's new?" When I evaluate catalog companies, these tend to be the beginning benchmarks for new products that I apply and then adjust based on sector demand. Interestingly, these minimum new product introduction rates have remained stable over the last twenty years or more, and this leads me to believe there is some inherent human threshold for 'newness' that must be satisfied. If that is true, it means that we are programmed to look for change and new things. If a consumer catalog is produced in four seasonal printings, each one will require minimally fifteen percent new products in order to reach the sixty percent annual new product threshold and satisfy the pre-programmed 'interest quotient.' This personal newness threshold is driven home to me every time I get on an airplane and try to browse the seat-pocket catalog. I keep seeing the same products offered and never get past page six. Of course, I fly *way* too much, but let's face it: if it isn't new, it isn't interesting!

Customers who have high recency, frequency and monetary value scores may have a high new product threshold. Perhaps the top RFM sector requires ninety percent new products annually to remain in that top performance tier.

Customers with low recency, frequency and monetary value scores may have a low new product threshold. Perhaps the bottom RFM sector requires zero new products because they are buying only one or two mature, commodity products and will never increase their purchasing.

The point: You won't know until you know. But when you do know, then you can do something extraordinary. Of course, all of these new product elements vary by channel. A multi-channel approach demands integrated new product development and introduction. In many instances, the online channel can be effectively and rapidly used to obtain a reading on new product interest and viability.

The other side of new product introduction, and the side that is often neglected, is old product retirement. We have all seen or heard of warehouses filled with two-headed product lizards that nobody wants to buy. Periodically, these moribund inventories are dusted off and trotted out as a corporate asset, generally when the business is, too late, put up for sale. It seems there are a lot of people who just can't get rid of old products.

Because there is a rate of new product introduction that sustains customer interest, there is a corresponding rate of old product retirement that sustains product relevance (as well as corporate profitability). To understand what that rate should be, first we have to understand the success rate of new products.

Direct marketers are getting better at new product development. Twenty years ago, it took ten new products to find one winner. Today, that ratio seems to be about five to one. For every five products introduced, one will be a winner, an 'evergreen' product that stays in the line. A business-to-business catalog company with 1,000 products (not SKUs) will need, minimally, 350 new products a year, or 35 percent, to maintain customer interest. Out of this annual crop of 350 new products, 70 can be expected to be successful and be retained (one out of every five). Actually, 280 other new products have been introduced that are not 'evergreen' successful (350-70 = 280). These 280 new products must be ranked against all old products and, wherever new products beat old products, they replace the old products. If the new product development skills and talent are good, there will likely be about 50 percent of the new products that outperform old products, or 140 products that can replace old, lesser-performing products.

The math then is: a 14 percent old product retirement rate; a 14 percent new product substitution rate; and a 7 percent 'evergreen' new product rate. Start with 1,000 products; add 350 new products; discontinue 140 new products; swap 140 old products for new products; keep 70 top-performing 'evergreens.' Total products equal 1,280 products for an effective gain of 280 products, or 28 percent. (1,000 + 350 = 1,350 – 140 = 1,210 + 70 = 1,280 – 1,000 = 280 or 28%)

The substitution of superior products for lesser performing old products is formulaic. The identification of the top performing 70 evergreen products is easy. The real difficulty is abandoning the 140 new products that don't measure up to any of the older products. The better the new product development talent and experience, the better the success rate becomes. If experience and talent can reduce the 140 unsuccessful new products by 50 percent, the overall success of the new product machine goes up. It isn't until you do the math and calculate what unsuccessful new product introductions really cost that you become convinced of the wisdom of hiring exceptionally skilled and talented new product people.

The total rate of old product retirement in the above example is 14 percent, or 140 products that need to eliminated each year. Whether these products are obsolete or perhaps need to be 'rested' and returned to the line will depend on their position in the product life cycle. This is why product life cycle analyses must be available before the new product development program is ramped up and the new product machine turned up to high. There is an order to all of this.

Knowing when to pull the plug on a new product is always difficult. Everyone in the catalog world has an opinion on how long a product should be tried before giving up and pulling it from the lineup. My personal belief, for business-to-business new products, is that it takes at least a full year and perhaps two years for some products in order to make that decision. Perhaps the best advice that can be given, especially to CEOs, is that all product managers want to know what the parameters are for any new product. When you establish defined product performance expectations, you are actually describing the 'walls' that a product developer and manager works within to meet the objectives of the business. Most people are fine as long as they know where the walls are; take away the walls and they roam all over the place. For example, it is far better to say:

"New products will have twenty-four months to meet the following performance benchmarks: 1) fifteen percent return on investment by year two; 2) gross margin of fifty-four percent by year two; 3) six percent annual price increase; 4) unit sales of five hundred annual rate by year two; 5) no more than $7,000 inventory burden; 6) no more than $2,000 R&D and research costs; 7) less than five percent returns rate by year two; 8) must be shippable by UPS at a profit of not less than two percent. Achieve these objectives by the twenty-fourth month or eight catalog cycles and the product remains in the line. Miss three or more of these objectives in the first year, and the product will be discontinued by the twelfth month."

Now, those are walls! Twelve or eighteen months from now, no one can ask, "What part of this didn't you understand?" This is *exactly* what product managers want and wish someone would give them.

NEW PRODUCT INTRODUCTION AND RETIREMENT: PICKERING

New products get everyone excited. They are on the cover, they generate buzz, customers clamor for them. New products are sexy.

There is big business in older products. Last year's models can frequently be obtained from suppliers at a fraction of the cost of when they were the latest and the greatest. And, there is a segment of buyers in the marketplace that don't want a product when it is brand new, don't want to be on the bleeding edge. They want to get it when the price is on the way down; they are looking for a deal. Admittedly, this is frequently the case in consumer marketing more than in business-to-business, but there is applicability in both.

Websites get it. If you look at most merchandise-oriented direct marketing websites there is a special section devoted to closeouts, special deals, or whatever the catch phrase may be. These are frequently the most clicked on portions of the website. Duluth Trading, as one example, does a great job on their site with closeouts.

Many catalogers get it, particularly those whose products are seasonal. In the beginning of the season, the newest products are featured on the covers and up front in the catalog. There may be no special deals or they may be relegated to the deep inside, perhaps on the order form. But later in the season, the special deals come out, the discontinued, last year's model. Frequently they can even make it up to a special section or signature that is wrapped around the core catalog. Bike Nashbar does an exceptional job of marketing closeouts in their catalog.

There aren't many marketers that make an entire business concept out of discontinued items, through there are a few, such as overstock.com. This is one of those opportunities that the seasoned direct marketer can spot and seize. You can earn good margin and usually attract customers who are attentive to your offerings and have a better than average propensity to repurchase.

PRODUCT AND GROSS MARGIN: LIBEY

First, a definition:

Gross margin is the ratio of gross profit to sales revenue.

Gross margin = revenue – cost of goods sold ÷ revenue

For example, if a product sells for $49.00 and it costs $22.50, the gross margin is 54 percent ($49.00 – $22.50 = $26.50 ÷ $49.00 = 54%).

Catalog marketers have historically had gross margins of about fifty-four percent for all catalogs (blender effect); fifty-one percent for business-to-business catalogs; fifty-four percent for consumer catalogs; and fifty-three percent for hybrid catalogs. Of course, these may vary by sector, but on a blended basis they will be fairly representative of actual gross margins.

The overall gross margin, however, is the sum of the individual product gross margins, an average of the gross margins of products that are above and below the fifty-four percent benchmark. Maintaining a stable gross margin requires constant adjustment to either selling prices or cost of goods. Increasing the overall gross margin requires a variety of tactics, which may include vendor price concessions (vendor bending), increasing prices, importing, private labeling, or changing the product gross margin mix. While increasing overall gross margin is difficult, any success produces an immediate increase in earnings and, as a result, an immediate increase in business valuation, an important factor when preparing the business for the exit strategy or harvest event. A one-dollar increase in earnings can translate to a six-dollar or more increase in valuation. Drop $170,000 of improved gross margin to the bottom line and the value of the business can go up by over $1,000,000.

The hierarchical segmentation of all products by gross margin provides valuable information. A descending hierarchy of the highest gross margin products to the lowest gross margin products can be viewed in comparison with a variety of other hierarchies. One would be the hierarchy of product sales. Are the top selling products coming from the top gross margin products? Another comparison would be the hierarchy of top performing recency, frequency and monetary value customers. Are the top performing customers buying the top performing products? A third comparison would be manufactured products versus purchased products, especially for business-to-business direct marketers. Are the internally manufactured products producing higher gross margin than the products purchased for resale? The same question could apply to domestically sourced products versus imported products, or private label products versus branded products. For any of these hierarchical comparisons of product gross margin and some variable, the top performing segments and comparisons are important, but the bottom performing segments are equally important. Knowing as much information about the worst performing products and the customers buying those products is essential to the proper alignment of product gross margin. *The point: Gross margin versus sales is either improving, remaining the same or eroding; only one direction is acceptable.*

For each channel, the various hierarchies of gross margin and performance are analyzed separately. The online comparisons will likely be different from the catalog comparisons, and telemarketing may be very different from either online or catalog. Each channel has an optimal gross margin-sales-customer segment hierarchy. The Masters know what that optimal combination is and how to force it through product mix, advertising, channel allocation, sourcing, cost of goods focus, and pricing tactics.

All of these hierarchical comparative analyses are performed quarterly. Over twenty rolling quarters, the five-year view of trend can be seen by disciplined plotting on the classic *x* and *y*-axis chart. Visual proof of the trend in product gross margin, in gross margin of the top selling products, in gross margin of the top RFM customers, in gross margin of 'make versus buy' products, and other key comparisons, is the only way to truly understand the direction of the business. Most of us are visual; we *see* key information better than we process it mathematically. One of the great skills of Direct Marketing Masters is the discipline to chart performance factors over time in the visually revealing format of the *x* and *y*-axis chart.

PRODUCT AND GROSS MARGIN: PICKERING

Margin is important because it's what keeps us honest. Without margin we are simply having a theoretical discussion: does product category *A* produce good customers? We think so; they have a high propensity to repurchase and they have high lifetime dollars. Without margin, however, we don't *really* know if they are good customers.

The simple fact is this: when analyzing prospecting campaigns there are few marketers who are looking at margin. There are some, though these are generally single product offerings (solos) where there is one margin. To judge effectively the quality of prospecting and to make sure that we are filling the faucet with good customers, we need to look at the margin, the profit that those customers produce.

The measurement of prospecting as it relates to margin does not have to be done immediately after the campaign is closed. There is a good argument that right after a campaign is closed is a *poor* time to do this analysis. Most marketers are investing in prospecting efforts, so performing margin analysis as a campaign closes is simply which list or campaigns or seasons did we lose the least amount of money. Analyzing a campaign or season after there has been twelve months or more purchase history allows a true yardstick to be applied to a prospecting effort. Did we produce customers that had a high propensity to repurchase, and did these subsequent purchases move margin into the positive? What lists or segments produced the most margin? These are the questions that give deeper insights to the health and success of a company.

Margin can be difficult to track, especially over time. Few marketers are blessed with a constant cost of goods sold (COGS). And in addition to the fluctuation of COGS there is a variety of ways of applying the costs: first in, first out (FIFO), last in, first out (LIFO), and so on. Some marketers choose to take an average COGS and apply it across *all* products. This is fine if all products have a fairly close COGS across all categories, but most direct marketers that I have seen don't have a close COGS across all categories, especially if they private label some product. And by close I mean within five percentage points or less.

For those marketers with unlimited time and unlimited financial and technological resources, there is virtually no substitute for applying the COGS of the product at the time it was sold. For those of us in the real world, there are some other techniques. COGS is frequently similar for product categories, so that is one way to apply it. Another is by supplier: map the SKUs to the OEM that supplied them and apply that COGS to those purchases.

Once you have related COGS in some fashion to products purchased, you can develop margin measures by customer, product category, season or year of customer acquisition, etc. Having this margin information at the most micro level possible gives you—the marketer—the best possible idea of the success or challenges in your marketing effort and the best arguments to justify the marketing budget when that time comes. Knowledge is power and knowing margin—intimately related to product—gives power almost beyond compare.

AFFINITY CLUSTERS: LIBEY

Affinity is defined as an attraction to or liking for something; a force between things or people. *Clusters* are described as a number of similar individuals or things that occur together. In direct marketing, affinity clusters is a term that is applied to a variety of elements.

Products are found in affinity clusters. Analyze the transactional data and you will find 'star' products ('star' in the sense of our Sun). These are the big products, like a John Deere tractor, that drive other product sales, the 'planet' products: star John Deere tractors drive sales of planet products like mower attachments, trailers, snowplows, and garden tillers. The planet products drive sales of 'moon' products: mower attachments create add-on sales for blades, mulchers, aerators, baggers and blowers, sharpener kits and other orbiting goodies. Around moon products are 'asteroid' products: touch-up paint, replacement seals and gaskets, lubricants, disposable grass clipping bags, etc. The whole system is one big affinity cluster with the tractor in the center, planet products orbiting it, moon products orbiting the planet products and asteroids whizzing in and out of the moons. *The point: You have to know which products are stars and which are planets, moons and asteroids.* Unfortunately, most direct marketers don't know how their galaxy is structured.

When I visit a company and discover the operating system does not provide cross-sell and up-sell opportunities for individual customers based on product affinity clusters and purchase history, I almost always see an easy twenty percent increase in sales, or more. Back in the 1970s, I decided I wanted to really learn about small retail business. So, I bought a pet shop. The business offered every kind of pet: dogs, cats, birds, rodents, reptiles, tropical fish, saltwater fish, insects, and all the supplies that go with them. I built a Puppy Room, which was a ten by six foot, latticework gazebo structure with mirrors lining the lower half of all four walls. I'd put the little kids in there with a puppy and the parents would stand outside, leaning in over the top rails, watching their little loved one reflected in all four mirrors—all happy and giggly, playing with the adorable puppy. Displayed on the upper half of the back wall were all the add-on products every parent was going to take home with the new addition to the family. While they watched their little kid fall in love with the puppy, I was explaining all about the 'New Puppy Product Package.' If the dog was $300, the New Puppy Product Package for that breed was $300. If the dog was $400, the products were $400. Every employee knew that the puppy was only fifty percent of the sale. The puppy was the Sun; leashes, collars, harnesses and sweaters were Mercury; grooming products were Venus; food and feeding products were Saturn; housebreaking aids and products were Uranus; vitamins and flea collars and nail clippers were the Moons of Saturn; toys were asteroids; ah, the power of affinity clusters!

Creating the product affinity clusters around the driver products is time well spent. There is a hierarchy of product affinity clusters in every direct marketing business if you take the time and effort to discover what they are. First, isolate the 'suns' or driver products. Study every transaction for driver products and determine all of the products that are bought with that primary product. Aggregate them and create a hierarchy of 'planet' products. Repeat the process at the next level and create a hierarchy of 'moons.' Continue until you find the 'asteroids.' These affinity clusters provide huge opportunities for product bundling, add-ons, cross-sells, advertising groupings, online specials, and a variety of other innovative and productive merchandising tactics.

Once the affinity clusters are empirically defined and identified, overlay the affinity product hierarchies with recency, frequency and monetary value to determine which affinity clusters perform best with top RFM segments. Equally, which are bottom RFM magnets?

Once you have those hierarchies analyzed, do the same thing in each specific channel. Then, ask the question, "How do I integrate channel product affinity performance with RFM performance into optimal, multi-channel, product affinity performance?"

Affinity clusters are also found in pricing. If we look at infomercials, we find many offerings grouped at the $14.95 price point; numerous at the $19.95 price point; and a variety at the three or five payments of $29.95. Customers exist who purchase only products offered at $14.95 and others who purchase at both the $14.95 level and at the $19.95 price. These customers rarely purchase at the multiple payments of $29.95 offer. Two price affinity clusters are described and the targeting of broadcast time and exposure is designed to optimize each affinity cluster's viewing habits.

In the retail channel, price affinity clusters exist, as well. The cereal aisle in the grocery store carries brand name cereal and generic cereal, effectively the same product but with up to a fifty percent price difference. Price affinity customers purchase generic cereal and they also purchase generic soup, crackers, rice, cough syrup, aspirin, tissues, and other commodity products with significantly lower prices.

In the catalog channel, business products customers who purchase the lowest price, utilitarian envelopes generally also purchase the lowest price utilitarian mailing labels or file folders. Lowest price describes an affinity cluster of products that can be predicted based on purchase behavior. Other customers, who purchase custom printed, one hundred percent cotton rag, laid paper envelopes generally buy upscale file folder systems and other office products. Behavior, based on image and other factors, forces them into another, higher price affinity cluster.

When affinity cluster product data is analyzed and viewed from a variety of angles, it can be overlaid on recency, frequency and monetary value analysis to determine which affinity clusters are driving the business. Top performing RFM segments may, in fact, be comprised of low price affinity cluster customers. Whether this is positive or negative requires using a third hierarchical overlay: gross margin.

Each channel will potentially have affinity clusters that are unique or overlapping. The ability to understand affinity clusters of different types in different channels is essential to the structuring of position, value propositions and offers. Equally important is determining whether the affinity clusters can be migrated. If a customer is acquired at a price affinity of $14.95, can that customer be migrated over time to $79.95? If a customer is acquired at a product affinity of 'asteroids,' can that customer be migrated to 'Suns?'"

One of the most productive affinity clusters is one identified by speed. Customers often buy based on delivery time. These tend to be customers who do not purchase based on price and they are willing to spend more money to get the product faster. Once the hierarchical analyses are done to list the top performing customers by delivery speed affinity clusters, specific speed offers can be deployed to service that affinity. A good example of this in business-to-business direct marketing is imprinted or personalized products that are used at trade shows or conventions. By isolating the customers who are *always* late in placing their orders, an affinity cluster emerges that thrives on speed of delivery positioning and offers.

Other affinity clusters only require imagination. Style in interior design forms affinity clusters around traditional, contemporary, modern, art deco, French country, log cabin, and other looks. Status in automobiles forms affinity clusters around luxury, economy, hybrids, off the road, SUV, retro, sport, and others, including the Hummer which represents an affinity cluster of 'drivers most likely to paint their faces with NFL team colors and grunt loudly in public.' But, if you want to sell noisemakers and spicy raccoon jerky, this is the group. Ideology forms affinity clusters. Liberal and conservative describe two clusters; Libertarian and Socialist two others. Affinity clusters are found in religion, education, membership groups, residential type (homes, town homes, apartments, starter castles, etc.), ethnicity, hobbies, the arts, and an endless potential for differences and sameness. *The point: Knowing how affinity clusters influence your business and which affinity clusters are important is critical to multi-channel direct marketing strategy.*

AFFINITY CLUSTERS: PICKERING

Some topics just make you fall all over yourself because you have so much to blurt out. Affinity clusters is one of those topics.

Mastering an understanding of affinity product clusters is something that almost every successful direct marketing company does—and something that almost every unsuccessful direct marketing company *cannot* do. Lacking this understanding can lead to unwise product line additions, foolish mergers or acquisitions, and even bankruptcy.

On the positive side, understanding affinity clusters can not only lead to increased profitability by developing relevant cross-sell offerings, but also point to profitable opportunities for new catalog or website titles, seminar offerings, even good potential acquisitions.

The process is rather simple and you will find the way that works best for you. First, look at all the best customers defined by an RFM segmentation that includes margin performance. Next, look at which combinations of product categories the customers purchased. Third, look at all the combinations and permutations. This will require some statistical acuity, but nothing too strenuous. The clusters will become obvious. There may be *driver products* within your product offering, though not necessarily. What is important is to know and understand those drivers.

If you perform a web search to find retailers who sell the Apple iPod, you will find a few dozen authorized outlets. Computer hardware is notoriously low margin. If you then look for those who sell iPod accessories, there will be hundreds upon hundreds. This is a great business, because the margin on accessories is higher, even if the total amount is less than the driver product. And if you can develop a specialized product that becomes the 'must have' accessory, you can write your own ticket. So look outside your own product offerings for the affinity stars, these can be the treasures of the planets and the moons and the asteroids.

Star products don't even need to be currently manufactured. If you have a Jeep Scrambler and it needs repair (and what Scrambler could not benefit from some TLC?), you almost certainly have looked at J.C. Whitney. They have an offering of products that makes them more than a retailer; they become a universal reference source for information. A Jeep Scrambler in need of repair, a J.C. Whitney catalog, a Chilton's guide, a set of Craftsman tools, and you might not see your brother-in-law for months!

Direct marketers who have an extensive product line sooner or later will ask the question: should I launch a separate title or website? Frequently this is done by first discovering an unserved or underserved market. There can be reward in that, and the most logical place to look is within your own customer base.

When looking at your RFM segmentation and overlaying this with product and SIC (or some other descriptor of business, interest or demographic) you likely will find a profitable segment. This segment spends well, has a good propensity to repurchase, but only orders from a few of your product categories. Further, you find that compared to the prospect universe available, you haven't penetrated very far into this group of customers. This is a ripe opportunity to dedicate a new title to this group.

Launching a new title to better serve a special group requires a tight focus. By knowing the affinity of the products that cluster around this group, the Master Marketer can pare down the products in this catalog or on this website. Additionally, new products or product groups can be introduced to this market that normally would not have enough appeal for the entire customer base. Further, promotion efforts, such as dates of catalog drops or email blasts, can be tailored to the needs of this group.

All this potential lies before you only if you thoroughly understand product affinity clusters. If you do, you *can* spin straw into gold.

PRODUCT AND RFM OPTIMIZATION: LIBEY

A number of practical concepts have been explored in the product realm of multi-channel direct marketing beginning with the product life cycle and extending through product categories, new product development and introduction, gross margin, and product affinity clusters. If you are addressing all of these practical elements of your product foundation, you are exceptional. For almost all companies, business-to-business or consumer, holes will exist throughout the product program. Determining which holes to fill is the critical discretionary decision. For me, the answer has always been simple: *I gain the greatest growth in earnings and business valuation when I know what products my RFM segments are buying.* It's actually that simple. If you can accomplish nothing else, figure out that little bit of analysis, because the key to the money machine is in the overlay of product on the recency, frequency and monetary value hierarchies.

Segment your customers into the classic four RFM groups: Stars, Cows, Mystery Meat and Dogs **(Figure L5.5)**. First analyze the products being purchased by the Stars. Then analyze the products being bought by the Dogs. Find more Stars. Stop doing Dogs.

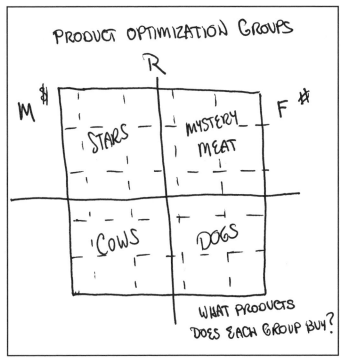

Forget about Cash Cows for the moment, because they will always be Cash Cows. Focus on the Mystery Meat because they were once Stars when they were buying regularly and, if you can get them back, they will be Stars again. That's it. That's all the strategic planning you need. Go do that and you will make a lot of money, your business will be worth more, and when you bring it to me to sell, we'll get a lot more for all of your hard work over the years.

PRODUCT AND RFM OPTIMIZATION: PICKERING

Understanding product, especially as it relates to RFM, is easy conceptually, but not so easy to put into practice. The rewards are clear: increased sales, increased margin, increased profitability, and decreased risk when launching a new title.

It isn't easy to understand product, especially as it relates to RFM. You can understand recency without understanding frequency or monetary. You cannot begin to understand the current state of your businesses with out understanding product and RFM. Understanding RFM and product will allow you to better forecast business cycles and identify new opportunities. Understanding RFM and product allows you to graduate from being a tactician, able in the arts of segmenting the file, to being a strategist, able to chart the course for your business. Both are important, but knowing RFM and product allows you to write your own ticket.

Chapter 6 Channel

CATALOG: LIBEY

Any discussion of multi-channel direct marketing must begin with the catalog channel. Any discussion that focuses on the size of the catalog channel and other macro estimates of growth will be outdated in a matter of months. It is wiser to find current statistical data on the catalog channel as it is required. Here, it is wiser to focus on the philosophical and conceptual elements of the catalog as a viable channel within direct marketing.

Catalogs have been around for a very long time. One of the first recorded references to a printed catalog was in the twelfth century. Monks working in scriptoriums produced illuminated copies of the catalog on vellum and they were carried by priests in the summer and fall of the year to abbeys throughout Europe. The catalogs contained drawings and descriptions of religious relics, which could be obtained by the abbeys as items of veneration for the faithful, for a price. The finger bone of a saint, the heart of a martyr, scraps of holy shrouds, chalices, splinters of the cross and other religious antiquities were offered along with add-on handcrafted reliquaries to house the treasures. Purchases were paid for in advance and the priest returned to headquarters with the orders and the cash, loaded up the products and delivered them on the return trip, along with a new catalog and the 'spring' offers. The cardinal elements of this earliest of catalogs remain the same today: 1) a good list; 2) good products; 3) a good offer; 4) circulation; 5) fulfillment; and 6) the first known bounce-back and package insert.

Almost eight hundred years later, catalogs have become a very big part of the global commerce. In the United States alone, we estimate there are over twenty thousand catalogs of all types: business-to-business, consumer and manufacturing. The catalog is an established, respected and effective method of selling. The reason for its success is, I believe, because of its contemplative nature. Looking at a catalog of products is, largely, a personal and relaxing endeavor. The catalog shopper is engaged by photography, descriptive or specification copy, attainment of a dream or successful achievement of an application, all contemplative and pleasant intellectual activities, whether personal or business-related. That just doesn't happen in a Wal-Mart.

While the contemplative nature of the catalog has endured, the call to action has shifted progressively from mail to telephone and now to online response. Online ordering, in response to contemplative catalog shopping, accounts for half of the orders, yet eighty percent of those online orders are driven by a paper catalog. At the same time, the total number of catalogs produced is increasing. Online ordering will continue to gain over mail and telephone, but the catalog will remain a primary driver of those online orders. Eventually, online catalogs will edge up in popularity, partly because of generational acceptance and familiarity, but also because of irresistible catalog economics. Suffice it to say, the online world will grow in importance, but the paper catalog world will retain its relevance and importance for many more years. It is not the catalog channel *or* the online channel; it is the symbiotic blending of both—as well as other channels—that drives the future of direct marketing.

Were I to venture a guess as to the mix in twenty years, I would think physical catalog response would be at the ten to fifteen percent level with online response at the eighty-five to ninety percent level. This means, of the eighty-five to ninety percent online orders, probably fifteen percent will be driven by a paper catalog and the remainder driven by search and online catalogs. Worst case, paper catalogs will still drive about twenty to twenty-five percent of orders. However, the direct industry will be magnitudes larger and the total number of orders will have increased dramatically. The larger number of orders will be obtained across numerous channels, one of which will be the enduring and ever-viable catalog channel.

With a positive long-range outlook for catalogs, common sense demands that, at the minimum, optimized RFM analyses be accomplished for catalog channel customers to derive the greatest possible understanding of the trends in their historical purchasing behavior. The added benefit of being better able to allocate resources to the catalog channel on a basis proportionate to earnings is a plus. If the catalog channel is twenty-five percent of your business in the future, and if industry growth produces a business that is four times your present size over twenty years, then the catalog channel alone could equal the same or more than your entire business today. *The point: Catalogs are important to your future and knowing as much as you can possibly know about your catalog customers is like having life insurance.*

CATALOG: PICKERING

We have lived through the Orwellian coming of 1984, the end of the world as we knew it in 2000, and we have lived through the projected complete demise of the catalog in favor of the web and email. The catalog is a tough old bird and has survived all these events.

Nonetheless, there are changes as well as constants with catalogs. For one thing, a stand-alone catalog, as we knew it in the 1960s or

1970s, with all responses coming via mailed in order form, is dead. There was debate in the late 1970s and early 1980s about the appropriate use of 800 numbers: do we include them and pay large phone bills or do we have regular numbers and reduce, but 'qualify' the inbound callers? History has shown that investing in making things easier for the customer to give you their money pays off.

Order forms today look much different. They used to be in the middle of the catalog (always) easily ripped out and usually included some sort of envelope. Today they are usually, but not always, in the middle, but aren't really intended to be detached. The order form has morphed into a vehicle to communicate shipping charges, delivery information, and sizing charts. In the 1980s, there was a story, perhaps apocryphal, about a new circulation manager who ordered an entire season's worth of catalogs without an order form. It was the most elementary of mistakes. Today, it would scarcely be noticed.

The move toward using catalogs to drive order placement via toll-free calls was a great boon for catalogers. It became a built-in opportunity to cross-sell or up-sell and, at the minimum, the ability to provide 'high-touch.' The newer channels of outbound telemarketing, web, and outbound email have similar opportunities inherent in them.

The cliché that says that the only constant is change is certainly true. Direct marketing has always been attractive to entrepreneurs because of the low barriers to entry. You don't necessarily need to set up distributors or retailers; all you need is product (not even inventory) and a catalog, website or telephone. That is true now more than ever.

With the increasing clutter that comes along, more and more offerings make knowing and putting into practice the basic lessons of direct marketing all that more important. We have had less than ten years to find our way through the new channels of web and email. There will likely be five or ten more years before integrated multi-channel campaigns are the norm. By that time, we will likely have new channels of communication, payment, and delivery.

As Harry Truman said, "There is nothing new in the world except the history you do not know." Knowing the history and principles of direct marketing as applied to catalogs will allow you to apply tried and true principles and have a reliable guide to the new channels.

ONLINE: LIBEY

As with the catalog channel in direct marketing, it is useless to discuss the present status of the online channel because the data will be out of date within forty-eight hours. Once again, the macro philosophical and conceptual elements of this ever-evolving channel is about all that can be offered.

I began saying the Internet and the web were dying in 2004. Mid-year, I realized that the only thing the web offered in the future was more of the same. Any time an evolutionary process offers only more of the same, its run is over. Evolution doesn't want more of the same; evolution wants change. In fact, evolution *has* to have change in order to evolve.

The next web, the next thing, is something yet unnamed, but what I call the WorldNet. Access will encompass every known communication device, including computers, iPods, Blackberries, Treos, OnStar, cell phones, televisions, satellite systems, literally any device that connects to something. There will be no need for subscription service; no roaming or geographic limitations. Wherever you are, you'll access a vast hyper-connected world and have the capability of obtaining anything you can imagine. Credit cards will be obsolete; credit units will be instantly exchanged for goods and services anywhere on the globe. The WorldNet is being built right now; it will be reality in your and, perhaps, my lifetime. Imagine the web as ubiquitous as air or light. The WorldNet will be everywhere and will access everything, instantly and universally. And the WorldNet will be the 'next thing' in the history of multi-channel direct marketing. The WorldNet will also create the next descriptive change for our industry: UniChannel Marketing—totally direct; totally integrated; all conceivable access points and all conceivable sales channels. Email becomes Unimail and it is delivered by televisions, OnStar screens, radios, kiosks in the park, any hotel room, on your iPod, over your watch, through your home security system, at your theater seat, anywhere, anyhow you want to access and accept information.

The WorldNet will be a post-search world. Search engines will be organically integrated into your personal systems in the same way Google's Desk Top Search does your hard drive now. Search will jump channels from online to television to cable to hand-helds. All products will be both horizontal and vertical as to source and price; 'local' will have a whole new meaning for fulfillment; dropship will be the only concept remaining; few merchants will actually own inventory.

Over time, the WorldNet channel will require more of your channel-allocated advertising dollars. All advertising channels will expand in total dollars spent, but the WorldNet channel will demand more as a percentage of overall expenditures, and these will include remnant spending for what remains of the old online approaches, the remnants of search engine marketing, paid search and pay per click, if any.

Shopping in the online WorldNet future will be *highly* organized. The comparative pricing and product aggregators of the first decade of the century will seem archaic compared to the product comparison architectures of the future global access systems. Individual customer product preferences and histories will follow us wherever we go and whatever we access; purchasing and shipping processes will be transparent and all of the relevant credit and shipping address information will be automated within our encapsulated 'WorldNet accounts.' The annoying and repetitive administrative parts of the purchasing process, such as having to fill out billing and shipping addresses, will be eliminated. More important, effective security controls will emerge that reduce identity fraud and theft to negligible levels.

Not only will the process of shopping be highly organized, but the tracking and analytics of the individual and collective shopping histories will be equally organized and highly sophisticated. List performance and segmentation analyses will attain levels only dreamed about, far beyond optimized RFM, extending into affinity clusters, predictable purchasing patterns, 'market basket' approaches to product propensities, and geographic targeting that concentrates on local preferences for product selection, price competitiveness and access channels.

Why should you accept the plausibility of these concepts? Reread this section and then reflect on the fact that virtually nothing I have described in the last seven paragraphs even *existed* twenty years ago. These evolutions—or similar ones—are inevitable.

The present online channel is, then, nothing more than a birth canal for your future UniChannel direct marketing business. That future business already is waiting on the other side, but you have to go through this existing, albeit already obsolete, online channel to get there. You have to do it over the next few years; you have to evolve. You *must* have the experience of search engine optimization, linguistics and word purchasing replacing other forms of access, price aggregation, and comparative product dissection, all of the tectonic technological constructs that demand an increase in your velocity of change, even if they will soon be superseded by other, newer channel modalities. Why? So you will understand and be prepared for what will be.

Welcome to the future!

ONLINE: PICKERING

Online almost defines the term buzzword. People want to know if your business is 'online.' Ask people what they mean by that and you will get myriad different responses.

In the very late 1990s and early part of the twenty-first century, many businesses tried to migrate online or simply start there. What we found were enormous challenges to overcome, and ethics and rules to develop.

What we found was that online, if you look at that as a website, is not the magic bullet that some thought it was. A great site will not replace a catalog. Unlike a catalog, a great site will just sit there unless acted upon by some other force to drive people there. That is when you see the combination of catalog, search engine marketing, outbound email, space advertisements, television, and radio start to drive traffic to the site. It is not simply enough to build it.

So, for all of its perceived advantages, such as no cost of paper or postage, the website is in some significant ways less powerful and less capable than the catalog antecedent. What this is really showing us is that, as we live in a more connected world, we must more closely connect and integrate our marketing messages to that they are mutually supporting and reinforcing.

Regardless of what media drives a person to purchase, or what channel they purchase through, one thing is certain: so long as there are customers there will be a need to segment the best ones for communication and valuation purposes. The cornerstone for that has been and will continue to be RFM.

CATALOG-ASSISTED ONLINE: LIBEY

The online channel will eventually morph into the WorldNet channel, but until that evolution emerges, we must work with the existing reality: catalog-assisted online direct marketing. For some period of years, the online and catalog channels will remain inextricably linked. Catalogs drive buyers to the websites, and that behavior must be better understood by direct marketers.

If catalogs are to better assist in the multi-channel transition, we have to learn a great deal more about the interaction between the catalog and the web. Doubtless, there are 'triggers' that cause buyers to get up and walk to their computer, catalog in hand, to go online. What are those triggers? When do they occur and what causes them? Are specific pages more active triggers than others? Is there a relationship between pagination and trigger actions? Do printed calls to action, such as "Go online now and see special pricing," create additional transchannel activity? Is there a consumer 'window of hours' in the day where the catalog drives more web shopping? Is there a similar business-to-business window of hours? Is the half-life of the catalog becoming shorter due to the relationship with the web? How do top RFM customers use the catalog, and will they go directly to landing pages if the extended URLs are printed under the catalog price blocks or as a photo caption? There are thousands of questions to be answered about the catalog-web symbiosis. When we began the Golden Age of the Catalog, in the 1980s, similar questions were being asked about the buyer and the relationship with the physical catalog; in fact, all of our contemporary wisdom about catalog creative has sprung from those early days a quarter-century ago. Now, we are simply extending the behavioral analysis and asking what goes on when the catalog and the website are conjoined.

Direct marketers often seem to have either way too much information or not enough information. As a consultant, I am always wary of those companies that can produce truckloads of data at will; generally, they cannot isolate simple truths about their business out of the tons of analyses. Opposite the paralytic analytics are the companies that have no idea what is going on in the business, and there are many. These companies have minimal systems to give them even minimal information. Fortunately for both of these extremes, the truly important questions are almost always simple and fairly easy to answer. For instance:

1. What percent of the buyers use a physical catalog when placing a web order?

2. Is that percentage increasing, staying the same or decreasing?

3. What percent of the top RFM segments use a physical catalog when placing a web order?

4. Is that percentage increasing, staying the same or decreasing?

5. What products are primarily associated with a catalog-assisted web order?

6. What products are primarily ordered online without a catalog?

7. For those orders that are catalog-assisted, what are the top three triggers?

8. What is the relationship between the catalog price and the online price?

9. Where in the catalog pagination should web drivers be located?

10. When the catalog tells the reader that additional products not in the catalog can be found on the website, does that drive more web sales?

These are only ten simple questions out of hundreds that must be asked, but few direct marketing companies are able to answer even those questions definitively. Yet, we have truckloads of data on click rates, hundreds of consultants and vendors who only focus on 'usability studies' and a near-obsession with measuring functionality. Unfortunately, we don't know about the stuff that creates sales. But, it has always been thus. I am reminded of the days when we did catalog page eye tracking studies to see how the pages were being read. The CEOs who commissioned those expensive studies usually couldn't tell you who their best customers were and what products they bought. *The point: If you are to maximize the catalog-website interrelationship, you better know all about the stuff that really matters.*

In 2005, for advanced multi-channel direct marketers, approximately fifty percent of all orders were being received online. Of that fifty percent, eighty percent were being driven by a paper catalog. Over time, the total orders received online will increase and the percentage driven by paper catalogs will decrease (**Figure L6.1**). One day, there may be an economic crossover reached where it is no longer profitable to use paper catalogs, but that day is some distance in the future. Until then, direct marketing companies must allocate their resources on a constantly changing basis to keep in step with the constantly changing catalog-online relationship. Remember, it is not the *contacts* that change, only the form of the *media*. Whether a name is mailed or emailed is immaterial; there will still be contacts. The real difference is in the form of prospecting.

To me, the catalog industry has always been much like an apple orchard. Somehow, buyers get out to the orchard; in years past, they came by horse and buggy and then they began shifting to automobiles. Our companies have always been the trees. Our products have always been the apples. Now, more buyers are going to the orchard via the Internet. Our companies are still the trees. Our

Figure L6.1

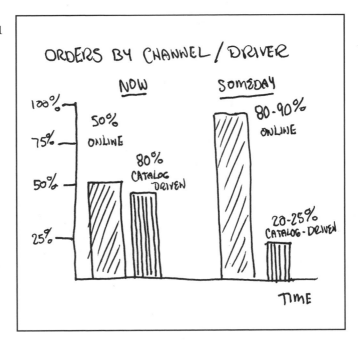

products are still the apples. The only thing that has changed is how the buyers get to the orchard. However, consider the inevitable logic. Riding to the orchard on a search engine will be cheaper than riding to the orchard on a mailed paper catalog. More visitors will come on the search engine. Fewer visitors will come on a catalog. We will still require names but they will come from new sources in different ways. Nothing will really change; yet, everything will change. And it will all grow, become larger, and our companies will expand beyond anything we could have imagined.

CATALOG-ASSISTED ONLINE: PICKERING

For many direct marketers, catalog-assisted online marketing has been the norm. This is quite obviously a good thing, for it allows you to use the strengths of both media.

As discussed, websites are great, but cannot create customers organically as a catalog can. And most direct marketers who have a catalog have more products than they can put in a catalog, even a large house file catalog. So, there is a great potential for catalogs and websites to provide mutual support.

Most older economy direct marketers have done very little tracking of the cross-pollination between catalogs and websites. We are only now reaching a point where a significant amount of catalogers are trying to capture a key code from a mailing tied to an order placed on the website. This is building block stuff, without this you are operating in the dark and might as well be placing space ads.

More advanced catalogers are performing occasional analyses examining what percentage of web buyers have received a catalog during the thirty or sixty days prior to a web purchase. Although I would encourage catalogers to do this regularly for themselves, the answer is always the same: an overwhelming majority of web purchasers are receiving catalogs a short time before they make a purchase.

A smaller number of even more advanced practitioners can tell you things like the spend is less on website purchases, or that web customers tend to order fewer line items. Very little analysis has gone into the difference between product categories purchased from catalog versus web or *why*. If you start to drill into that, you can quickly outpace your competitors.

Even though the cost of technology continues to go down in many important ways, there has been in many companies a decrease in the velocity of technological innovation on their web and catalog offerings. Many years ago, we started clicking on pictures to see an enlarged view. Several years ago we began being able to click on different colors to change the color of the sweater in a picture on a website. Recently developed is the ability to click a button and talk live to an operator. What is next?

Maybe Philadelphia is next. Recently Philadelphia announced plans to begin building zones of free wireless internet access in their downtown. The effects of this are profound. Aside from perhaps signaling the change of the ISP business to one of public utility, it shows that there are going to be changes in consumer purchasing (perhaps more impulse purchases if the web is available more places with greater bandwidth), greater levels of education (decreasing the digital divide), and myriad other changes.

If Philadelphia is the harbinger of things to come, we direct marketers need to think more than ever about geographic influences. Are the areas we are promoting in connected with high-speed internet access? What is the utilization?

Households with computers increased about fifty percent from 1998 to 2003, according to various sources. However, we have only just reached the point where a majority of households have computers. And high-speed, reliable internet access is many places, but it is not universal. Also, we are just beginning to see the first retirees who are comfortable with computers. More and more growth is to come.

The USPS has begun pilot programs assigning IP (Internet Protocol) addresses not only to houses but also to the devices within the houses, such as individual computers, fax machines, etc. This is not the death-knell of catalogs, but a sign of the continuing integration of the channels. Companies that think that they have finished integration of the catalog and the web are likely finished themselves. There is much opportunity left to develop the technologies and techniques to make these channels support each other.

PAY PER: LIBEY

I will indulge in further heresy and predict that the 'pay per' concept in online direct marketing will all but disappear soon. My reason for believing this is that I have never seen a middle tier able to make money in an environment of continuing margin erosion. It is financially more viable to manage the purchase transaction yourself than to pay someone else for some, most or all of the marketing or purchasing act. Whenever price is the primary differentiator, the middle tiers disappear. To say this another way, there really aren't enough slices of pie anymore.

This belief of mine does not extend to affiliate relationships, which are, after all, only dealer or wholesale structures in a new context. My belief concerns the pure pay per click, pay per click through, pay per sale, and the various other pay per arrangements. In some cases, bogus clicks and fraud create distrust and excess cost; in some cases, verification and tracking cost and effort overwhelm the value. I believe that—given time—direct marketers will always migrate from a dependent relationship to an independent control; they will soon invest themselves in the pay per skills and harness them to their own full benefit. *The point: It's cheaper to learn the channel than to buy the channel.*

SEARCH ENGINE: LIBEY

There are five essential and fundamental pillars to the process of finding a new customer: 1) prospecting lists; 2) cooperative databases; 3) collaterals (inserts, off-the-page, other); 4) email; and 5) search engine marketing.

While the integration of these five source components for new customer acquisition is critical, sophisticated list testing and investment prospecting remains as the primary source of our new customer acquisition strategies. In recent years, the emergence of cooperative databases with advanced modeling have raised the bar, but they still require the fundamental response, compiled and circulation list efforts by catalogers to drive their effectiveness. Email has begun to be productive and effective when executed correctly by experts who truly understand its structure and implications. While spam continues to be detrimental, the final email outcome will prove this a valuable and essential component of the integrated approach to finding new customers. Collaterals are having a new-revival, perhaps due to their relative dormancy over recent years.

But, the recent buzz in cataloging has focused on the recognition of how important a linked catalog-Internet strategy is to the process of uncovering and retaining customers. As we have said previously, eighty percent of all Internet orders are driven by a physical, paper catalog and a large percentage of those are catalogs mailed to prospects on a good list, targeted to specific prospects in specific segments and specific market sectors. Using a strong catalog prospecting program, driven by strong lists, causing prospects to go directly to the website is one of the great serendipitous events to ever happen to our industry. The Internet has *not* made cataloging or lists obsolete yet; in fact, it has strengthened both the list and the catalog as foundational pillars of the industry. Now there is a newer and equally beneficial source of new customers that is worthy of understanding and integrating into the mix: search.

Gaining hourly in importance is the pillar of search engine marketing. I would offer that this new addition to the arsenal of the multi-channel direct marketer will continue to grow in effectiveness. You as managers responsible for finding new customers, regardless of where they are or where they come from, will increasingly integrate search engine marketing into your overall list, investment prospecting and circulation planning. I call this the Dynamic Optimal Search Engine Marketing System, or DOSEMS, because I believe it actually *is* a system, and it has to be *dynamic* or ever-changing, as well as *optimal* for productivity and return on investment.

Dynamic means the DOSEMS never grows old. Dynamic implies a moving target that is predicated on relevant changes in technology, the catalog company, the customer universe and the marketplace. If you create a DOSEMS that is static, it will simply remain locked in whatever year it is developed. With the DOSEMS, it is mandated that you build in capability and capacity for change. This means you are going to have to spend money to buy knowledge and vision to assure you are building a dynamic system and not a static system, and you will have to assure you are investing in architecture that can deliver that change.

Optimized means fully furnished and fully productive. Optimized implies multiple components of DOSEMS including: keyword market intelligence; best practices integration; organic tracking and reporting; keyword optimization campaigns; keyword verification; link popularity trending; linking optimization strategies; search engine saturation trending; meta-data optimization; indexing improvement; and analytics and ROI reporting. A truly optimized DOSEMS means you are obtaining the maximum possible productivity from the DOSEMS relative to return on investment.

Search Engine means the thousands upon thousands of data aggregators ranging from the massive Google to the tiny Gourdle (a search engine for people interested in gourd carving). There's a search engine for anything you can name. But, the only search engines that matter are the ones your customers use to find you and your product or service. Now, imagine that your niche is a constantly changing whirlpool of interest and focus on products. Your customers go to different places to find different products at different times based on logic, whim, access and memory. See why I begin with the term 'Dynamic' followed by 'Optimized' and then 'Search Engine'? It's not about the search engines; first, it's about dynamic change that is always optimized and which focuses on the customer finding and accessing your catalog, website, retail store or other channels. It is *absolutely not* about you putting yourself out there to be found and then sitting back and waiting for hits.

Marketing means the amalgam of all those things we do to sell a product. It's market segmentation, list identification, testing, targeting, branding, merchandising, copy, content, graphics, design and layout, circulation, and everything else that we lump into the catch-all called marketing. Marketing is everything you can possibly do to link the integrated, physical catalog and the online website, and other channels, to sell a product. It is the primary *objective* of the 'dynamic,' 'optimized,' 'search engine' effort, and in that order. As catalogers, we have an advantage over any other channel because marketing in all its glory is what we have been doing for several hundred years.

System means an organized, ongoing process with objectives and accountability. Developing a DOSEMS is *not* a project; rather, it is a core business within the overall catalog business. It is a key factor, a prime directive, a cardinal element and an investment. If you think of your facility, you could not be in business without a plumbing *system*, or a heating and air conditioning *system*, or an electrical *system*, or a telecommunications *system;* and you cannot be in business without a Dynamic Optimized Search Engine Marketing System. In other words: it is forever and it is expensive. Deal with it.

Like anything else, the DOSEMS requires planning. If you think of it as an inevitable strategic system that inserts your company into the path of qualified customers who are looking for products you sell, the necessary planning objectives become compelling and logical.

Increased Profitability. It is logical to expect that the DOSEMS will reduce costs and increase the speed of return on investment as well as producing increased profitability. Given the almost infinite segmentation capability and the targeting, the number of effective campaign cells increase and market penetration increases, provided the universe is large enough to sustain those variable cells. Your business becomes larger faster.

Branding. If you have true product brands, the DOSEMS allows widespread brand reinforcement. In-depth keyword analysis and linking can expose targeted and segmented ready-to-buy customers to not only the specific product they want but to your specific better branded product. Where the brand is also promoted by a strong catalog and online presence, the power of the brand and the DOSEMS is magnified.

Targeting. The DOSEMS allows for specific positioning from multiple access points of your catalog. You put your products directly in front of actively searching, ready-to-buy customers who want the precise product you sell. Not only does the dynamic form of positioning assure you of a more qualified customer, but also of a higher percentage chance of making a sale. When that targeting is complimented by a physical paper catalog, the odds of a successful sale increase dramatically. The secret of the DOSEMS master is to continually revise and redeploy the access points of the target positioning to follow the constant shifting and changing of the customer and prospect variable search choices, and to do so while integrating prospecting databases, cooperative databases and sophisticated list strategies.

Segmentation. The DOSEMS is highly flexible. You can slice and dice, add or delete engines or parameters to develop the capacity for specific segments of your market. If you want to find Safety Directors inside the trucking industry, those segmentations can be effectively described in the DOSEMS protocols. As a part of the optimization routine, the outcome segments to any market can be almost infinite. When coupled with masterful list and database usage, the percentage chance for precise segmentation is significantly enhanced.

Flexibility. For all of us who come out of a targeting, segmenting and testing background that can take four catalog cycles, two years and added cost to discover one key variable, the enormous flexibility of the DOSEMS is highly attractive and cheap. Because it is an online, electronic, immediate medium, the ability to define and redefine, segment and resegment, price and reprice, test and retest variable campaigns by market or product, or both, is an instantaneous occurrence with instantaneous results and a much faster return on investment. The secret of the DOSEMS master, however, is to choose relevant and maximally productive and profitable campaigns and not to let the seductive attraction of 'you can test anything' become addictive. And to *never forget the importance* of the larger testing requirement of the primary source of new customer names: response lists.

Feedback. Provided you have a market and products that generate sufficient, specific searches by qualified buyers, no other marketing channel can give you feedback and results faster than the DOSEMS. Compared to waiting months or even years, the DOSEMS campaign can be read, adjusted, augmented and redeployed often in days or weeks. The secret of the DOSEMS master is to keep the information and the resultant wisdom on a relevant basis. Feedback is only valuable if it *means* something. It is no different from the old secret of the catalog master concerning testing: *The point: Test shouts, not whispers.* Whatever you do with the DOSEMS, make sure it matters.

Keywords and Markets. I am convinced that DOSEMS technology will create new demand for trained linguists. The formulaic word descriptions of your catalog, products, services and your markets have patterns and cycles. Linguists are trained to understand these etymological linkages. The objective of this component is to identify every possible single and combined word description and phrase describing your business, as spoken or thought, by all segments of customers and prospects. Often, these are odd words, phrases or industry short cuts. Looking for the leading finance industry guru might include near-slang words like, 'financial silver-back' or the 'investment *eminence gris,'* as examples. The possibilities are endless and demand minds that are in synch with language and words, particularly the natural language and words of specific, targeted customers. As a further example, linguists are trained to know that a particular form of sandwich is called a torpedo in one part of the country, a grinder in another, a po-boy elsewhere, a hoagie in New Jersey, and probably three other names somewhere else. If you sell that sandwich, you better have keyword markets tightly defined with the right primary keywords. Remember, a searcher only sees your HTML link title and your meta-description tag, or an abstract. That's it. They don't see all your wonderful graphics content or copy. They don't see individual pages with your heart and soul in full view. They see a few *words,* a few *key words* that either cause them to click on you or pass you by.

Search Engine Submissions. Early in the beginning of search engine technologies, the only way to be noticed was to submit your keywords and meta-tags to every search engine individually. Then, search engine submission services sprouted up that would do the work for you. Today, these free and paid submission routes are still available, but are no longer terribly effective due to the emergence of paid inclusion and pay-for-placement alternatives. Mastering the free submissions is essential and does no harm, but no longer is the pillar of search engine effectiveness. The problem with this elemental form of submission is there is no real measurement of effectiveness. You submit your keywords and information, hit the 'submit' button, and then wait for something to happen. It is not a proactive or dynamic process.

The components of a well-designed and dynamic DOSEMS are constantly changing, falling out of favor and being replaced with new approaches. Presently, paid search and various 'pay per' elements are found in comprehensive DOSEMS. Again, I believe these will be replaced with independent approaches that are totally controllable by the multi-channel direct marketer. The hyper-dynamic rate of change in search engine technology makes it impossible to provide a stable road map for this channel. Anything I might say here will be obsolete in a week. However, it is patently clear to me that search engine marketing is as important as database marketing was in the early 1990s. If we scroll ahead to 2016 and the twenty-fifth anniversary of online marketing, one of the formulating elements leading to success will have been search engine marketing.

Regardless of the present or ultimate form of search engine marketing, there will be measurements of effectiveness. One of those measurements should be a hierarchical listing showing what search access point the greatest number of customers come from. Perhaps Google will be number one with Yahoo number two, and so on down the list until the very minor search sources are found at the bottom. With that hierarchy, you can overlay it on your recency, frequency and monetary value hierarchies to discover what quality of customer is derived from the various search engines. You may be surprised. Perhaps an obscure, small search engine only accounts for two percent of your new search customers, but it delivers four times the average order value than the number one or two engines. *The point: Search is a comparative RFM measurement that cannot be ignored.*

TELEMARKETING: PICKERING

Outbound telemarketing is dead, right? Wrong. With the advent of the National Do Not Call Registry, many things in telemarketing changed. Some opportunities arose.

The days of carpet-bombing consumers with telemarketing calls extolling the virtues of this credit card or that one are over. Actually, they really weren't here at all. Telemarketing is expensive and many of the companies that over-did the outbound telemarketing learned quickly and scaled back the practice. Either that or they went out of business or were acquired.

The combination of the Do Not Call Registry along with a move toward sourcing more telemarketing jobs offshore has helped make telemarketing continuing and viable. The registry has helped identify and eliminate those people highly unlikely to respond at all out of the pool of prospects. Good for them, and good for the marketers. The move offshore of many telemarketing jobs is less clear. To be sure, it offers businesses the possibility of decreased costs. It also exports some jobs from the United States to places like India, the Philippines, and elsewhere. This is a fact of life in an economy that is globally connected.

To get the full measure of the potential of moving telemarketing activities offshore requires the same types of efforts that are required in the U.S. There is no substitute for training; in fact, the need is obviously greater when going off-shore. If the cost of making a call from India is one-third that of the cost in the U.S. and the effectiveness is fifty percent, there is some savings potential there. But, what if you had intensive training with your people on the ground in Bangalore three or six months a year? You could move the effectiveness to seventy-five percent or perhaps even on par with U.S. sourced calls. That is a great pay-off, but it requires hard work and finding the right people. Those people are hard to find, but if you can develop them it is a very worthwhile investment.

Opportunities continue to exist for in-bound telemarketing. In-bound calls are opportunities to actually interact with a customer, have a dialog. There is no better time to cement a relationship or make a cross-sell.

Thoughtful managers, directors, vice presidents and even presidents will make a point of periodically listening to calls. Quick calls are always a goal, take as little of the customer's time as possible. The intention for brief calls often leads the TM customer service representative to give short shrift to any cross-sell opportunities, or not make them at all. This underscores the need for regular training on cross-selling and up-selling, good systems to provide relevant cross-sell suggestions, and incentive programs. We have even reached the level of sophistication that effective cross-selling can be performed by automated means while the customer is holding for a confirmation number.

Telemarketing is something easily glossed over today but offers great opportunities for the Master Marketer to bring all channels to a high level of integration and effectiveness.

EMAIL: LIBEY

The email channel, I believe, is encapsulated within the context of three other channels: 1) catalog; 2) telemarketing; and 3) online. By this, I mean that email must be a part of the tactics of those three channels to be maximally effective. By definition, then, email is a permission-based channel.

Consider Amazon or Expedia. Confirming emails for orders placed and travel arrangements booked are immediate and acceptable to the customers; in fact, emails are *part of the process*. That is what *encapsulated email* means to me: part of the process. When it is part of the process, the process can be expanded because you have access and acceptability. The email can be a process element for catalog purchasing, telephone purchasing, or online purchasing. The email can also up sell, cross sell or present specific, time-limited offers. It can do these things because there is the established acceptance of the email by the customer. In this context, email is good; in almost any other context, email can be negative.

One of the great advantages of the email channel is immediate customer access. If a direct marketer is allowed to access an individual customer with pertinent information, product announcements, or other customer-defined, personal reasons for contact, that customer will read the email and will read it with a predisposition of interest. I happen to be an avid reader of everything published about Sherlock Holmes. When Amazon sends me an email about new Holmesian publications, not only do I read them, but I buy the products. Email and product affinity comfortably co-exist; therefore create and deploy email offers to product affinity clusters.

Several hierarchies can be constructed around the email channel. First, intensify efforts to capture email addresses, perhaps work and home, for all top performing RFM customers. Second, create the product hierarchy for those customers. Third, create email offers that integrate the top RFM segments with the top product affinity clusters. Fourth, begin the segmentation of top RFM customers and *individual* products and deploy fully individualized email offers.

Where sufficient customers exist, split these hierarchies into the respective catalog, online and telemarketing channels (or others) and compare for email performance. Does email work best when the top customers are catalog channel customers or online customers? Is the online channel email performance better than the telemarketing channel customer? Once you know the performance hierarchy for email *by channel,* you can optimize your allocation of email resources to take maximum advantage of the return. *The point: The email channel can benefit from RFM hierarchical analyses and segment prioritization.*

The other side of the email channel—non-encapsulated email—is less clear. Here, there is no 'part of the process' precedent; email is speculative, spam-like. The customer relationship is not accepted and access is not automatic. Much of the future of the channel is tied to privacy concerns and, perhaps, future legislation. Yet, email prospecting, where good names and addresses exist, has made significant advances in recent years. Logic again points to the future when the email address all but replaces the physical address for contact strategy, but that is a long way in the future; first, we must navigate the regulatory and privacy waters. Non-relationship email is, unfortunately, mostly about questionable offers; relationship email is all about product and merchant integrity, and that is where the future lies for the multi-channel direct marketer.

EMAIL: PICKERING

The thought of email killing land mail died about the same time the Internet bubble burst. Perhaps the 'irrational exuberance' about email being a magic bullet contributed to the bubble's burst. Meaningful discussion about email can only happen when we look at the prospecting and customer communications (house file) sides separately.

The current state of prospecting via email has been relatively stable the last couple of years. The number of quality, opted-in names on prospecting lists is small (a fraction of the land mail universe) but growing. Email lists continue to be substantially higher priced per thousand than land mail lists and generally no merge-purge can be done. Mailing a list at a time with no deduplication harkens back to mailing lists in the 1960s and 1970s.

It is difficult for many multi-product merchandisers to effectively prospect via email. It can be very effective for offers that are more singular: buy one product, subscribe to a newsletter, etc.

Continuing to communicate with customers via email is incredibly effective. In this instance, there is relevant purchase history available to make effective product offers. Embedded links can direct customers to specific landing pages (taking the place of key codes) so that meaningful tracking can be done.

Few marketers segment email addresses in any way. Even though most email records (once on the customer file) have a physical address, little or no analysis is done on demographics (age, income, etc.) or firmographics (SIC, employee size, etc.). Frequently this is because the number of customers with email addresses is so small.

One of the most often asked questions is how can a list owner get more records with email addresses? The email append services generally can give only a very small number of appends; generally this is not cost effective. There is the further issue of ethics: is it acceptable to append email addresses to customer records? Right or wrong, more and more direct marketers are simply not risking it.

The simple way is best: ask for the email address at the time of order no matter what the channel. Asking may not be enough, so make it worthwhile to the customer to give it. Provide tracking and confirmation information to them via an email. Tell the customers that you send relevant and money-saving offers to your best customers via email and you would like to include them in that group. If all else fails, offer them a discount off of their next order if you can email them a coupon. Any logical cost to acquire the address will be offset by increased retention of the customer and list rental revenue, if the email list is on the market.

When a meaningful number of customers have email addresses, RFM and optimal RFM segmentation should be performed. At this point, the mechanics are obvious: coordinate land mail campaigns with emails to alert the customer a catalog is on its way, and track RFM based on the presence of an email address. The same principles that helped direct marketers this far will guide us through email and whatever lies ahead.

AFFILIATE: LIBEY

The affiliate marketing channel relies on others to refer orders to you. Conceptually, that is a big difference from others *selling* your products, which is the *dealer* channel, or *wholesale*. Affiliate marketing is *cloning*.

The basis for affiliate marketing is, of course, commissions. Affiliates earn a commission for marketing your product and directing sales to you for fulfillment. Immediately we see that gross margin is reduced in this channel. In theory, the additional volume of business makes it possible to sustain the lower gross margin.

The wonder of American ingenuity is that we can always find a way to divide up the pie so that many can enjoy a small piece of dessert. We have organizations that will solicit and manage the affiliate relationships for you for a cut. We have affiliates who have other affiliates. To some extent, affiliate marketing has become a lot like multi-level marketing with 'downlines' and everyone being paid on someone else's efforts.

The primary benefit of the channel, however, is rapid market reach. You can get your company or products into niches you never knew existed and that you may never have found. Affiliate marketing creates share; the more reach, the more recognition; the more recognition, the more orders you get. Plus, many of those orders will come directly to you in the future, bypassing the affiliate.

If you have two hundred affiliates, probably only twenty or so of them are doing eighty percent of the affiliate sales. You need a way to focus on the affiliates that matter and that is RFM. Every affiliate has recency, frequency and monetary value information that can be scored. It is simple to create an affiliate RFM hierarchy. With that hierarchy, you can do two things: 1) identify which affiliates to allocate resources to; and 2) compare the affiliate channel hierarchy against the RFM hierarchies for all channels and determine where affiliate marketing scores on an intra-channel basis. Maybe it does better than catalog. Maybe the return on investment in affiliate marketing is better than the return on investment in pay per search marketing. *The point: Know where and when to use affiliate marketing, and who to use as affiliates.*

RETAIL: LIBEY

Ah, the nemesis of direct marketers. "To open retail stores, or not to open retail stores, that is the question." For some, it is Nirvana; for others, it is Hell. Direct marketing has a number of successful retailers; it also is littered with unsuccessful attempts. By and large, retailing seems to be a channel that is best begun by retailers. There seems to be more success with retailers who expand into the catalog and online channels than catalogers who expand into the retail channel. Perhaps retailers learn cataloging more easily than catalogers learn retailing.

Of course, exceptions are found. I look at truly great multi-channel marketers, such as Northern Tool + Equipment, and I find strong leadership in all channels driven by a simple, yet brilliant entrepreneurial vision: *Sell more stuff to more people any way we can.* Their retail channel is superb. Their online channel is superb. Their catalog channel is superb. They are among the very best multi-channel direct marketers as well as retailers. For Northern Tool + Equipment, the retail channel was a natural. Founder and CEO Don Kotula was *born* a multi-channel marketer and there is none better. For him, any and every channel is an opportunity to be fully developed in order to fulfill his company's mission: *Sell more stuff to more people any way we can.*

Direct marketing and retail seem to be converging. Direct marketers see the growth available to them through retail. Retailers see the database marketing advantages and customer service skills available to them through direct. There is an inevitable overlap emerging driven by the mega-retailers such as Wal-Mart, Target, Home Depot and others.

Retailers are focused on circles of market area twelve miles wide. They like to have stores inside those twelve mile circles so they overlap. Catalogers are focused on single names all over the country. Eventually, retailers will focus outward and catalogers will focus inward. Retailers will learn national circulation techniques and catalogers will learn to market in twelve mile concentrations. At that point, convergence will have arrived. The wild card in this converged future is the online channel. If direct marketers can dominate the online channel, they win; if retailers dominate the online channel, they win. The battleground, however, is clearly the online channel. Everything else will be fought to a draw. *The point: Sell more stuff to more people any way you can.*

That being said, recognize that not all retail customers are alike. The single most significant analytic advance that retail can make is to overlay recency, frequency and monetary value analysis on top of the retail purchasing history. Some retailers are becoming sophisticated in RFM analytics but, for the largest portion of retail, little sophistication exists. For the multi-channel direct marketer expanding into the retail channel, RFM analytics are routine. The same hierarchies of RFM performance, in all their diversity, exist for retail customers as they exist for catalog and online customers. The best multi-channel direct marketers will adopt not only hierarchical comparisons between the retail channel and the other channels, but in-depth RFM hierarchical comparisons between *each* retail location.

The final comment will be met with great disbelief. As of this writing, less than three percent of all catalog companies are single channel having only a catalog. Ninety-seven percent of all catalogs are multi-channel. Within twenty years at the outside, fifty percent or more of the multi-channel catalog companies will include retail stores. Less than fifty percent of all multi-channel catalog marketers will *not* have retail stores. It does not require too much of a stretch to conclude that the direct marketing industry will be much more consolidated at that point.

WHOLESALE: LIBEY

The wholesale channel is a cornucopia of opportunity for multi-channel direct marketers. Because of the many opportunities, this could be the 'sleeper' channel of the next twenty years that produces numerous mega-companies with multiple channel domination.

Consider the logic of wholesaling. By and large, wholesaling is a faceless channel creating few inter-channel constraints. Catalog and retail customers have no awareness of wholesalers and the risk of alienating customers is minimal. Wholesaling to channel competitors is one way of sharing in the competitive pie. Wholesaling to the irritating, low-price 'net gnats' that compete with you online is almost refreshing. Direct marketers are already expert at fulfillment and distribution. In recent years, they have become far more sophisticated in supply chain logistics. Wholesaling is easily integrated into the various systems and operational structures already in place. You are shipping ones and twos now; there is no reason why you can't ship thirty-sixes and seventy-twos. It's not a foreign concept. Many of the relationships you have now are the same suppliers you would use in a wholesale operation. As purchasing volume increases, your gross margin increases which helps your direct channel business. On the wholesale side, gross margin drops, but volume grows. The key is fixed costs and productivity. If you can add a wholesale component without significant increases in labor or facilities, you benefit from the synergies at all levels.

For importers, the wholesale channel allows for larger purchases at better cost. Consolidators are able to put together larger shipments and purchase at prices that are more favorable. And, to some extent, being able to set prices at the wholesale level creates advantage over competitors in other channels.

On the marketing side, direct marketers already know the products and how to sell them to end users. The addition of wholesale sales is not a giant step. Plus, direct marketers can use the various direct channels to develop the wholesale side of the business.

Numerous business-to-business direct marketers have entered the wholesale channel quietly over the past few years. Consumer direct marketers are slower, but there are a few. As price becomes more prevalent as a trigger, expanding the channel mix as well as gross revenues becomes increasingly attractive. With increased costs for direct channel operations, such as postage and paper, the relative cost-efficiency of wholesale marketing becomes attractive.

The final impetus for the wholesale channel, to me, is the logical, concentric expansion of market share. Vertical integration from manufacturing to wholesale to retail has fallen out of favor; yet, there are a number of very smart direct marketers who *are* vertically integrated and who *do* manufacture, wholesale and retail the same products, some even operate successful dealer networks, as well. *The point: In a consolidated environment, the wholesale channel is an opportunity not an impediment.*

CHANNEL AND RFM OPTIMIZATION: LIBEY

After product, channel has to be next to be optimized with full RFM information. The benefits are too great to ignore. For some, the RFM optimization is fully furnished with the achievement of knowledge to the channel level. At that point, we know who is buying most recently, who is buying most frequently, who is spending the most money, the products they are buying, and the channel they buy from. We also have a five-point reference for hierarchical comparative segmentation analyses. The number of potential comparative analyses is large, more than even the most advanced companies can manage. But success in RFM optimization is built upon the single question, "What if . . .?" If we could get there, what would we have? More than we have now.

CHANNEL AND RFM OPTIMIZATION: PICKERING

Channel has great potential to improve the ability of RFM to discriminate high potential customers from those with lesser potential. At this point, the mechanics of that analysis should be apparent.

Whereas there is much product information in any marketing database, there is less information on channel. Important information gets lost coming from the web server to the marketing database or from the call center or from wherever fax orders arrive. The biggest challenge to RFM + channel is not a lack of understanding of how to do it, or even a lack of appreciation for its importance. More than anything else, the ideal of optimization suffers from a lack of good information and organization. Meeting that challenge will help turn reams and reams of data into actionable information, knowledge and wisdom.

Chapter 7 Position

PRICE: LIBEY

Positioning is the perception the marketplace has of your company based on at least six elements: price, quality, service, speed, selection and access. Other positioning elements exist, but these six are most often central to a multi-channel direct marketing position. Looked at another way, position is a vantage point from which prospects and customers determine whether they want to do business with you. As an example, what do you think of when you see a Wal-Mart ad? Now, what do you think of when you see a Williams-Sonoma catalog? Those two *very* different perceptions are the sum of your beliefs and vantage points of each company based on price, quality, service, selection, access and, in this comparison, image. Position tends to be either in-your-face or elusive. Some companies are masters of defining and presenting a clear position; some are tentative and fuzzy about what and who they are.

In an ideal world, position determines almost everything. If a company opts to be known only for low prices, as does Wal-Mart, that choice of a single position determines the flimsy, cheap plastic bags, the eyesore-blue color of the stores, the littering of the surrounding neighborhood, the rare cleaning of the carpets in the entryways, the purely utilitarian shelving and lack of attractive displays, uninformed, part-time, minimum-wage employees, the absence of meaningful customer service, and the overarching aura of lowest-common-denominator-mediocrity that so typifies the Wal-Mart experience. In contrast, the multi-position choices of Williams-Sonoma determine taste, style, elegance, informed and friendly staff, high-design, spotlessness, extreme customer services, and the overarching aura of highest quality and value. Decisions about creative, logos, training, website design, packaging, products, wages, location—literally, everything—begin and end with the corporate position. That's in an ideal world. In reality, position is partially ignored and the elements get confused.

When doing the preliminary interview work with CEOs to begin the process for long range strategic planning, I always ask two questions:

1. What is your exit strategy? Until the objective of the end is known, we cannot create a strategy to get there. You operate businesses very differently depending on whether they will be sold to a competitor, sold to an investment group, given to the children, structured as an employee buy-out, or liquidated for cash. For each end game, there is a different strategy for almost every interim business decision and direction.

2. What is your position? Once the exit strategy and the end game are known and described, the position necessary to get there with the greatest amount of business valuation can be determined and all tactical and strategic decisions flow from there. If it's all about price, certain things become important. If it's all about service, certain other things become important. The integration of channels is determined by the position. The design of catalogs is determined by position. The

product selection is determined by position. Position is the elephant we ride on to get to the Taj Mahal.

One of the positioning points is price. Three price positions are found: 1) high price leader; 2) mid-price player; and 3) low price leader. The first sets the price standard for the market or product group; the second hides in the weeds and adjusts; the third battles for share on price. None of the three is the best position and none is the worst position; each is a viable position provided all other positioning elements are in synch and integrated properly.

If all of direct marketing were organized as a circus, then the companies that position themselves on price would be the high flyers, the aerialists, the trapeze artists operating without a net. Price always performs in the center ring and is not very forgiving. With a price position, you are always holding your breath. Have you ever noticed that the businesses that operate on pure price, such as commodity traders buying and selling corn, wheat, pork bellies, foreign currencies, crude oil (or any other classic 'good'), buy and sell on fractions of a cent? A transaction on the Chicago Board of Trade for twenty contracts of wheat (100,000 bushels) may be done for as little as one-quarter of a cent gain per bushel. The profit per trade is only $250, but if you do that over and over one hundred times a day, you make $25,000 a day. Of course, the floor trader standing next to you is probably willing to do the business for one-quarter of a cent less. When you are the high price or the low price leader, there is always someone who will do the business for a fraction of a cent less. That is the problem with the price position.

The mid-price player position takes you out of the center ring. Unfortunately, that means you are just another act and are relegated to the side rings. As the price leaders parry and dodge, the mid-price player works the spread and makes a little more or a little less depending on the price extremes. Most business-to-business direct marketers like to be mid-price players, never appearing on the radar screen at either the highest or the lowest price. There is a nice bit of business to be done just working 'the middles.' After all, that's where most of the buyers will be found. At least until the unholy Wal-Martization of America is complete.

The turn of the century will be remembered as the time when price became primary in the mind of the American consumer. Prior to the advent of online technology, price comparison was a *physical* and *intellectual* effort involving on-site or telephone research. With Internet access, price comparison has become an *automated* and *technological* process involving search engines and shopping aggregators. What previously took perhaps weeks, now takes only nanoseconds. The effect of this is, of course, that most purchases going forward will involve price comparison, thereby forever establishing price as the primary driver of commerce, an evolution of the buying process that remains to be evaluated for its future positive or negative effects.

A curious *ménage a trois* exists between price, product and channel that is seldom understood or explored. A company like Northern Tool + Equipment sells many products with price ranging from a few dollars to thousands of dollars. There are binoculars for $9.99 and big NorTrac tractors for $7,999. If you examine price, you may find that price levels define the purchase channel. Most people want to climb up on the tractor and drive one before buying, and, for them, that means a retail channel is essential. Tasco binoculars can be sold online or in the catalog. A hierarchy similar to RFM is indicated. Take price point groups ($1-$100; $101-$200; $201-$500; $501-$1,000, etc.) and overlay them on channel transactions. Which channel is responsible for the bulk of sales between $1 and $100; which for $201-$500; and so on? The three-way clustering of price, product and channel may be quite surprising. Online price thresholds have increased over time; diamonds are routinely purchased online for $10,000 or more. The benefit to be gained is in the alignment of product and channel presentation, or perhaps channel exclusivity. There is a great deal of manipulation needed to maximize the relationship between these three elements. If price is the position, then price, product and channel must be understood totally.

Another aspect of price as a position is universe. In that context, price cleaves into only two segments: the luxury market and all others. If we accept Wal-Mart's ubiquity and realize that low price appeals to nearly everyone in society, then the only other remaining market is the luxury customer who would never be caught dead in a Wal-Mart. Price position defines the competition. If the luxury universe is small, each competitor has to battle for share. If the low price universe is enormous, each competitor is a 'me-too' and can attract share more easily. Problems occur when the strategic position is not compatible with the available target universe. A high-end, luxury business with a strategic growth target of two billion dollars may never be able to reach that level of sales because there are fewer and fewer people in the universe who are *not* driven by price. Similarly, a low price leader could fail miserably in an attempt to penetrate the high-end, luxury market simply because too few luxury buyers will purchase from a 'down-image' company.

Whether the multi-channel direct marketer can successfully maintain a variety of price positions is an interesting question. In my opinion, multiple price positions under one brand or company name, but operating in different channels, trains the customer to migrate to the low price channel, a margin eroding strategy. If you price your products higher in a catalog, with a lower price incentive for ordering online, and you also merchandise a separate clearance or low price website, you will ultimately drive the bulk of the customers to the low end and train them to wait for the clearance offerings. That will only work if it is your expressed strategic decision to exit the high and middle price positions for the low price position and compete for greater share in a larger universe.

A multiple price position *can* be maintained, however, when the separate positions are held as unrelated brands or company names. A catalog can secure the high end of the market under one brand or company name. Online price savings can be offered under a separate name or brands, and the low price, clearance market can be served with either flyers or an online site, or both. Clearly, products will be different in each channel and at each price position. A number of direct marketing companies who employ this positioning strategy also maintain separate mailing addresses, company profiles, even key employee information for each operation. Fulfillment and operations may be completely consolidated, but the customer is never aware of that fact. The active principle of this price positioning strategy is to compete with yourself to expand market share in segments you otherwise never would have benefited from. *The point: Sell more stuff to more people any way you can, at all prices.*

QUALITY: LIBEY

Quality and price are inextricably linked. Re-read the previous section and simply substitute the word 'quality' for 'price' and it fits with only a few nuances. As a buying concept, quality is much more of a positive position than price. Quality *justifies* price. Quality is a non-threatening position.

The classic 'good, better, best' is a multiple quality position that never quite focuses on price. Price is only implied. Without the blatant and in-your-face price, the buyer is allowed to quietly and privately decide on 'high quality,' 'mid-quality' or 'economy quality.' How much nicer that sounds than 'expensive,' 'run-of-the-mill' or 'cheap.' Quality is more of a psychological position than a rigid price position; quality can be finessed. For these reasons, a quality position may be a better way to arrive at the same positioning goal as price. Think of contributions to charity. Donors never mention an actual amount. They say things like, "We are major supporters of the symphony," a quality-of-giving kind of statement that conjures up images of great, bulging bags of cash and a bevy of eternally grateful bassoonists. Indirectly, the positioning is clear.

The three categories of quality position structure are much more compatible than those within pure price positions. The three are:

1. Single quality position. Most often, these are luxury, standard or mid-quality, and economy. Here, the direct marketer chooses a single quality grade of product across all channels with no price strategy differences.

2. Multiple quality position. Here, the direct marketer offers—within each channel—product choices in the 'good, better, best' categories. A single product may have three quality grades and three different price levels and will be merchandised similarly across all channels.

3. Multiple quality and channel position. Here, the direct marketer offers 'good, better, best' products separately in different channels or under different names. The 'best' products may be offered by catalog and be branded under a unique brand name. The 'better' products may be offered online under another name and brand. The 'good' products may be offered in an auction format online only and have only generic product names. Because of the channel opaqueness, price levels can be disparate.

Thinking back to the RFM hierarchies of product price and customer segments of RFM performance, consider a slightly different comparison. Identify your individual products (not SKUs, but primary products) as high quality, mid-quality, or economy, or use good, better and best. With the hierarchy structured that way, overlay the top performing RFM customers and correlate the products they purchased to the quality level. Are the top RFM customers buying mostly best products, better products or good products? Are the lowest performing RFM customers buying mostly good or economy products? Are the cash cows buying mostly better or mid-quality products? If these relationships of quality and segmentation were looked at over twenty rolling quarters of history, what would the trends look like overall and in each channel? With that historical perspective, you are ready to consider the strategic question for a quality position: where is the business going relative to quality? If the customer trend is to lower quality and no product or price concessions to that trend have been made, you are losing share. If the trend is to higher quality and no product enhancements have been made, you are losing share. If the trend is going nowhere, you are losing share. *The point: Quality, as a position, is always migratory. Lead, follow or lose share.*

SERVICE: LIBEY

By service, I do not mean customer service or fulfillment service; they are a given, not a position. I mean *expertise*. A position driven by expert knowledge is a strong position.

Found most often in business-to-business, multi-channel direct marketing, service revolves around unique knowledge. The founders are often professionals in specific career fields, such as health care, water treatment, human resources, and compliance within a narrow industry. Their exceptional knowledge is a resource for others in that particular field and their companies become the trusted destination for products and services. A good example is USABlue-Book, a catalog serving the municipal water and wastewater market. The company's experts are operating engineers and actually know how to run a water department and how to install and use the equipment and products they sell. For local water departments and wastewater plants, they are consultants on call. In consumer marketing, the service position is found generally within narrow interest markets, such as hunting, fishing, equestrian, hobby supplies, and others where specialized knowledge or technique is involved. A good example would be a direct marketing company selling specialized glazes for pottery. Potters unsure about kiln temperature and the effect on a particular glaze would rely upon the company for precise information on how to control temperature for the glaze being sold. In both examples, the service position is best described as providing 'go-to' and 'how-to' information.

A service position is valued over a price position when the product is specialized. The price position is valued over the service position when the product is a commodity. It is difficult to support a service position when the product is rolls of cheap packing tape. It is easy to support a service position when the product is a custom-produced DNA reagent. Stated another way, the gross margin of a service position product is usually higher than the gross margin of a non-service position product.

Through its exceptional customer service and its innovative customer access portals, Lands' End became a company associated with a service position as well as a quality position. The company began with a quality position and then evolved a customer service position and a customer access position where expertise was immediately available, live on the telephone or live online. The result is a double-barreled position that creates a high barrier to entry and above average customer retention.

To arrive at an understanding of where service fits, it is necessary—once again—to create a hierarchy of RFM and overlay it with a hierarchy of product segmented into service-dependent products and non-service-dependent products. Every product can be classified as either service reliant or non-reliant. When this segmentation is overlaid on the top performing RFM customers, what is the service profile? Are your best customers purchasing predominately service-dependent products? If so, is there a service position culture within the company to support this finding? At the other extreme, are your worst performing RFM customers purchasing predominately service-dependent products? If so, what is that expensive service emphasis and focus producing from this poor-performing customer segment? *The point: Is the service position in line with the economics?*

If the customer seeks out your company because of your service, what channel is the primary service channel? Is it inbound telephone? Is it live online response? Is it extensive specification and usage information published in the catalog? Is it retail store visits? By segmenting product by service classification and overlaying it on RFM performance, you will see who buys service and who does not buy service. For those who buy service, knowing the preferred channel is essential. If all of the service requests are coming on low gross margin products and coming over the telephone, there would appear to be a need to create alternative service access systems that will answer these needs at a greatly reduced cost. This will free up knowledgeable, expensive staff for developing and supporting high gross margin relationships and product sales.

SPEED: LIBEY

One wonders whether speed is a position any longer. The direct marketing world in recent years has almost universally settled in on the three to seven working days range of delivery with options for overnight and second day delivery. The position of speed has really been usurped by FedEx and United Parcel Service. Their definitions of delivery speed and the costs of delivery have homogenized the speed position until it is perceived by the customer as being a FedEx or UPS position and not that of the merchant. The only thing left for the direct marketer is to offer free delivery, reduced delivery costs, or a bargain upgrade to overnight or two-day delivery, all of which reduce profitability. If viewed dispassionately, FedEx and UPS have done direct marketing a favor by taking away control of the delivery speed and cost position. They have leveled the playing field and created a non-issue. Speed and cost are what they are. The customer can only control them if they want immediate overnight delivery at additional cost. The merchant can only control them by discounting or giving away shipping charges. The only actual position to be exploited by direct marketing is within the retail channel (where it exists) with in-store pick-up. And even then, a cost exists for speed. I just looked at a book on Barnes & Noble. It was listed for $5.60 online plus shipping or I could order it for in-store pick up for $9.95.

Where I *do* believe speed matters is when a product is being compared online. When the product is identical, the comparison hierarchy tends to be price and delivery speed, in that order. Where price is identical, speed wins. Where speed of one merchant is faster than another, speed wins provided price is *about* the same. Where price is lower and delivery speed is significantly longer, it becomes a toss-up depending on the amount of the price difference. When a price is discounted but comes to about the same amount as another online merchant when expedited shipping is added back, I will order from the other online merchant whose price and shipping are not artificially manipulated. The determining issue has shifted from speed and price to trust.

Years ago, I was in the fresh seafood catalog business, lobsters and clams and diver's scallops by overnight delivery anywhere in the U.S. Quality and speed were interchangeable positions. If the customer wanted the very best Maine lobster, quality was the position. If the customer wanted live lobsters for tomorrow's dinner, speed was the position. *The point: Speed is a supporting position.* The seafood business taught me one of the only two truths I have learned in my many years in business: never be in a business with a living inventory. The other truth is never, ever, under any circumstance, pass up the opportunity to use a bathroom.

SELECTION: LIBEY

Selection as a position is seductive. It is seductive for the customer because everything you could ever want is available. It is seductive for the direct marketer because everything you could ever want is available. For the customer, the position means *choices.* For the direct marketer, it means *inventory.*

Selection often becomes a position accidentally. We realize one day that the catalog has become so large that we are now the selection-leader. Where this phenomenon is actually 'bloating,' the position is dicey. Where it is planned and managed, the position is powerful.

Selection is more often a position found in business-to-business direct marketing than in consumer direct marketing. It lends itself to components and parts, yet consumer sectors that are seasonal, style or fashion-driven can be positioned on selection also, such as hunting and fishing, jewelry and beads, hobby and crafts, and knitting and quilting. The premise of selection is to exclude competition based on breadth and depth of product. Selection uses inventory as a barrier to entry. One of the justifications for product depth has always been, "It looks like we have a full line." True, but there is a cost associated with that product breadth and depth. When the product life cycle is out of control and the inventory tips into obsolescence, the business is in jeopardy, and this so often occurs in direct marketing companies that are positioned on the slippery slopes of selection.

One of the biggest unknowns with selection is how to measure it as a position. When you have fifty SKUs, eighty percent of the customers will buy ten of them. When you have one hundred SKUs, eighty percent of the customers will buy fifteen of them. When you have 5,000 SKUs, eighty percent of the customers will buy five hundred of them. Having forty extra, non-selling products is very different from having 4,500 extra products, especially just to 'look like we have a line.' Selection goes directly to product life cycle management. The classic RFM hierarchy is laid against product sales and the matter of selection is objectively evaluated.

Selection by channel must also be considered. Where is the cost of advertising a large selection more efficient: in the catalog or on the website? In which channel is the return on selection investment highest? Selection relative to retail square footage versus website storage versus catalog pages is entirely quantifiable and the return on investment can be calculated. For catalogers, advertising and selection are normally quantified by square inch analysis, but 'squinch' never quite gets to the issue of *depth* of product selection. For direct marketers to master this position, we will learn from retailers. The mystery about selection that baffles many direct marketers was long ago solved by the grocery industry. This position is best studied from outside the direct marketing industry, because we simply have so little experience with the requisite metrics.

ACCESS: LIBEY

Positioning our businesses on customer access is a very new position. In the recent past, there was mail. In the 1980s, the telephone came into its majority. In the late 1980s, the fax became a form of access. Since then, online access has rapidly gained favor and shares almost half of customer access with telephony and some residual mail.

But, the real revolution in access as a position is the recognition that customers should be given the opportunity to do business with our companies as *they* determine. Access is a customer position, not a merchant position. The customer determines how much access the merchant must have and whether access is the key ingredient. The customers took over this position about 1995-1998. In that three-year period, the customers told the direct marketers how they were going to access their businesses in the future. Some direct marketers heard them and began expanding their channels, particularly the online channel. Some did not. As this is being written, about three percent of all catalogers *still* don't have a website. They are the ones who probably don't have a toll-free telephone number yet either.

Where are the orders coming from? Segment all orders by access channel. Look at first-time orders by access and then subsequent orders by access. Observe the migration. Are customers coming in for the first order by catalog and telephone and then migrating immediately to online access? If so, that tells you something.

Create the classic RFM hierarchy of top performing customers and overlay on it the original source of their orders. Are the best customers coming in by catalog or online? Are the worst customers coming in by catalog or online? But, most important, how do those top performing and worst performing customers access you *after* the first order and what is the subsequent trend?

While it is a given that all forms of access must be offered to the customer, it is also a given that all of those access activities, over time, will funnel down into one or two *primary* continuing channels of access, and those will most likely be telephone and online. What you have to know is the migration or percentage change in the catalog-assisted, online access. When catalog-assisted online access begins to migrate to pure online access without the physical, paper catalog assist, you have to be aware of that change and positioned to capture the shift in access that the customer is signaling.

POSITION AND RFM OPTIMIZATION: LIBEY

In French cuisine, there are numerous classic sauces, but there are only five Mother Sauces, those from which all other sauces begin. Position is similar in the creation of a great multi-channel direct marketing company. There are three Mother Positions: price, quality and service. Some believe you can only have two of the three; I believe you can have all three, but only one can be dominant. I also believe an integrated position is required across all channels, although there is room for nuances.

Of all positions, I fear price and selection the most. Either of them can harm a business quickly. The eternal legacy of direct marketing, regardless of the channel, is quality and service. It is how we emerged and grew as a powerful and universal industry. You cannot go wrong with a position of quality and service; you can quickly go wrong with price and selection; speed and access are simply part of the necessary structure. Your decisions about position come down to maintaining quality and service and carefully evaluating price and selection. It's really that simple.

I will close with a tantalizing 'what if' question: What if you could assign every customer with position and access codes that identified the position that first attracted them and the position that kept them coming back and identified their choice of access?

By creating an optimized RFM hierarchy of top performing Stars and worst performing Dogs, as well as Cash Cows and Mystery Meat, you could overlay on them position and access, and position and access migration.

What if . . . ?

Chapter 8 Market

CORE MARKET: LIBEY

Core markets are the bread and butter, the heart of the business. They are described as specific groups of businesses, such as elementary teachers, veterinarians, golf pros, safety managers, or restaurants; and consumers, such as grandparents, quilters, aging men, pre-teens, or young mothers. As direct marketers, we describe our core markets by describing our core customers and our core products: "We sell auto body shop supplies to auto body shops." Sometimes we qualify our core market: "We only sell to body shops west of the Mississippi," or, "We specialize in body shops that restore antique cars." Sometimes, we qualify and limit our core market: "We only sell to body shops west of the Mississippi that restore antique cars." In each description of the core market, the universe has become smaller and smaller until it has become a niche market. Direct marketers thrive on niche markets, especially when they are easily identifiable, accessible, involve high gross margin consumable products, have no seasonality, and are recession-proof. If the products can be drop-shipped, that's an added plus.

The auto body market description above is an example of what I call the *reductive market strategy*. The core market—auto body—is first reduced geographically, then by specialization. The core market distills from, say, seven thousand shops to one thousand shops. The reductive market strategy begins with those one thousand shops and develops the antique car restoration parts and supplies business to its fullest potential. When that niche is fully developed, the reductive strategist will drill down to the next niche: Studebakers. "We sell to body shops west of the Mississippi that restore antique Studebakers." The core market has been further reduced from one thousand shops to maybe ten shops, a sub-niche that may or may not be large enough to be profitable. The reductive strategy implies more and more products for smaller and smaller niches. If the core auto body business has five thousand SKUs, the full Studebaker restoration business may have ten thousand SKUs dedicated to replacement parts for all of the models and model years Studebaker ever produced. The reductive market strategy begins with the broad core market (auto body) and ends with niche dominance: "We're the King of Studebaker Restoration." It starts with broad knowledge and experience and drills down and focuses to turn that knowledge and experience into niche dominance.

The opposite strategy, I call the *inductive market strategy*. Here we begin with the fully furnished Studebaker restoration niche. The niche is then expanded, perhaps by geography or specialization. The Studebaker restoration market may be expanded east of the Mississippi and Ford antique restoration parts are added west of the Mississippi. Once the Studebaker and Ford antique parts markets are dominated, Packard is added, and Cord, and then Chevrolet. At some point, the antique auto restoration market is fully furnished and the inductive strategy would call for expansion to the contemporary market and the general bodywork and parts business for all cars.

Each of these core market strategies is dependent on universe and product. The universe has to be of sufficient size to sustain the business and there must sufficient product demand, regardless of the direction chosen. Also, each of the core market strategies has a specific learning curve. It may be easier to accomplish the reductive objective of becoming the King of Studebaker Restoration by starting at the general auto body level and working deeper into the specialty niche. Broad knowledge tends to apply downstream. It may be more difficult to become the inductive King of Auto Body by starting as the King of Studebaker Restoration and working toward the broad core market. Specific knowledge may not always apply upstream. Both core market strategies can be debated for their growth potential and efficacy; however, the only quantitative measurement is a detailed financial model of both approaches to determine which produces the greatest return on investment.

Regardless of the approach, direct marketers benefit from a market analysis utilizing recency, frequency and monetary value information. In business-to-business companies, use the RFM hierarchy of performance and overlay it with a hierarchy of Standard Industrial Classification. This will reveal whether the core market is well defined or diffuse. If the top performing RFM customers are within the core market definition and SICs, then the core market strategy is likely correct. If, however, the top performing RFM customers are from SICs outside the core market, there is good reason to assess the market strategy. Similarly, a core market and performance correlation for the low performing RFM customers may be equally revealing. A second overlay of product hierarchy will provide additional insight into the core market strength or weakness. Top performing customers that come from the core market SICs but are not buying core market products would indicate the existence of product obsolescence, pricing pressure, channel migration, or possibly all three.

In consumer businesses, a similar RFM hierarchy of top performing customers overlaid with specific demographic profiling may provide information that indicates a core market shift. As an example, a beauty and skin care business targeted to women twenty-five to thirty-five years old may migrate to women thirty-five to fifty-five years old, a very different universe having very different product interests. Evidence of such a migration must be explored for the cause. Possibly product managers have skewed new products to older women, or prospecting circulation has expanded to older segments, or older women have a growing interest in younger women's products. *The point: Your core market must be analyzed constantly to understand migration trends, shifts, or competitive deterioration, and RFM will assist you in creating that awareness.*

The core market can be a trap. Over the years, I have heard many owners and CEOs say they have never gone outside their core market. Where the core had a large universe, this intense focus has often been beneficial and the companies have prospered. Where the core universe was small, the constant focus on the core market has often stunted growth and, thereby, valuation. Frankly, I believe the core market strategy is quite often a reflection of an owner's philosophy about growth and achievement. I will reprise some thoughts on this philosophic quandary and discuss the strategic merits of 'big' versus 'small.'

For a number of years now, I have been asking CEOs and owners of direct marketing companies a difficult question: why do you have to grow? I have endured the look that says, "This guy's not too bright." I have received the empty stares and the minds devoid of another possible viewpoint. I have heard the silence and the unformed replies. It is simply inconceivable that a direct marketing company—or any other type of business—should not grow. After all, continuous growth is the basis of all wealth building. Without growth, the valuation of a company declines. It's what we learned from Keynes and Drucker: "We *must* grow next year because that's . . . well . . .what we do!" Maybe. Maybe not.

The growth knotholes for direct marketing companies are legendary. The first is at $1 million, then $5 million, next at $10 million, then $20 million, a big jump to $60 million, then $100 million, and increments of $50 and $100 million thereafter. Each knothole of growth requires significant changes of people, technology, channels, management, circulation, facilities, and market and product concentrations; in fact, all aspects of the company. If the truth were known, what we *really* do is manage knotholes.

Each successive growth knothole, in turn, becomes successively more difficult to manage. People problems become more time consuming and thorny; channel management becomes complicated and macro and micro analytic; technology problems become more complex and abstruse; talent and skill issues consume time and attention; management becomes more politicized and distant; circulation and contact strategies require ever-widening resources and thinking; facilities are ever-expanding and more expensive; logistics and globalization become overwhelming; markets are elusive and ever-changing; products require a constant battle against margin creep and staleness; and one soon forgets what exactly it was we set out to do.

We can argue that the first three knotholes are probably necessary. Businesses having sales of less than $10 million just don't pack on the requisite valuation to assure a sufficient 'cash out.' After all, one really doesn't want to have to live with the kids. But, at $20 million, a business having a sound footprint should be throwing off, say, $3 million a year in adjusted EBITDA. At a seven time multiple, it is worth $21 million. What's wrong with that? Where is it written that one must go on to the $60 million knothole, probably $5 million in earnings at that point, and a $35 million valuation? What is the difference between $21 million and $35 million, really? When it comes time to cash out, the amount starts to be somewhat irrelevant after a certain level. What may be more relevant, however, is the cost to get through the $60 million knothole. And that would be, not insubstantially, the cost in risk, time, stress, emotional well-being, pressures of responsibility, and other quality of life issues.

Suppose, briefly, that we ignore the common wisdom and eschew growth. Let us assume that we have a $20 million business producing $3 million in EBITDA and, after taxes and reserves, we have $1.5 million in personal income. Under the 'grow or perish' theory, one would endlessly expend enormous energy, time and resources to achieve a fifteen percent growth, top and bottom line. Under the anti-knothole theory, one would now devote equal amounts of energy, time and resources to maintaining, strengthening and perfecting the core market and the business at its current levels. In effect, doing more of what you do well, a strategic approach that develops true mastery of a niche business. Theoretically, this allows more time, energy and resources for meaningful endeavors outside of the business while providing a stable and secure business environment for owners and loyal employees. And you get to keep all of the $1.5 million each year instead of plowing it back into the business.

The anti-knothole theory demands, as its ante, focus and concentration on people, technology, management, channels, circulation, facilities, markets and products *in a known core market and universe*, and that can't be all bad. This places one in the constant position of refining and improving a known quantity, rather than exploring and mining an unknown quantity. In short, *value is added through solidity*. In difficult economic times, or in a major cyclical reversal, this may be a potent recognition.

If you eliminate chasing growth, you can refocus your efforts on the proven trident of direct marketing: circulation, products and channel integration. In the constant growth chase, these foundational elements are rarely, if ever, brought to an optimum peak performance. There is never sufficient time to shore up list segmentation, RFM and circulation testing to reach the point of absolute mastery; the growth chase soaks up too much time and energy and all of the concentration is spent on people, finance, cost-controls and integration. When automated growth is eliminated, optimization of circulation is liberated. Time is made available to consult extensively with your list broker and to develop comprehensive circulation strategies and testing approaches that create absolute, proprietary circulation solidity and optimal investment prospecting in each channel. Similarly, time and energy is available to focus on a fully furnished analytic understanding of customer retention, behavior and affinities, all of which lead to greater integrated, multi-channel marketing mastery. And, perhaps most important, time is freed up to allow you to zero in on product life cycles, new product development, remerchandising of existing products, analysis of product performance, product profitability, better purchasing for margin enhancement, and reduction and elimination of product obsolescence, all of which lead to product mastery and further improved earnings, *which you get to keep.*

This strategy improves what is already successful rather than diluting the existing success for the unknown and elusive promise of growth. Doing more of what you know better is also likely within the capability and capacity of existing, talented managers who would be more motivated and happy doing what they know and what they do well. There is little here that can do harm.

In difficult times, this core market strategy makes sense. In difficult times, one digs in and preserves. In good times, one explores and expands, primarily through adjacent market expansion and acquisitions. The factor that determines the strategy is *money.* Those that have sufficient money to both navigate the economic cycles *and* to invest in growth will do so; those that do not have sufficient money to do both are best advised to maintain, strengthen and preserve what they do have.

The classic customer migration strategies apply, as well. High cost companies with high customer acquisition costs and high RFM customers come under pressure from low cost companies. Low cost companies attempt to steal your good customers and trade off their poor customers. If you are fighting to retain valued customers and to protect your position, it is counterproductive to acquire new, low value customers simply for the sake of growth. In good times, you can afford to create new customers for growth, but in difficult times, you may only be able to afford maintaining your best customers. It's all about choices and timing.

For many direct marketing companies faced with an increasing financial cost to obtain growth, as well as an increased emotional cost, it may be advisable to consider whether growth is, indeed, an appropriate strategy. Notice, however, that earnings must remain at optimal levels for this choice to make sense. If earnings begin to decrease, the inherent value of the direct marketing company begins to decrease, and that would be undesirable. But a stable business, having solid foundational elements, producing above average earnings, maintaining its market and competitive position, and focused on preservation rather than growth . . . ? Could be attractive to many owners and potential acquirers I know, heresy or not. It's worth pondering at any rate and it just might lead to a life-lengthening strategic change.

CORE MARKET: PICKERING

Core markets are critical, but most of us are not in the room (or at the company or in some cases even born!) when it is decided what core market(s) the business is going to focus on. Many times, there isn't too much explicit thought or discussion given to it. On day one, right after they tell the new circulation manager where the copier is, they explain who or what the core markets are.

The rub is that core markets are dynamic. Core markets can change in response to defined actions by the marketers; mail pieces are targeted to a greater percentage of one hundred plus employee sites than has historically been the practice, so more one hundred plus employee sites come on the house file.

A very useful exercise is to look at the house file and try to define the core audience by looking at the top performing RFM segments. How does your definition line up against what the traditional school of thought says is the core market?

Core markets can of course be a self-fulfilling prophecy and, in fact, they often are. A company only targets small employee sizes, so that is all that appears on their house file. This is not necessarily a bad thing if the premise was developed on good data. And despite best efforts, promotion pieces will get to some non-core audience prospects, so there will be a mix.

Core markets are particularly important when developing a prospecting circulation plan. There are two schools of thought on list testing, let's call them the shotgun and the rifle shot. The shotgun approach is generally based on getting as much universe as possible and tests big lists with big rollout potential. If a list works, that is good, as there are big universes. This can work for some offers that have more universal appeal, like credit cards or office supplies. Even then, however, some selectivity is necessary.

The rifle shot approach applies significant segmentation and selection criteria to test lists in order to give the test the best opportunity to work. If the core is defined as SICs 15-17 and fifty plus employee sizes, those selections are made on test lists whenever possible. Gender, household income, employee size, response model—any combination of selection attributes can be used. Some will be selection criteria that can be used against almost any list; gender would be an example of one such attribute. Other selections are specific to certain types of list, like direct-mail-sold-to-publisher on subscription lists. Even more finite selections that are list specific can be made, like product purchased. A competent broker will be attuned to all of these.

The more specific rifle shot approach is more appealing to most direct marketers, especially because the cost of prospecting is almost always regarded as high. As with so much in life, balance is key. Segmentation so specific that it gets down to test cells of thirty-seven names not only does not produce consistent and repeatable results, it doesn't leave universe enough to circulate to if the test pans out.

Keeping the core market definition consistent between prospecting and house file circulation is critical to the success of the company. Both efforts form a symbiotic relationship. If a market performs well for prospecting (usually measured by response rate, though sometimes by AOV or dollars per thousand of circulation), but doesn't yield profitable, long-term customers for the house file side, it is deadly for the overall effort. If a segment is particularly profitable on the house file side but there is a negligible universe for prospecting, there is not going to be the ability to replenish the customers lost through attrition. Balance must be achieved between the two efforts and this requires regular and extensive comparisons between the house file core customer groups and the prospecting core customers. You would be thunderstruck to see how many companies never attempt such analysis. Some companies that I have worked with periodically switch assignments: the individuals responsible for prospecting begin doing house file and the converse. This takes great fortitude and will likely cause some bumps in the road, but the potential rewards in terms of better overall circulation and more well-rounded employees are enormous.

ADJACENT MARKET: LIBEY

Adjacent markets exist side-by-side with core markets. If the core market is antique Studebaker restoration shops, an adjacent market is antique Corvette restoration shops. If the core market is larger, say, auto body shops, an adjacent market is brake shops or transmission shops. If the core market is broad, auto repair, an adjacent market could be airplane maintenance or boat repair.

Adjacent markets tend to be horizontal with some overlap (**Figure L8.1**). If the core market is health care, for example, an adjacent market may be health care record keeping. Since all health care professionals have to keep records, the adjacent market overlaps concentric markets such as physicians, veterinarians, dentists, and

Figure L8.1

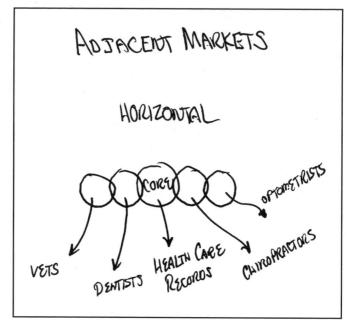

chiropractors. Another adjacent market might be health care uni-
forms, also an overlapping market. A third adjacent market might
be health care practice furniture. Each of these adjacent markets
have a logical basis for expansion: universe. When we look at the
giants of direct marketing, such as Patterson Dental Supply, we
find an adjacent market strategy serving the dental, the companion
pet veterinary and the rehabilitation markets. Similarly, NEBS, the
venerable business forms direct marketing company, serves tilers,
plumbers, electricians, HVAC, landscapers and other adjacent markets within the broad contractor market.

Consumer adjacent markets are often less horizontal and logical, more circular (**Figure L8.2**). The popcorn and flower markets,
as an example, are both served by 1-800-FLOWERS and would
seem to be an illogical fit until you understand that the core market
is actually gifting. In that context, their brand line-up makes sense:
Popcorn Factory, Plow & Hearth, HearthSong, Magic Cabin Dolls,
Cheryl & Co. cookies and 1-800-FLOWERS.

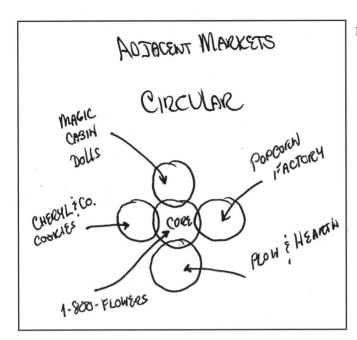

Another perspective on adjacent markets can be obtained with Amazon.com. Since beginning with books, the online marketer has expanded to twenty-nine adjacent markets, not all logical. Books and music are clearly logical, as are DVD/VHS. But books and tools is illogical, as are pet supplies, apparel and kitchenware. Amazon's definition of adjacent markets is broad, almost 'general department store' in nature. Yet, all of the adjacent markets are home related and all can be serviced online.

In contrast, multi-channel direct marketer Barnes & Noble views adjacent markets quite differently. The core book market is supported by used, out of print and textbook markets. Music is a major retail department as well as an online market. Considerable retail space is devoted to the coffee bar and specialty baked goods, soup and sandwiches. The adjacent market strategy is much more horizontal and overlapping than we find with Amazon. Barnes & Noble is retaining its core market while adding adjacent markets that are quite logical.

When adjacent markets and RFM segmentation and optimization are examined, Amazon is far more advanced than Barnes & Noble. After more than twenty years of shopping at Barnes & Noble, they have no idea who I am and what my interests are, nor do they have any way of contacting me as a customer. Why? Because I have never signed up for their membership program. I spend between $2,000 and $3,000 almost every year in the retail stores, but am still a nameless customer they know absolutely nothing about. Compare that to Amazon, which knows more about me and my interests than any company or person on the face of the Earth. Amazon does everything we talk about in this book and more. Amazon actively manipulates my RFM behavior, my affinities, my linear purchases, literally everything I do in my relationship with the company, and optimizes my lifetime purchases and my lifetime net profitability. As a result, I spend more with Amazon than I care to think about. But, I only buy books and the odd CD. I'm a core market guy and probably will never be an adjacent market customer. Yet, I buy cappuccino, music, new books and used books from Barnes & Noble. *The point: If you want to expand to adjacent markets, first decide whether you really mean adjacent markets or adjacent products.*

ADJACENT MARKET: PICKERING

Adjacent markets can occur or they can be developed. With more channels and more advertising vehicles being deployed by direct marketers today, there is more opportunity for adjacent markets to develop unintended and unaided.

There is nothing whatsoever wrong with adjacent markets that naturally occur. Think of it as marketing Darwinism (my grandfather used to call these occurrences 'volunteers'). Adjacent markets can develop from the most unlikely of places.

WD-40 was developed as a degreaser and penetrating solvent intended for use on engines and other machinery. As such, the core market was defined as people who service machinery. However, many anglers swear that WD-40 is a great bait for bass fishing. The bass fishing market is probably not the audience that WD-40 started out to serve, nor was attracting bass the problem they hoped to solve. Yet WD-40 is extensively used in that way.

What does WD-40 do with this unusual opportunity? It could do nothing. Or it could start to package the product differently, perhaps in smaller containers that are more easily taken with the angler. It could also start to look for advertising opportunities reaching those who both work on machinery and enjoy fishing as a hobby,

Among direct marketers, government agencies and educational institutions often occur as an adjacent market. And it only makes sense. What building has more office space than any other in the world? The Pentagon. What do you think its budget is for things like cellular phones, office supplies, floor mats, computers, light bulbs, and the plethora of things used and consumed in an office?

An adjacent market, by definition, is not, or was not, the core market or the intended market. Therefore, to move effectively into a adjacent market, the tactics must be reviewed to see if they are as applicable in the adjacent market as in the core. April may be a great month to mail the core market, but it is probably a poor time to try to send a mail piece or an email to anyone at the I.R.S.

Adjacent markets are usually defined using the same variables and descriptors used for core markets. For business-to-business marketers, the language generally includes variables like SIC, employee size, and job title. Consumer marketers may look at age, income, special interest, ethnicity, gender, USDA growing zone, and the like. It is important to develop definitions that are executable in the real world. If you want to define a market by SIC, but that variable only has coverage on twenty percent of your file, is that really a useful definition? It probably makes sense to investigate how to increase the coverage of that variable and see if the market definition still works.

CONCENTRIC MARKET: LIBEY

Concentric market expansion is the 'tree ring' strategy of growth. The core market is the center core of the tree. Each successive market is logical, concentric and vertical. Concentric markets imply unique products with little or no overlap **(Figure L8.3)**. As an example, the core market is spices. The first concentric market is soup mixes. The next is salad dressings. The next is BBQ rubs. The next is stocks and demi-glazes. The next is dried mushrooms and fresh herbs. Through the addition of concentric market rings, the core market has migrated and expanded from spices to culinary ingredients. Customers who began with an interest in spices logically have an interest in the add-on concentric markets. This is an example of tight, product-focused, concentric market definition.

Another view is to begin with culinary ingredients and add concentric markets such as candy-making, baking, vegetable gardening, tabletop fashion, and organic foods. Here, the market is expanded both vertically and, to some degree, horizontally.

Figure L8.3

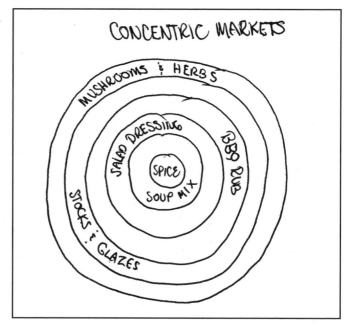

A third view is to incorporate all of the sub-markets above into three vertical concentric market expansions beginning with the culinary enthusiast market, then a concentric expansion to the restaurant market, and the third to the commercial food preparation market. This is a concentric strategy based on universe scalability.

What we don't have in the concentric market model is a mixing of the cooking enthusiast market and a totally unrelated market like, say, wigs. We also don't have a market mix of hunting and fishing with scrapbooking, even though both are hobbies. Non-concentric market expansion is dangerous.

Market expansion, whether core, adjacent or concentric, is about *focus*. Over the years, I have developed an enormous respect for the handful of owners and CEOs who have managed to remain tightly focused on their niche markets. In nearly every instance of extraordinary success, the touchstone of those success stories has been focus. Focus allows you to say, "No." Focus keeps you from investing in things that do not further the narrow objectives of the company. Many such expansion or investment opportunities are good ideas and well conceived, but have little to do with the primary objective of the business. When you arrive at the outcome, it has little relevance to sustaining the core of the business.

Focus can be elusive. A microscope lens provides a tight focus, but so does a wide-angle lens or a telephoto lens. The choice of focus has to be appropriate for the end-game objectives of the business owner. If a narrow focus on a product niche is demanded by the goals and objectives, a wide-angle focus on concentric market expansion and multi-channel development may not be the right lens for the job.

Consider the legendary focus of, say, New Pig on spill absorption, or of Black Box on micro-acquisitions. Both of these direct marketing companies have attained success because of an unwavering focus on a niche, a product line, a strategy, and a channel. Think of Crutchfield and its early near-maniacal focus on making it easy for customers to upgrade and install automobile audio systems for every make and model of automobile. Consider the Trappist monks at the Abbey of Gethsemani (www.monks.org) and their disciplined focus on the quality and consistency of their incredible fruitcakes, year to year. This is the type of focus that produces success. It's seldom exciting or glamorous, but it sure does work.

Focus is, to me, *the* single most important thing for success. Wherever focus has wavered or broadened beyond sustainability, the direct marketing companies have failed. Whenever the strategic focus has included peripheral goals and objectives, the primary goal and objective has been diluted and usually lost. Whenever product, position, quality or market focus has been abandoned for multi-foci, the competition has walked away with the market. I can find no other element as pivotal as focus in predicting the ultimate outcome of a multi-channel direct marketing business (except the cleanliness of the bathrooms). In nearly every instance of the seventy plus strategic plans I have facilitated for catalog companies over the past twenty-five years, focus has been the core issue to be resolved for the future. The focus may be on core, adjacent or concentric markets, channel integration, new product development, acquisitions, customer retention, circulation penetration, or other tactics; however, central to any strategic planning success, is the recognition that the focus must be intense and unwavering on the key strategic objectives.

CONCENTRIC MARKET: PICKERING

We have all have seen the concentric market drama play out. Sometimes it is a winner, all too often it is not. One thing that that would help to improve the batting average on these efforts is paying more attention to RFM. By chapter eight this should not come as a surprise.

In many cases, concentric markets are developed via acquisition or merger. The result is a group of what used to be several different companies now supposed to act as one more or less cohesive unit. This infrequently happens, but when it does it can be quite powerful.

A centralized marketing database that combines and aggregates all customer data *will not* ensure success of a concentric market approach for a multi-divisional company; but the lack of centralized information *will* ensure a difficult time and missed opportunity.

Mergers and acquisitions often occur because reducing redundant costs (which generally means people) better leverages assets across multiple divisions. Within direct marketing one of the most costly assets to acquire is the file of customers. Therefore, it is imperative to effectively share the customer base across divisions to make a concentric market theory work.

RFM segmentation and analysis must be expanded to include P (product) and D (division). Two customers who are worth the same amount within the last twelve months and have the same frequency will likely respond differently if one has purchased from only one division and the other customer has purchased from three divisions.

Creating an enterprise-level customer marketing database can sound like a very daunting task, and it assuredly can be made into a daunting task. However, at this level, less detailed information is needed; it isn't important to know that someone bought a yellow sweater and how much that specific item cost, it is simply important to know that they have bought from the sweater product category and have spent a total of $325 in the last twelve months.

Cost cannot be disregarded, but it will take a certain amount of investment to develop an enterprise level database. This is an *investment,* and one you would make expecting that it will yield a return every year. It is possible—and should be requisite—to track the costs of an enterprise level marketing database versus the amount of sales generated by effective sharing of the customer file asset.

Growing a market will take an investment of money and resources, primarily in the form of assigning skilled people to accomplish this task. Investing in growing the top line and the bottom line will result in growing the business and enhancing the valuation.

MARKET AND RFM OPTIMIZATION: LIBEY

It is difficult to correlate market with recency, frequency and monetary value. Unlike product and channel, market (along with position) is difficult to quantify. Perhaps there is a way to segment customers as being 'in-market' or 'out-of-market,' but that remains to be discovered; if so, it clearly would open up new approaches to prospecting. The SIC hierarchy overlaid on RFM hierarchy remains the best method for obtaining a read on the market relevance. If the Mother Sauces were to be produced, they would include RFM plus product and channel. That's where the bulk of the flavor will be found. RFM plus position and market correlations will give you navigation landmarks and keep you on course and cause you to see opportunities. But, straightforward optimization of RFM performance across all channels for all products will provide you with sufficient information and insights to grow your business effectively, rapidly and profitably if, indeed, that is the future you choose.

As we conclude, however, it is my hope that we have challenged traditional thinking about the uses of recency, frequency and monetary value. In this robust multi-channel direct marketing milieu, we have suggested numerous ways RFM can provide insight and knowledge about your business; it only remains for you to begin the disciplined tracking and gathering of the data and then to convert it to useful information. With reliable information, the next step separates the masters of direct marketing from all the others: *thinking*. Information considered with thought leads to wisdom, and wisdom produces great strategic ability and rewarding business valuation.

MARKET AND RFM OPTIMIZATION: PICKERING

Regular, rigorous, thoughtful RFM analysis will reveal much about all types of markets: core, adjacent, and concentric. This is a high-level, deep-thinking endeavor that is beneficial for the entire company.

I once worked with a leader of an organization who periodically requested in-depth analyses of markets, opportunities, current performance, and the like. Although the individual did pay close attention in the presentation to all the data, analyses, and information that the marketing group brought together, there was a deeper strategy in mind. That leader told me that, even if he immediately forgot all that the marketing department labored to produce, it was a worthwhile use of time because it got the marketing managers, directors, vice-presidents, and even the analysts thinking about the larger issues, seeing the bigger picture, not just worrying about the day-to-day efforts of feeding the marketing machine.

The insights produced by performing some or all of the RFM analysis and segmentation that we have suggested are very valuable. They will produce a deeper understanding of your business and provide a road map around pitfalls that leads you to wondrous opportunities. The additional reward will be developing the practice of looking at the larger issues and implications and making the transition from reacting tactically to thinking strategically.

ABOUT THIS BOOK

The text of this book is composed in 11-point ITC Galliard, a typeface designed by Matthew Carter in 1978 for the International Typeface Corporation and based on the work of the sixteenth-century letter cutter Robert Granjon.

The paper used is 60# Nature's Natural, a fifty percent post consumer recycled paper, processed chlorine free. The book's printer, Thomson-Shore, Inc., is a member of Green Press Initiative, a nonprofit program dedicated to supporting authors, publishers, and suppliers in their efforts to reduce their use of fiber obtained from endangered forests.

Jacket design, text design, and production management by Angela Schmitt of West Des Moines, Iowa.